Global Issues in Commercial Law

By
Kristen David Adams
Professor of Law
Stetson University College of Law

Claude D. Rohwer
Professor Emeritus
University of the Pacific, McGeorge School of Law

AMERICAN CASEBOOK SERIES®

WEST®

A Thomson Reuters business

Mat #40778234

American Casebook Series is a trademark registered in the U.S. Patent and Trademark Office.

© 2010 Thomson Reuters

    610 Opperman Drive
    St. Paul, MN 55123
    1–800–313–9378

Printed in the United States of America

ISBN: 978–0–314–19993–5

To four California pioneers: Orpha, Salome and two Lenas.

C.D.R.

To Jeff, for whose love, patience, and perspective
I am thankful each day.

K.D.A.

Preface

These materials are designed to supplement standard materials designed for a commercial law class by presenting international and comparative issues and topics in a manner that will enrich students' understanding of domestic law. This book could also be used as the text for a seminar in international commercial law. The various chapters stand alone, and class assignments can include one or several as the professor chooses. Some chapters can be used to provide greater depth to a student's understanding of sales law. For example, Chapter 1 provides a comparative analysis of the treatment of several basic sales law issues under the UCC, the CISG, and the Ontario Sales Act, which is representative of Canadian law. A better understanding of the interpretative methods that might properly be used to interpret and apply the CISG can be gained from a study of Chapter 2. Various issues and impacts resulting from a contractual choice of forum are introduced in Chapter 3.

Several chapters have as their purpose an introduction to or a better understanding of specific subjects that may not be highlighted in the typical commercial law materials, such as interest and usury (Chapter 4), commercial agencies and franchises (Chapter 5) and bankruptcy (Chapter 9). In Chapter 6 the specific topic is claw back laws and related laws dealing with the responses of several nations to the extraterritorial application of foreign (primarily US) laws. This opens the door to an examination of the diplomatic and economic issues that place limits on the exercise of extraterritorial jurisdiction. Chapter 8 introduces the basics regarding letters of credit and documentary sales, important topics in any modern commercial law course. Finally, Chapter 7 deals with microfinance, a topic that is of particular interest in developing countries and increasing interest in the United States.

The authors have included excerpts from various kinds of sources to give students some exposure to each, wanting students to see that treatises, cases, and statutes from other jurisdictions may be written and presented differently from United States domestic law. The questions, comments, and problems that are presented throughout can be assigned to students or used to facilitate class discussion as the professor desires.

The authors gratefully acknowledge Vice President and Dean Darby Dickerson, Associate Dean Mark Bauer, and Professors

Brooke Bowman, Peter Fitzgerald, and Joseph Morrissey of Stetson University College of Law, each of whom provided comments on some of these materials in draft form. We also wish to express our appreciation for the efforts of Professor Franklin Gevurtz and Dean Elizabeth Rindskoff Parker of University of Pacific McGeorge School of Law for their highly successful efforts in promoting the concept of the Global Issues series and to Reuters–Thomson West for committing to get these books published and distributed. Finally we wish to express our appreciation for the support of Stetson's excellent Office of Faculty Support Services, particularly Dianne Oeste, and the fine research work performed by current and former Stetson students Nicole Armstrong, Tim Berryman, Mustafo Davlatov, Rebecca Farrar, Erin Isdell, Maria Helena Ordoñez, Megan O'Shea, Yuliya Swaim, and Jeff Swerdlow, and by Dennis H. Flesch, Pacific McGeorge class of 2010.

Acknowledgements

Nina J. Crimm, Post–September 11 Fortified Anti–Terrorism Measures Compel Heightened Due Diligence, 25 Pace L. Rev. 203, 208–210 (2005). Reprinted with permission from Pace Law Review.

Professor Franco Ferrari, Specific Topics of the CISG in Light of Judicial Application and Scholarly Writing, 15 J.L. & Com. 1, 117–125 (1995). Reprinted with permission by the Journal of Law and Commerce.

Keith Epstein & Geri Smith, Compartamos: From Nonprofit to Profit: Behind its Gentle Image is a Tough, Highly Lucrative Bank, 4064 Bus. Wk. 45, 45 (2007). Reprinted with permission from Business Week.

Mark H. Haller & John V. Alviti, Loansharking in American Cities: Historical Analysis of a Marginal Enterprise, 21 Am. J. Legal Hist. 125, 136–141 (1977). Reprinted with permission from The American Journal of Legal History.

Hawkland UCC Series § 1–103:6 [Rev]. Sections 1–103:7 [Rev] and 1–103:8 [Rev]. Reprinted with permission by West, a Thomson Reuters business.

International Institute for the Unification of Private Law, UNIDROIT Principles of International Commercial Contracts, Preamble (2004). Reprinted with permission by the International Institute for the Unification of Private Law (UNIDROIT).

Daryl J. Levinson, Collective Sanctions, 56 Stan. L. Rev. 345, 395–396 (2003). Reprinted with permission from Stanford Law Review.

Ulrich Magnus, General Principles of UN–Sales Law (1995), available at http://cisg.law.pace.edu/cisg/text.magnus.html. Reprinted with permission from the author.

Marguerite S. Robinson, The Microfinance Revolution: Sustainable Finance for the Poor 9 (2001). Reprinted with permission by World Bank.

Thomas J. Salerno, Reorganization of the Financially Distressed Business in the US—Just How Far Afield Is It from the Rest of the World?, Global Insolvency & Restructuring Yearbook

2008/2009 71. Reprinted with permission by the author and Euromoney Institutional Investor PLC (London).

Phil Smith & Eric Thurman, A Billion Bootstraps: Microcredit, Barefoot Banking and the Business Solution for Ending Poverty 41 (2007). Reprinted with permission by McGraw Hill Publications.

Muhammad Yunus, Nobel Peace Prize Acceptance Speech: Poverty is a Threat to Peace (Dec. 10, 2006), available at http://nobel prize.org/nobel_prizes/peace/laureates/2006/yunus-lecture-en. html. Muhammad Yunus is the sole author of text and this has been reprinted with permission © The Nobel Foundation 2006.

Application and Agreement For Commercial Letter of Credit, http:// www.saehanbank.com/resources/lc%20application%20form.pdf. Application and Agreement for Commercial Letter of Credit has been reproduced with permission from Saehan Bank.

Application and Agreement for Commercial Letter of Credit, http:// www.calbanktrust.com/products/products/ibg/jpdfs/LCAPP 0906.pdf. Application and Agreement for Commercial Letter of Credit has been reproduced with permission from California Bank & Trust. California Bank & Trust will not undertake to notify the author of any change, revision or amendment to the form, nor will it make any representation or warranty of its appropriate use in any jurisdiction other than the state in which the bank operates.

Global Issues Series

Series Editor, Franklin A. Gevurtz

Titles Available Now

Global Issues in Civil Procedure by Thomas Main, University of the Pacific, McGeorge School of Law
ISBN 978–0–314–15978–6

Global Issues in Constitutional Law by Brian K. Landsberg, University of the Pacific, McGeorge School of Law and Leslie Gielow Jacobs, University of the Pacific, McGeorge School of Law
ISBN 978–0–314–17608–0

Global Issues in Contract Law by John A. Spanogle, Jr., George Washington University, Michael P. Malloy, University of the Pacific, McGeorge School of Law, Louis F. Del Duca, Pennsylvania State University, Keith A. Rowley, University of Nevada, Las Vegas, and Andrea K. Bjorklund, University of California, Davis
ISBN 978–0–314–16755–2

Global Issues in Copyright Law by Mary LaFrance, University of Nevada
ISBN 978–0–314–19447–3

Global Issues in Corporate Law by Franklin A. Gevurtz, University of the Pacific, McGeorge School of Law
ISBN 978–0–314–15977–9

Global Issues in Criminal Law by Linda Carter, University of the Pacific, McGeorge School of Law, Christopher L. Blakesley, University of Nevada, Las Vegas and Peter Henning, Wayne State University
ISBN 978–0–314–15997–7

Global Issues in Employee Benefits Law by Paul M. Secunda, Marquette University Law School, Samuel Estreicher, New York University School of Law, Rosalind J. Connor, Jones Day, London
ISBN 978–0–314–19409–1

Global Issues in Employment Discrimination Law by Samuel Estreicher, New York University School of Law and Brian K. Landsberg, University of the Pacific, McGeorge School of Law
ISBN 978–0–314–17607–3

Global Issues in Employment Law by Samuel Estreicher, New York University School of Law and Miriam A. Cherry, University of the Pacific, McGeorge School of Law
ISBN 978–0–314–17952–4

Global Issues in Environmental Law by Stephen McCaffrey, University of the Pacific, McGeorge School of Law and Rachael Salcido, University of the Pacific, McGeorge School of Law
ISBN 978–0–314–18479–5

Global Issues in Family Law by Ann Laquer Estin, University of Iowa and Barbara Stark, Hofstra University
ISBN 978–0–314–17954–8

Global Issues in Freedom of Speech and Religion by Alan Brownstein, University of California, Davis School of Law and Leslie Gielow Jacobs, University of the Pacific, McGeorge School of Law
ISBN 978–0–314–18454–2

Global Issues in Income Taxation by Daniel Lathrope, University of California, Hastings College of Law
ISBN 978–0–314–18806–9

Global Issues in Intellectual Property Law by John Cross, University of Louisville School of Law, Amy Landers, University of the Pacific, McGeorge School of Law, Michael Mireles, University of the Pacific, McGeorge School of Law and Peter K. Yu, Drake University Law School
ISBN 978–0–314–17953–1

Global Issues in Labor Law by Samuel Estreicher, New York University School of Law
ISBN 978–0–314–17163–4

Global Issues in Legal Ethics by James E. Moliterno, College of William & Mary, Marshall–Wythe School of Law and George Harris, University of the Pacific, McGeorge School of Law
ISBN 978–0–314–16935–8

Global Issues in Property Law by John G. Sprankling, University of the Pacific, McGeorge School of Law, Raymond R. Coletta,

University of the Pacific, McGeorge School of Law, and M.C. Mirow, Florida International University College of Law
ISBN 978–0–314–16729–3

Global Issues in Tort Law by Julie A. Davies, University of the Pacific, McGeorge School of Law and Paul T. Hayden, Loyola Law School, Los Angeles
ISBN 978–0–314–16759–0

Summary of Contents

Table of Contents

Table of Cases

The principal cases are in bold type. Cases cited or discussed in the text are roman type. References are to pages. Cases cited in principal cases and within other quoted materials are not included.

Global Issues in Commercial Law

Chapter 1

CHOICE OF LAW: SUBSTANTIVE CONSIDERATIONS

When disputes involve more than one jurisdiction, one of the first things a judge or arbitrator must do is to decide what law applies to the transaction. If the parties have agreed upon and stated their choice of law, their choice of law will ordinarily be respected.[1] When the agreement fails to provide for the applicable law, determining what law is to be applied can be a very complex, costly and time consuming proposition. Experts do not even agree upon the proper name for this issue. (It is called "conflict of laws" in the US but "private international law" in most other countries.) The rules are complex, much disputed and in most cases leave room for debate and interpretation.

There are numerous practical considerations regarding choice of law. Perhaps most obvious is the fact that different laws will create substantive differences by imposing different rights and duties upon the parties. For example, they will often permit different reactions such as the permissible responses of a buyer when delivery of goods is delayed, and they will require different levels of

---

1. Many foreign jurisdictions permit wide latitude to the parties in their choice of law. However, most US jurisdictions have traditionally limited choice of law to that of a jurisdiction which bears a reasonable relation to the transaction. The 2001 revisions of the Uniform Commercial Code (hereafter UCC) in § 1–301(c) would have changed this to bring American law more closely in conformity with foreign law at least for cases governed by the UCC. However, this subsection was rejected by the states that adopted the 2001 version of Article 1 and in 2008 the Official Text of the UCC was revised to require that there be a "reasonable relation." *See* § 1–301(a). Thus, if there was a transaction governed by the UCC that provides for performance in Utah, made between an Arizona supplier and a Nevada construction company, the parties could effectively agree that their transaction would be governed by the law of Arizona or Utah or Nevada but not some other state that had no reasonable relation to the transaction.

breach and perhaps different procedures to permit avoidance of a contract.

The significance of the differences among various laws that may apply should be considered initially even before a contract is formed. This could impact the decision relating to drafting of forms as well as a formal contract. One must know the substance of the applicable law in order to properly draft the contract and to advise the client when problems arise during the course of performance. In the event of litigation, the primary handling of the case must be entrusted to one who knows the substance of the applicable law and the procedures that it brings into play.

THE HYPOTHETICAL—A US–CANADIAN TRANSACTION

Your client Minn Corp (Minn) produces animal feed in the State of Minnesota. Northern Feeds (NF), which has a similar business in Ontario, Canada, is replacing much of its machinery including a large pelleting machine which NF has advertised in a trade journal for sale for C$100,000 (Canadian dollars) Minn has need for such a machine and the price is reasonable. The Minn plant foreman went to NF's plant in Ontario and inspected the machine. Minn advises you that it wishes to negotiate a contract to purchase this machine with a slightly reduced price if that can be obtained.

In a transaction involving sale of goods between a buyer in Minnesota and seller in Ontario, Canada, what law will apply to this transaction? What law do you want?

If the agreement does not contain an effective choice of law provision, the applicable law will be the United Nations Convention on Contracts for the International Sale of Goods (Vienna 1980), hereinafter CISG.[2] Application of the CISG will likely cause concern to the everyday Minnesota lawyer because few practicing lawyers claim expertise in that law. The CISG has no official comments to explain or provide guidance, and there are few American cases that apply and interpret the CISG. Many lawyers contract out of the CISG at least in part due to the fact that it is unfamiliar turf. This brings us to a choice between what might be referred to as "domestic" Minnesota law (the UCC) and "domestic" Ontario law (Sale of Goods Act, R.S.O. 1990, c.S.1). One might expect that the Canadian counsel will want Canadian law and you will want Minnesota law and the UCC, and there are practical reasons to support your respective desires. However, various factors involved

2. CISG Article 1(1)(a). Both Canada and the USA are "Contracting States" thus the CISG is the law of both Minnesota and Ontario applicable to transactions that come within Article 1(1)(a). Note that when it ratified this Convention, the US excluded Article 1(1)(b).

in this choice including the potential advantages to your client of one system or the other may influence your decision.

PROBLEM 1a   Risk of Loss

This will be a contract for specific ascertained goods, a used pelleting machine. It is located in the seller's plant in Ontario and your client contemplates that after entering a contract of purchase, it will send a truck to Canada to pick up the machine. Seller has agreed to remove the machine from its mill to an adjoining warehouse and prepare it for Minn to pick up. What if a fire destroys the machine before it arrives in Minnesota? When will the risk of loss shift from the seller to the buyer? When must your client make certain that it has appropriate insurance coverage to protect against damage to or destruction of the machine? If the machine is damaged or destroyed after risk of loss has passed, Minn must still pay for it. The important concern is that risk of loss could pass to your client before it comes into possession of the machine. Minn's insurance coverage may not cover equipment in a foreign country that Minn has contracted to purchase but has not yet received unless this specific risk is recognized and appropriate insurance coverage negotiated.

Under the CISG, Articles 66 and 69 are in point. (Do you see why Article 67 does not apply?) Risk of loss passes when?

Under the UCC, § 2–509(3) should control unless there has been a breach. Is the seller a "merchant" for purposes of this section? Study § 2–104 and particularly comment 2 which directs courts to use the broadest definition of "merchant" to determine the seller's status for purposes of passage of risk. If the seller is not a merchant, when does the risk pass? Does the UCC define "tender of delivery?" (See § 2–503.) What facts might make § 2–510 applicable here? (See § 2–610.)

Unlike the UCC and the CISG, Ontario law focuses on passage of title. The Ontario Sale of Goods Act provides:

R.S.O. 1990, Chapter S.1

§ 18   Property passes where intended to pass

(1) Where there is a contract for the sale of specific or ascertained goods, the property in them is transferred to the buyer at such time as the parties to the contract intend it to be transferred.

(2) For the purpose of ascertaining the intention of the parties, regard shall be had to the terms of the contract, the conduct of the parties and the circumstances of the case.

§ 19 Rules for ascertaining intention

Unless a different intention appears, the following are rules for ascertaining the intention of the parties as to the time at which the property in the goods is to pass to the buyer:

Rule 1.—Where there is an unconditional contract for the sale of specific goods in a deliverable state, the property in the goods passes to the buyer when the contract is made and it is immaterial whether the time of payment or the time of delivery or both is postponed.

Rule 2.—Where there is a contract for the sale of specific goods and the seller is bound to do something to the goods for the purpose of putting them into a deliverable state, the property does not pass until such thing is done and the buyer has notice thereof.

. . . .

. . . .

§ 21 Risk passes with property

Unless otherwise agreed, the goods remain at the seller's risk until the property therein is transferred to the buyer, but, when the property therein is transferred to the buyer, the goods are at the buyer's risk whether delivery has been made or not, but,

(a) where delivery has been delayed through the fault of either the buyer or seller, the goods are at the risk of the party in fault as regards any loss that might not have occurred but for such fault; and

(b) nothing in this section affects the duties or liabilities of either seller or buyer as a bailee of the goods of the other party.

Assume that while it was still in the possession of the seller, the pelleting machine was destroyed by a fire which occurred without fault of either party. What additional facts would you need to know or what legal determinations would you have to make to determine who had the risk of loss under the three different legal systems? Note Rule 2 under § 19 which provides that for property in the goods to be transferred, they must not only be specific and ascertained but must also be in a deliverable state. Recall that our hypothetical contract provides for the seller to perform certain acts relating to the pelleting machine before it can be picked up.

Jerome v. Clements Motor Sales Ltd. (1958) O.R. 738 (Ont. C.A.) involved a contract for the sale of a specific car. The seller was to perform some repairs which were almost completed but the seller had not yet installed a working battery. The Ontario court held that the car was not yet in a deliverable state so property had not yet passed and the risk remained on the seller.

To the extent that risk of loss is a concern, which law is best for the buyer?

If negotiations lead to an agreement to apply Ontario law, what must you warn your client about insurance coverage that might not be a concern if the UCC or the CISG were applicable? The more inclusive property damage policies cover property in which the insured has an insurable interest. When property and thus risk of loss passes to the buyer under Ontario law, the buyer has an insurable interest. Contracting to purchase the machine could be argued to constitute an insurable interest, too. However, while some policies give worldwide coverage, most Inland Marine policies limit coverage to property located in the United States.

Passage of property in the goods under Canadian law is a fundamental concept that affects issues other than passage of the risk of loss. When property has "passed" to the buyer, the goods are the property of the buyer. If seller refuses to tender or deliver the goods, an action may be brought in replevin or an action may be bought for specific performance without regard to whether the goods are unique or special in any way. So also, if buyer refuses to take delivery, seller may maintain an action for the price as the contract has been performed.

PROBLEM 1b   Right of Inspection and Notification of Defects

In the given facts, Buyer has already sent an employee to Ontario who has inspected the machine. However, Seller is to remove it from the plant and prepare it for shipment which might make further inspection reasonable or necessary.

Regarding inspection and notice of defects the Ontario Sale of Goods Act provides:

R.S.O. 1990, Chapter S.1 § 33

(1) Where goods are delivered to the buyer that the buyer has not previously examined, the buyer shall be deemed not to have accepted them until there has been a reasonable opportunity of examining them for the purpose of ascertaining whether they are in conformity with the contract.

(2) Unless otherwise agreed, when the seller tenders delivery of goods to the buyer, the seller shall, on request, afford the buyer a reasonable opportunity of examining the goods for the purpose of ascertaining whether they are in conformity with the contract.

The CISG contains an interesting compromise of provisions found in the German Commercial Code (Handelsgesetzbuch or HGB) and the American UCC.

HGB § 377 provides:

Duty to examine and object to defects

(1) Where the sale is a commercial transaction for both parties, the buyer must examine the goods promptly following delivery by the seller insofar as this is practicable in the proper course of business, and if a defect becomes apparent, promptly advise the seller.

(2) If the buyer fails to advise the seller, the goods are deemed to have been approved, unless there is a defect which was not apparent during the examination.

(3) Where such a defect becomes apparent at a later time, notice must be given promptly following the discovery, otherwise, the goods are to be deemed approved, also with regard to this defect.

(4) The timely dispatch of notice suffices to preserve the buyer's rights.

(5) Where the seller has maliciously concealed the defect, he may not assert these provisions.

The UCC gives the Buyer a "reasonable" time to inspect (§ 2–606) and notice of defects must be given "seasonably" (§ 2–602(1) and § 1–204(3)).

The CISG draws one part from each law. Article 38(1) provides for inspection "... within as short a period as is practicable ...", but Article 39 gives a "reasonable time" after discovery or "should have discovered" for giving notice.

Of course, national traditions as to timeliness can affect the interpretation of the factual question as to what is "prompt" or "reasonable" or "as short a period as is practicable." The case decided by Oberlandesgericht Koblenz on 11 September 1998 which is set forth below on page 12 deals with time allowed for inspection and notice as well as a discussion of some CISG warranty law issues.

PROBLEM 1c Duty to Accept Goods; Right to Reject Goods

Many factors can apply to determine whether a buyer has the right to reject goods. This can involve issues relating to title and encumbrances, delay in tender or delivery, quantity discrepancies, and/or quality of the goods. A related question involves the buyer's right to conduct an inspection before it must accept or reject the goods. Finally there is the question of what constitutes acceptance. (And under the UCC, even after acceptance there is a unique rule that can permit revocation of that acceptance (§ 2–608).)

Because it involves transactions of an international nature, the CISG is often applied to sales where the seller is shipping to a buyer at some distance and often in another country. A rejection of the goods by the buyer will thus often leave the seller with the awkward task of finding a reasonable way to dispose of goods at a distant location in a foreign country. It is thus not surprising that the CISG denies the right of rejection for minor problems. Refer to Articles 46 through 52 to find the full pattern of provisions that limit the buyer's right to reject or avoid the contract. However, with regard to quantity, the CISG rules are unusually strict (Article 29).

There is still the possibility that there are defects yet to be discovered with the pelleting machine. Assume that seller damages a conveyor belt on the machine in the process of moving it out of the plant and preparing it for handing over to Minn Corp. Assuming that the damage can be repaired, could this defect be classified as a fundamental breach justifying rejection under the CISG? (*see* Articles 25 and 49.)

Under the UCC, this is a single lot contract (§ 2–307) which brings into play the perfect tender rule (§ 2–601). Thus any defect in tender discovered prior to acceptance (§ 2–606; *and see* § 2–602) will justify rejection if made in good faith. Furthermore, even after acceptance, there is another window of opportunity to return the machine for a refund and possibly damages under the unique UCC concept of revocation of acceptance (§§ 2–607(4) and 2–608).

Ontario law relating to acceptance and rejection of goods and contract avoidance uses vocabulary with meanings that are unfamiliar to American trained lawyers or students. Ontario draws a distinction between "conditions," express or implied, the failure of which will justify avoidance of a contract for the sale of goods, and "warranties," express or implied, the failure of which gives rise to damages but not the right to reject the goods or avoid the contract.

As defined in § 1 (R.S.O. 1990, c.S.1):

> " 'warranty' means an agreement with reference to goods that are subject of a contract of sale but collateral to the main purpose of the contract, the breach of which gives rise to a claim for damages but not to a right to reject the goods and treat the contract as repudiated. ('garantie')"

Thus, to determine whether a buyer has a right of rejection or a right to avoid the contract, one must determine whether the breach in question relates to an implied condition (which permits rejection or avoidance) or an implied warranty (which gives rise only to a right to damages and nothing more). In distinguishing between the two, one finds guidance in sections 12 and 13 which provide:

§ 12 Breach of stipulation

(1) Where a contract of sale is subject to a condition to be fulfilled by the seller, the buyer may waive the condition or may elect to treat the breach of the condition as a breach of warranty and not as a ground for treating the contract as repudiated.

Stipulations which may be a condition or a warranty

(2) Whether a stipulation in a contract of sale is a condition the breach of which may give rise to a right to treat the contract as repudiated or a warranty the breach of which may give rise to a claim for damages but not to a right to reject the goods and treat the contract as repudiated depends in each case on the construction of the contract, and a stipulation may be a condition, though called a warranty in the contract.

Where breach of condition to be treated as breach of warranty

(3) Where a contract of sale is not severable and the buyer has accepted the goods or part thereof, or where the contract is for specific goods the property in which has passed to the buyer, the breach of any condition to be fulfilled by the seller can only be treated as a breach of warranty and not as a ground for rejecting the goods and treating the contract as repudiated, unless there is a term of the contract, express or implied, to that effect.

§ 13 Implied conditions and warranties

In a contract of sale, unless the circumstances of the contract are such as to show a different intention, there is,

> (a) an implied condition on the part of the seller that in the case of a sale the seller has a right to sell the goods, and that in the case of an agreement to sell the seller will have a right to sell the goods at the time when the property is to pass;

> (b) an implied warranty that the buyer will have and enjoy quiet possession of the goods; and

> (c) an implied warranty that the goods will be free from any charge or encumbrance in favour of any third party,

not declared or known to the buyer before or at the time when the contract is made.

There are general and specific lessons to be drawn here.

First, in international transactions, vocabulary is often a serious problem. In negotiations and in contract drafting, terms such as "warranties" may be employed by the American client or lawyer and by their foreign counterparts with each party intending a very different meaning.

Second, passage of title has very limited legal significance under the UCC. However, by contrast "the time when property passes" has great legal significance under the law of Ontario as well as in most other legal systems. In addition to matters relating to title and security interests which are not the subject of the present discussion, passing of the property can transfer the risk of loss (Problem 1a above). As provided in § 12(3), the passage of the property in the goods to the buyer can terminate the right to reject the goods. And note that in many sales situations, this passage of the property can occur before the buyer has an opportunity to inspect.

Third, Ontario's § 12(3) permits a negotiated provision allowing for termination for breach of a condition after acceptance. This is one of many examples of negotiating opportunities that are available only to those draftspersons who are quite familiar with the law under which they are operating.

Finally, note the policy distinctions made in the Ontario law between the right to sell, a condition the breach of which gives rise to the right to rescind, and the right to quiet possession and receiving goods free of "any charge" or encumbrances, which are merely warranties the breach of which only give rise to a right to damages.

Note that if this hypothetical problem involved an installment transaction, that is, "one which requires or authorizes the delivery of goods in separate lots to be separately accepted," the standards for rejection under the UCC would be far different. Rejection is proper only where the "non-conformity substantially impairs the value of that installment and cannot be cured." Termination of the entire contract requires that the non-conformity or default "substantially impairs the value of the whole contract" (§ 2–612). Thus in comparing the CISG, the UCC and the Sale of Goods Act, the UCC provides the easiest standard for rejection in a single lot contract. However in the case of an installment contract, the UCC presents the most difficult standard of the three different laws.

PROBLEM 1d A Drafting Problem

Assume that domestic Ontario law applies. Your client is not satisfied with the sufficiency of the inspection made by its employee but wishes to test the pelleting machine in operation in Minnesota and to reserve the right to return it if it does not operate properly. Based upon the discussion above, draft the language that you would recommend for inclusion in the contract regarding inspection and acceptance or rejection. You should include specifics regarding time of payment and risk of loss.

PROBLEM 1e Terms Relating to Quality of Goods (Warranties and Conditions)

Review UCC §§ 2–313, 2–314, 2–315. It is commonly accepted that these are three distinct warranties consisting of:

an express warranty arising from an affirmation of fact or a promise, a description of the goods, or any sample or model;

an implied warranty of merchantability when the seller is a "merchant with respect to goods of that kind"; and

an implied warranty of fitness for a particular purpose arising where the seller is aware that the buyer is looking to the seller's skill or judgment to select suitable goods for the buyer's disclosed purpose.

Analyze the provisions in CISG Articles 35 and 36. While organized and presented in a different manner, one can see provisions that parallel the UCC.

§ 2–313 (Article 35(1) and (2)(b) and Article 36(2));

§ 2–314 (Article 35(2)(a), greatly simplified and without the specific merchant requirements);

§ 2–315 (Article 35(2)(b) with a shifting of the burden of proof regarding reliance.)

While similar, differences between the CISG and the UCC may be critical in the purchase of the pelleting machine. This is a used machine being sold by the seller Northern Feeds which is apparently engaged in the feed packaging business and thus arguably knowledgeable about such equipment. NF is perhaps a merchant within the general definition of that term (§ 2–104(1)) because although he is not one who "deals in goods of that kind," it might be said that "by his occupation (he) holds himself out as having knowledge or skill peculiar to the practices or goods involved in the transaction . . . ." (See § 2–104, Comment 2.)

However though this may be a colorable argument, it is not likely that NF comes within § 2–314 as a "merchant with respect to goods of that kind." Though NF purchased this pelleting machine, is currently selling it, and is likely to buy a new machine in the future, NF is not in the business of buying and selling such machines. Such transactions are merely incidental to its business of packaging animal feeds. One who makes an isolated sale of goods is not a "merchant" for purposes of 2–314. Read the comments to that section, focusing upon comment 3. See also the rather inconclusive statement about second-hand goods.

Under CISG 35, does NF give a warranty that the pelleting machine is fit for ordinary use in pelleting operations? Would you conclude that Minn might get better warranty rights under the CISG than under the UCC?

Under Ontario law, assurances as to quality which the UCC and American common law refer to as "warranties" are broken into two distinct categories. Ontario law uses the term "conditions" to refer to assurances of quality the breach of which can justify rejection or contract avoidance. It refers to "warranties" as assurances of quality the breach of which gives rise only to the right to recovery of damages.

Sale of Goods Act,

R.S.O. 1990, Chapter S.1

§ 15 Implied conditions as to quality or fitness

Subject to this Act and any statute in that behalf, there is no implied warranty or condition as to the quality of fitness for any particular purpose of goods supplied under the contract of sale, except as follows:

> 1. Where the buyer, expressly or by implication, makes known to the seller the particular purpose for which the goods are required so as to show that the buyer relies on the seller's skill or judgment, and the goods are of a description that is in the course of the seller's business to supply (whether the seller is a manufacturer or not) there is an implied condition that the goods will be reasonably fit for such purpose, but in the case of a contract for the sale of a specified article under its patent or other trade name there is no implied condition as to its fitness for any particular purpose.

> 2. Where goods are bought by description from a seller who deals in goods of that description (whether the seller is the manufacturer or not), there is an implied condition that the goods will be of merchantable quality, but if the buyer has examined the goods, there is no implied condi-

tion as regards defects that such examination ought to have revealed.

3. An implied warranty or condition as to quality or fitness for a particular purpose may be annexed by the usage of trade.

4. An express warranty or condition does not negative a warranty or condition implied by this Act unless inconsistent therewith.

§ 16 Sale by sample

(1) A contract of sale is a contract for sale by sample where there is a term in the contract, express or implied, to that effect.

Implied conditions

(2) In the case of a contract for sale by sample, there is an implied condition

(a) that the bulk will correspond with the sample in quality

(b) that the buyer will have a reasonable opportunity of comparing the bulk with the sample, and

(c) that the goods will be free from any defect rendering them unmerchantable that would not be apparent on reasonable examination of the sample.

Other than the differences in vocabulary regarding conditions and warranties, what distinctions do you see between the UCC and the Sale of Goods Act? Do you see reasons for a buyer favoring one law over the other?

Oberlandesgericht Koblenz 11 September 1998

DATE OF DECISIONS: 19980911 (11 September 1998)

JURISDICTION: Germany

TRIBUNAL: OLG Koblenz [OLG = Oberlandesgericht = Provincial Court of Appeal]

JUDGE(S): Unavailable

CASE NUMBER/DOCKET NUMBER: 2 U 580/96

CASE NAME: German case citations do not identify parties to proceedings

CASE HISTORY: 1st instance LG Bad Kreuznach 12 March 1996 [affirmed]

SELLER'S COUNTRY: Germany (defendant)

BUYER'S COUNTRY: Morocco (plaintiff)

GOODS INVOLVED: Chemical substance (dryblend) used for production of plastic (PVC) tubes

---

Case text (English translation)*

Queen Mary Case Translation Programme

Translation by Todd J. Fox**

Translation edited by Ruth M. Janal***

FACTS OF THE CASE

The [buyer] is a Moroccan company that produces, among other things, plastic pipes. At the end of 1992, [buyer] purchased a used machine for the production of PVC-pipes from Company K. GmbH. The "extruder" machine was built in 1974. In addition, the [buyer] bought 55 tons of dryblend from the [seller] for the production of pressed PVC-pipes. According to the [buyer], the material arrived in the port of Casablanca on 15 December 1992. After setting up the extrusion machine, the [buyer] attempted to begin producing PVC-pipes on 18 January 1993. The production failed, since after a few minutes the PVC-material was badly burned at the pipe head. The [buyer] consulted the [seller] concerning the problem. From 13–15 February and 20–21 March 1993 representatives of the [seller] were with the [buyer]. However, afterwards the production of PVC-pipes was still not successful. The [buyer] sees the cause as defective raw material from the [seller] and is claiming damages. [Buyer] claims reimbursement of the purchase price for the 55 tons of dryblend in the amount of 85,800.00 DM [German marks], reimbursement of the related delivery costs of 12,100.00 DM, and reimbursement of costs in the amount of 51,648.73 DM spent in the consultation of workers of K. GmbH, the company that delivered the extruder machine.

The [buyer] maintains that the material from the [seller] is defective in that the temperature stability of the material is limited. [Buyer] asserts that the [seller] should have pointed that out, especially since the [buyer] indicated during the contract negotiations that it had acquired a complete used production line for the fabrication of pipes from Company K. This, [buyer] asserts, seemed

* All translations should be verified by cross-checking against the original text. For purposes of this translation, the Plaintiff of Morocco is referred to as [buyer]; the Defendant of Germany is referred to as [seller]. Amounts in German currency (*Deutsche Mark*) are indicated as [*DM*].

** Todd J. Fox is an Associate of the Institute of International Commercial Law of the Pace University School of Law. He received his LL.M. *summa cum laude* from Albert-Ludwig-Universität Freiburg.

*** Ruth M. Janal, LL.M. (UNSW) is a Phd. Candidate at Albert-Ludwig-Universität Freiburg.

not to interest the [seller] since [seller] did not inquire about details of the machine. The [buyer] requested that the [seller] be ordered to pay 153,655.09 DM with 10% interest from 20 April 1994.

The [seller] requested that the claim be dismissed.

The [seller] considers its material to be free of defects and claims to have already delivered this material for many years to other customers without objection. Furthermore, the [seller] maintains that the trouble in the production of PVC-pipes comes from the use of the antiquated extrusion-machine. [Seller] asserts that before the [buyer]'s order he gave the [buyer] a specification sheet with the characteristics of the delivered PVC. Thereafter, the [buyer] ordered the standard PVC from the [seller] without mentioning the type of machine the PVC would be processed with. Furthermore, [buyer]'s compensation claims should, in any event, be rejected because the [buyer] did not meet its duty to examine and give timely notice according to Arts. 38(1) and 39(1) CISG.

After consulting an expert opinion, the District Court dismissed the [buyer]'s claim. The Court held that the delivered goods were not non-conforming since the evidence showed that the [seller]'s material was suitable for the production of PVC pressure pipes with extrusion machines. According to the expert's report, the [seller]'s material is employable on currently common and usual extrusion machines. The particularity of the present case is clearly that the [seller]'s material is not able to be processed in the [buyer]'s machine since, due to its age, it evidently develops higher temperatures which exceed the temperature resistance of the PVC material. However, that does not make the goods that [seller] delivered non-conforming goods. That would only be the case if the [buyer] had expressly or impliedly made known to the [seller] the particular purpose of the material, namely its processing in [buyer]'s machine. According to [buyer]'s own representations, the [buyer] did not give this express indication. [Buyer] simply mentioned during the negotiations that it had purchased a production line from Company K. GmbH. The [seller] must not have inferred from this that the machine is an older machine for which its standard mix is not suitable. The [buyer] wrongly accuses the [seller] of not showing a closer interest in [buyer]'s machine. It is the [buyer]'s responsibility to specify the particular purpose rather than merely order the offered standard mix.

The further explanations in the District Court's decision are considered. In the appellate instance, the parties are further pursuing their first instance demands with supplementary and partially new statements. The [buyer] has reduced the amount of its claim. The [buyer] asserts that the dryblend that [seller] delivered is defective. [Buyer] maintains that it is not even within the frame of temperature resistance that is normally required for plastic production. The dryblend can allegedly not even withstand temperatures of 160 degrees. [Buyer] maintains that it examined the goods and gave notice of the non-conformity in a timely manner. [Buyer] asserts that it did not receive the shipping papers until 22 December 1992. These were then given to customs, which did not release the goods until 28 December 1992. Due to the particularities of the used extrusion machine, a reliable examination of the suitability of the dryblend could only occur through a test-run in the machine purchased from Company K. The installation of the machine bought in Germany could not take place from one day to the next. It was not until 16 January 1993 that technicians could arrive to assemble the machine. On 17 January 1993, the extrusion machine was production ready. Directly after installation of the machine, the [buyer] attempted to produce PVC-pipes with the dryblend. The attempt failed. The [buyer] telephoned Mr. M. of the [seller] and informed it of the unsuccessful attempt. At first, they presumed that the problem was with the machine. However, the technicians from Company K. examined the machine until 3 February 1993 and ascertained that it operated correctly and that the reason for the failure must be because of the dryblend. On 3 February 1993, the [buyer] immediately informed M., the authorized officer of the [seller], of this finding. The [buyer] maintains that the [seller] knew of the non-conformity of the dryblend, or at least [seller] could not have been unaware of such non-conformity. Alternatively, the [buyer] claims that, upon a breach by the seller of a duty to warn and advise, the application of Arts. 38 and 39 CISG is ruled out. [Buyer] further claims that the [seller], knowing the place of use, should have indicated to the [buyer] that usage of the dryblend could cause problems in older machines.

The [buyer] requests, in amendment of the appealed decision, that the Court order the [seller] to pay 149,548.73 DM in addition to 10% interest since 20 April 1994; in the alternative, [seller]'s exemption from judicial execution to be guaranteed through the surety of a bank.

The [seller] requests that the appeal be dismissed.

The [seller] asserts that the delivered dryblend is not defective. Rather, it is a current and usual mixture that has proved itself over many years in the marketplace. The [seller] did not know, nor was it discernible, that the [buyer] intended to produce PVC-pipes with a used and completely obsolete extrusion machine. [Seller] further asserts that the suit should be dismissed because the notice of the alleged non-conformity was not timely. Notice of the non-conformity was given at the earliest on 3 February 1993, more than two weeks after the first failure in production. [Seller] contests that the machine was not production ready until 17 January 1993. If that was the case, the [seller] asserts this would not be a sufficient excuse for the delayed notice. The [buyer] should have created the necessary prerequisites for a prompt examination. The [buyer], however, did not do this. Rather, [buyer] allegedly just let the delivered goods lie during a relative long period of time. The [buyer] allegedly knew since 7 December 1992 that the bill of lading was at S. Express in Casablanca. It is therefore [buyer]'s own fault if, according to its claim, it did not receive the goods until 28 December 1992, as the goods had already arrived in the port of Casablanca on 15 December 1992.

For the details, the content of the briefs as well as the documents deposited with the Court are considered.

REASONS FOR THE DECISION

The [buyer]'s appeal is without success. The District Court had correctly decided and the [buyer]'s appellate pleadings do not lead to a different result.

I. The [buyer] cannot demand the payment of 149,548.73 DM and interest from the [seller].

1. According to the correct reasoning of the lower decision, the United Nations Convention on Contracts for the International Sale of Goods (CISG) is applicable to the parties' contractual relationship.

2. The [buyer] maintains that the goods are defective and therefore refers to non-conformity within the meaning of Art. 35 CISG. However, under Art. 39(1) CISG the [buyer] lost the right to rely on a lack of conformity.

According to Art. 39, a buyer loses the right to rely on a lack of conformity if [buyer] does not give notice to the seller specifying the nature of the lack of conformity within a reasonable time after it has discovered it or ought to have discovered it.

According to Art. 38, the buyer must examine the goods, or cause them to be examined, within as short a period as is practicable in the circumstances. After expiration of the examination period (Art. 38) together with the notice period (Art. 39), the total period to notify the non-conformity, the buyer loses the right to object to the defect.[1]

a) The [buyer]'s notice of the claimed non-conformity was too late. It can remain undecided whether the notice did not take place at the earliest on 3 February 1993 when, according to the [buyer]'s

---

1. *See* Staudinger-Magnus, BGB, Art. 38 CISG Rn. 1; Art. 39 Rn. 30 (13 ed.).

statement, the [seller] informed the [buyer] that the production problems must be due to the dryblend. In any case, notice was not given before 18 January 1993. According to the [buyer]'s statement, the extrusion machine was not production ready until 17 January 1993. Directly after the installation, the [buyer] attempted production with the dryblend on 18 January 1993. The attempt was in vain. [Buyer] then informed the [seller] by telephone of the production failure. According to the [buyer]'s assertions, the [buyer] did not receive the goods until 28 December 1992. Taking the date of 18 January 1993 as a basis, the [buyer] consequently "demanded" almost three weeks for their examination. It therefore took a longer period of time than that which is usual. According to the [buyer], the dryblend could be examined in the extrusion machine. The fact that the production of PVC-pipes failed using the blend, which then caused the [buyer] to notify of the defect, could be quickly determined. The [buyer] itself claims that on 18 January 1993, one day after the machine was production ready, [buyer] informed the [seller] of the problem in production. Generally, a period of not more than one week is granted for the examination of the goods through a test-run.[2] Here three weeks had already gone by from the time the [buyer] claims to have received the goods (28 December 1992) to their examination (17/18 January 1993). This clearly exceeds the usual period of time for examination. The [buyer] unsuccessfully argues that it could not have its machine, the only one with which it could test the dryblend, in working order before 17 January 1993. [Buyer] maintains with this argument that a longer examination period than usual was necessary. The [buyer], however, has the burden of showing this.[3]

A specific showing is lacking, so that it also cannot be determined whether the circumstances did not permit the goods to be examined directly after delivery. In knowledge of its duty to give notice, the [buyer] had the burden to carry out the examination of the blend as soon as possible after the arrival of the machine, which was allegedly the only means by which an examination could be made. [Buyer]'s duty to notify could at most be preserved if, due to circumstances for which the [buyer] is not responsible, notice was not possible. This, however, cannot be determined.

Details concerning the exact time of delivery are lacking. The [buyer] stated only that the machine was delivered at the end of 1992. Also lacking are concrete statements concerning when the

2. *See* OLG (Regional Court of Appeals) Karlsruhe, Recht der Internationalen Wirtschaft (1998) 235, 236; Staudinger-Magnus, BGB, Art. 38 CISG Rn. 50.

3. *See* Staudinger-Magnus, BGB, Art. 38 CISG Rn. 65.

[buyer] arranged for the installation, which [buyer] maintains could occur in one to two days with the presence of expert technicians.

In the view of the court, even with an assumed receipt of the goods on 28 December 1992, the total period for examination and notice already expired on 18 January 1993: measured upon an examination period of one week, an additional period of a week for giving notice seems reasonable, particularly since the [buyer] itself explained in its notice of defect—given immediately after the machine was production ready—that this was to be expected and therefore was reasonable.

The total period for examination and notice would clearly be expired if the goods had already been at the [buyer]'s disposal. This is the case here. According to the [buyer], it did not receive the goods until 28 December 1992. However, it is uncontested that the goods were at the port of Casablanca at least from 15 December 1992. Since the [seller] notified the [buyer] on 7 December 1992 that the bill of lading was with S. Express in Casablanca, the [buyer] was put in the position to receive the dryblend from customs upon its arrival and the goods could have been at its disposal from this point in time. It was the [buyer]'s responsibility to timely acquire the shipping papers required for customs from S. Express so that the [buyer] could have received the goods upon their arrival instead of on 28 December 1992. The [buyer] did not sufficiently show that this would have been impossible despite the [seller]'s advance notification on 7 December 1992 containing two call numbers for S. Express, and the [buyer]'s inquiry over the express shipping service, allegedly unknown in Morocco. With over one month of time gone by, the total period of time for examination and notice, which should regularly be approximately fourteen days,[4] was plainly exceeded here.

b) The requirements of the exception provision under Art. 44 CISG are not present here. The buyer who relies on this provision has the burden of showing that the actual requirements for its application, especially those concerning reasonable excuse, have been met.[5] A sufficient showing is missing in the case at hand. For [buyer]'s excuse that the goods were not examined until 17/18 January 1993, the [buyer] unsuccessfully relies on its arguments that it could not acquire the blend until 28 December 1992 and that [buyer] was not able to set-up the machine from one day to the next. A prerequisite for a reasonable excuse is always that the buyer acted with the care and diligence required under the circumstances; that [buyer] reasonably reacted within the scope of its concrete possibilities.[6] However, as shown above in section **a)**, it

4. *See id.* at Art. 39 CISG Rn. 49.
5. *See id.* at Art. 44 CISG Rn. 27.
6. *See id.* at Art. 44 CISG Rn. 12.

can neither be determined that it would not have been possible for the [buyer] to already acquire the goods upon their arrival at port, nor that the installation of the machine on 17/18 January 1993 was still within the scope of acknowledged care and diligence under the circumstances. The [buyer] had not even stated exactly when it disposed over the machine in 1992 and when it arranged for the installation of the machine through Company K. The mere statement that an earlier date than 16 January 1993 for the arrival of Company K. technicians was not possible does not permit, for example, the determination of acknowledgeable business organization difficulties. As the purchaser of material intended for production of goods for which [buyer] knew that the material's examination required a test-run on a particular production machine, the [buyer] had the responsibility to make sure that the machine was timely prepared. This duty readily follows from the duties to examine and give notice which are for the protection of the seller and also include that the buyer properly organize the necessary test-run.

The lack of a proper organization of the test-run examination pursuant to Art. 38 is inconsistent with the requirement that the buyer examine the goods within as short a period as is practicable in the circumstances: the buyer's lack of organization is not to be taken into consideration with regards to the wording of the statutory duty to examine "within as short a period as is practicable in the circumstances." In this case, a proper organization of the examination of the goods cannot be determined; when and how the [buyer] organized the installation of the machine remains open. Accordingly, it cannot be determined that the [buyer] just "let the machine lie" for a particular period.

c) The [seller]'s reliance on Arts. 38 and 39 CISG is precluded when Art. 40 CISG applies. However, the [buyer] did not sufficiently substantiate its assertion that the [seller] knew of the dryblend's low temperature stability and that the use of the dryblend in older machines could cause problems. [Buyer]'s claim that the [seller] knew or could not have been unaware of the lack of conformity was therefore also not substantiated. Along with its assertion that the [seller] knew of the low temperature stability, the [buyer] merely evinces the [seller]'s knowledge of the blend's mixture, which was delivered to the [buyer] as ordered. The [buyer]'s conclusion, from its assertion concerning the [seller]'s alleged knowledge of possible problems connected with the blends use on older machines, that the [seller] therefore knew of the lack of conformity is without foundation. The [buyer] itself stated that it had only informed the [seller] that [buyer] had acquired a complete production line for the fabrication of PVC-pipes from Company K. The [seller] allegedly did not show interest in further details about the machine and did not inquire the [buyer] about it. The [buyer] later stated that it had informed the [seller] that the machine was second hand. The [seller] disputes this. However, even if the [seller] knew that the [buyer] wished to produce PVC-pipes with a used machine in Morocco, that does not mean that the [seller] imagined that the [buyer] intended production on an older machine, where the use of the dryblend could cause problems because of the machine's age. The [seller] is also not required to come to such a conclusion. As the District Court correctly explained, the [buyer] wrongly blames the [seller] for not having shown further interest in the machine. It was the [buyer]'s responsibility to specify the particular purpose and not merely order the offered standard mixture.

d) The loss of the right to rely on the lack of conformity of the goods would also apply if the non-conformity were based upon the breach of a duty to warn or advise by the seller. It cannot be found here that the non-conformity of the blend asserted by the [buyer] is based upon a [seller]'s breach of a duty to warn or advise. As shown above, the [seller] had no reason to advise or to warn. The mere knowledge of the [buyer]'s intention to use the blend on a used machine is not enough to impose a duty to advise during a purchase of standard mix. This is even more so the case in that the [seller] dealt with the [buyer] who is a producer. It cannot be determined that the [seller] had reason to know that the [buyer] was not at least as technically competent as itself.[7]

e) The exceptional case of a waiver of compliance with the notice provisions is discernibly not at hand here. Such a waiver is possible under the Convention.[8] Within the CISG's sphere of application, special circumstances of the individual case must show an obvious waiver.[9] The [buyer] in the present case did not show such circumstances. Such circumstances are also not to be found in the admitted documents of the parties. It does not constitute a waiver when the seller merely inspects the goods or has conversations with the buyer in order to determine the legitimacy of a notice of defects, or when the seller does not immediately reject a notice as being too late.[10] Such was the case here. [Seller]'s workers were sent to the [buyer] in February and March 1993 in order to determine the legitimacy of the notice of defects. During this time, the [seller] wanted to oblige the [buyer] and help it to get production going. In doing this, the [seller] continuously considered the machine, and not the blend, to be the reason for the failure in production.

---

7. *See id.* at Art. 35 CISG Rn. 35.

8. BGH (Federal Supreme Court), Wertpapier-Mitteilungen (1997) 2313.

9. *See* OLG Karlsrue, Recht der Internationalen Wirtschaft (1998) 235, 237.

10. *See* Staudinger-Magnus, BGB, Art. 39 CISG Rn. 18.

3. The loss of the right to rely on the lack of conformity of the goods leads to a dismissal of the claim since the [buyer] cannot successfully assert any of the Art. 45 CISG remedies.

II. The decision on costs is guided by § 97(1) ZPO [German Code of Civil Procedure]. The decision on the provisional enforceability is based on §§ 708 No. 10, 711 ZPO. The sum in dispute in the appeal and the [buyer]'s request for relief is in the amount of 149,548.73 DM.

Questions

1. Re-read Articles 38 and 39 of the CISG focusing upon time lines for inspection and notice and apply them to the events in this case. Starting with "within as short a time as is practicable under the circumstances" under the facts of this case, when should this time have been found to begin to run? Viewed from the buyer's perspective, is 17 January the correct date? Is 3 February the correct date?

Had this case been tried in Morocco, would the court likely have found that inspection should have occurred in December?

What if these facts were presented to a US judge?

When did the buyer "give notice to the seller specifying the nature of the lack of conformity of the goods"?

Does it matter that the seller's technicians were the people who were testing the goods?

2. Are you satisfied with the process by which the court concluded that the goods complied with the warranty contained in article 35(2)(a)?

What facts caused the court to conclude that 35(2)(b) was not applicable? Since the machine was being delivered contemporaneously with the plastic and was being installed with the assistance of the seller's technicians, what more would be needed to find that the "particular purpose" was "impliedly made known to the seller at the time of the conclusion of the contract"?

3. Under UCC § 2–314 an implied warranty of merchantability is given by a *"seller who is a merchant with respect to goods of that kind."* In our hypothetical transaction for the pelleting machine, is the seller a merchant with respect to pelleting machines?

Under the Ontario Sale of Goods Act § 16(2) "Where goods are bought by description from a *seller who deals in goods of that description* (whether the seller is a manufacturer or not), there is an implied condition that the goods will be of merchantable quality . . .". Is the pelleting machine seller one who deals in goods of that description?

The implied warranty provisions in Article 35 of the CISG apply to all sellers. Advantage buyer?

PROBLEM 1f Obligation of Good Faith

Assuming you have a choice, what rules of good faith would you like to see applied to the contract you are drafting?

Do you want the parties to be held to high standards or not?

Does it matter to you who will be deciding what conduct falls below the standard that the law fixes—a Canadian judge, an American judge, or an arbitrator?

If you have a jury trial, is the question whether a given course of conduct complies with the applicable standard of good faith a jury question?

The CISG has no mention of good faith other than in Article 7. This was a great disappointment for those who hoped to see a detailed imposition of standards of good faith upon participants in international commerce.

One would assume that the CISG drafters were concerned that the subjective nature of the interpretation of "good faith" would not contribute to uniform standards when applied by the judiciary or arbitrators in the different countries of the world. For example, does observance of "reasonable standards of fair dealing" include a duty to offer to renegotiate a contract when changes in world prices have caused the other party's costs to increase? One hears different answers to such questions in different societies.

The UCC provided for a "pure heart and empty head" test in Article 1 by limiting the question to honesty in fact with no external standards to be applied. (§ 1–201(19)) However, in the case of merchants involved in transactions in goods, the standard was honesty plus "observance of reasonable commercial standards of fair dealing in the trade." (§ 2–103(1)(b)) Those states that have adopted the revised version of Article 1 (§ R1–201(19)) now require that all parties comply with a standard of good faith defined as "reasonable commercial standards of fair dealing" in addition to honesty in fact. The phrase "in the trade" is no longer an appropriate qualification as this rule is no longer limited to merchants in its application.

Honesty in fact is a subjective standard that requires a measure of proof as to what was going on in the party's mind. The fact finder must find dishonesty. Observance of reasonable standards of fair dealing permits the fact finder to compare the conduct to an abstract standard of what is fair and reasonable. It is much easier to convince a fact finder that the evidence meets this burden of proof. "I may be unreasonable but I am not dishonest" does not provide a defense.

Ontario Sale of Goods law provides:

§ 1 Things done in good faith

(2) A thing shall be deemed to be done in good faith within the meaning of this Act when it is in fact done honestly whether it is done negligently or not.

There is no apparent reference to observance of reasonable standards of fair dealing—in the trade or otherwise. Unless expanded by judicial interpretation, this is the very minimal standard described above as involving a "pure heart and empty head."

With respect to good faith, which law would you prefer to have applied to your client's transaction and why?

Would your answer change if your client was known to engage in sharp practices on occasion?

Does it matter where and by whom the case would be tried?

PROBLEM 1g   Remedies

SPECIFIC PERFORMANCE

In the event that the seller, NF, breaches, would your client Minn ever want to seek specific performance? Recognize the practical implications of this decision. If any substitute machines are available, it is far better for your client to go buy one of those machines and get on with its business of processing animal feeds. You may decide to seek damages, but it is highly unlikely that Minn would want to do without the machine for an indefinite period of time while seeking to specifically enforce the contract.

There are many other practical reasons why parties do not seek specific performance even in countries such as Germany or France where specific enforcement is the basic legal remedy. This is true in all countries where there is a market economy and goods, even specialized items such as pelleting machines, are fairly readily available. The general attitude is, if the seller will not deliver, then the buyer should buy one elsewhere and worry about the damages later. Thus, in our hypothetical, if the seller fails to perform, the buyer is best advised to find a substitute machine elsewhere. The alternative is to continue to operate without the required machine for the period of time that it will take to obtain and enforce a court order for specific performance. Should the case fail for some reason (case lost in court, seller insolvency, machine disappears or is destroyed, etc.), the buyer suffers. From the seller's perspective, seeking specific performance is even more foolish. To do so, the seller must retain and care for the goods during the pendency of the suit with an ultimate goal of getting a judgment or court order for the purchase price and out of pocket expenses. When the price is finally paid, the seller becomes a reluctant bailee of the buyer's goods. Again, the case could fail for some reason such as the buyer becoming insolvent while the suit is pending, and seller is back at square one with an unsold machine.

The UCC adopts the traditional equity test permitting specific performance where the contracted goods are unique. However, it opens the door for judicial expansion of this remedy by adding the language "or in other proper circumstances" (§ 2–716). From a practitioner's point of view, if the existing factual situation gives one's client a good reason to want specific performance, § 2–716 probably will support the right to obtain that remedy if you present the case well.

Ontario law gives the court apparently broad authority to grant specific enforcement to the buyer. R.S.O. 1990, Chapter S.1 provides:

§ 50 Specific performance

> In an action for breach of contract to deliver specific or ascertained goods, the court may, if it thinks fit, direct that the contract be performed specifically, without giving the defendant the option of retaining the goods on payment of damages, and may impose such terms and conditions as to damages, payment of the price, and otherwise, as to the court seems just.

If property in the goods has already passed to the buyer, then delivery can be compelled under Canadian law by a replevin action or by an order for specific performance.

If the goods are specific and ascertained but property has not yet passed, the court may, if it thinks fit, direct that the contract be specifically performed. It is thus a discretionary remedy to be denied where damages are deemed adequate to fully compensate the buyer. Enforcement was denied in a requirements contract for the sale of coal to a steel mill (*Dominion Coal Co. v. Dominion Iron & Steel Co.* (1909) 1 A.C. 293 (P.C.), but enforcement was granted in a contract for the sale of a ship which had peculiar value to the buyer because he wanted it for immediate use (*Behnke v. Bede Shipping Co.* (1927) 1 K.B. 649. Canadian courts have not always required that the goods possess any unique characteristics. *Fraser v. Sam Kee* (1916) 9 W.W.R 1281 (B.C. Co. Ct.) involved a contract for the sale of potatoes. The seller was enjoined from selling to any other persons and the contract was specifically enforced.

As with UCC § 2–716, Ontario law and other Canadian law related to specific enforcement is sufficiently flexible that if one's client has legitimate need to have this contract enforced, the facts that support that need will be sufficient to justify a court ordering specific performance.

The CISG permits specific enforcement as a basic remedy (Articles 46 and 62), however where the seller has delivered non-conforming goods, the buyer may demand a conforming tender only if the seller's failure was material (Art. 46(2)). In addition, Article 28 contains a special rule which could affect actions brought in common law jurisdictions. This article provides: "a court is not bound to enter a judgement for specific performance unless the court would do so under its own law in respect of similar contracts of sale not governed by this Convention."

In some common law jurisdictions, Article 28 may prevent a party from specifically enforcing a contract for the sale of goods. However, under the current interpretation of Canadian law and of the UCC, if your client has reason to need to specifically enforce a contract for the sale of goods, the law will likely find sufficient reason to grant that remedy. Thus, from a practical perspective, specific performance of a contract for the sale of goods is as readily available in Canada and the US as it is in civil law countries or under the CISG.

GENERAL DAMAGES

Focusing first upon the buyer's remedies under the UCC, the most common remedy is for damages based upon cover purchase. UCC § 2–712 permits recovery of the cost of substitute goods minus the unpaid balance due on the contract. The substitute or cover purchase must be goods bought "in substitution for those due from the seller" and must be made in good faith, without unreasonable delay. This remedy was not generally recognized at common law or under the old American Uniform Sales Act and is one of the more successful innovations of the UCC. The CISG adopted a comparable damage formula in Article 75.

UCC § 2–713 permits recovery of the market price of the goods minus the unpaid balance due on the contract. While at common law this was the basic remedy, the UCC has been interpreted in many states to permit this remedy only where no cover purchase was effected. Liberal procedures are permitted for proof of market price (§ 2–723(2) and (3)) and this relaxed standard for proof of market price is yet another UCC innovation departing from the common law. CISG Article 76 has a comparable damage formula that is expressly made available only where no cover purchase was effected and can be applied only if there is "a current price for the goods."

If the UCC is applicable and FN breaches by refusing to deliver, Minn's most obvious self help would be to find and purchase a substitute machine. If it is a reasonable substitution, then the § 2–712 rules relating to cover purchase should apply and this provides a convenient formula to fix damages. If no such substitute is available, Minn must attempt to rely upon a contract market formula under § 2–713, but the absence of comparable machines in the market place makes finding a "market" price problematic. Section 2–723 is designed to alleviate this problem and buyer's arguments may be bolstered by provisions found in such sections as 1–102(1), 1–103 and particularly 1–106. The CISG provides Minn with similar damages.

Ontario law has no provisions concerning cover purchase that are comparable to the UCC or CISG. The section that permits damages calculated upon market price is limited to situations where there is "an available market" for the goods. This means a market to which one could look to find the current market price for the contracted goods. Because Minn is purchasing a used machine of a rather highly specialized nature, there would be no readily available market.

The Sale of Goods Act falls back on common law damage concepts derived from *Hadley v. Baxendale*, 9 Ex. 341, 156 Eng. Rep. 145 (1854).

Ontario Sale of Goods Act provides:

§ 49 Buyer may maintain action for non-delivery

(1) Where the seller wrongfully neglects or refuses to deliver the goods to the buyer, the buyer may maintain an action against the seller for damages for non-delivery.

Measure of damages

(2) The measure of damages is the estimated loss directly and naturally resulting in the ordinary course of events from the seller's breach of contract.

Difference in price

(3) Where there is an available market for the goods in question, the measure of damages is, in the absence of evidence to the contrary, to be ascertained by the difference between the contract price and the market or current price of the goods at the time or times when they ought to have been delivered, or, if no time was fixed, then at the time of the refusal to deliver.

CONSEQUENTIAL DAMAGES

This could be the major remedy issue for Minn. If Minn's existing equipment is broken or otherwise inoperable and this is interfering with current production and sales, delay in obtaining and installing an operable machine could involve significant damages. Facts relating to this question and the seller's knowledge of such facts will be of significance in any claim for the recovery of those damages.

When applying rules relating to consequential damages for breach of contract, all common law systems are to one degree or another based upon or at least influenced by *Hadley v. Baxendale*, 9 Ex. 341, 156 Eng. Rep. 145 (1854). Whatever the correct holding of this confused and confusing case decided by a nondescript court with at least one judge who should have recused himself having previously represented the defendant, the rule that is drawn from this case today is reasonably clear: Parties to a contract are not liable for damages that they did not have reason to foresee at the time when the contract was made.

The UCC has codified a foreseeability rule applicable to consequential damages in § 2–715(2)(a). The notion that a party was not liable for consequential damages unless it tacitly assumed responsibility for such damages was rejected (See comment 2 to § 2–715.)

CISG Article 74 provides for damages including loss of profit suffered as a consequence of the breach. The second sentence of this article bears repeating as it could be used today in an American hornbook as a statement of the US common law rule or the UCC rule.

It provides:

> Such damages may not exceed the loss which the party in breach foresaw or ought to have foreseen at the time of the conclusion of the contract, in the light of the facts and matters of which he then knew or ought to have known, as a possible consequence of the breach of contract.

Ontario Sale of Goods Act section 49(2) quoted above adopts the "first rule" of the Hadley case relating to damages that "directly and naturally result in the ordinary course of events." There is apparently no provision for consequential damages which fall under the Hadley "second rule" where the defaulting party knew or ought to have known were a possible consequence of the breach. Any recovery of consequentials is thus dependent upon application of common law principles. (See Fridman, Sale of Goods in Canada (5th Ed.),Thomson Canada Limited.)

Chapter 2

INTERPRETING AND SUPPLEMENTING THE CISG

I. COMPARING UCC SECTION 1–103(B) WITH CISG ARTICLE 7

This chapter introduces the basic interpretive methodology to be used when applying the CISG.[1] The discussion begins by showing how the UCC and CISG approach the matter somewhat differently.

Uniform Commercial Code § 1–103(b) provides the general rule that courts must apply when seeking to determine whether the UCC preempts certain common-law claims. Section 1–103(b) provides as follows:

UCC § 1–103

Construction of UCC to Promote its Purposes and Policies; Applicability of Supplemental Principles of Law

* * *

(b) Unless displaced by the particular provisions of [the Uniform Commercial Code], the principles of law and equity, including the law merchant and the law relative to capacity to contract, principal and agent, estoppel, fraud, misrepresentation, duress, coercion, mistake, bankruptcy, and other validating or invalidating cause supplement its provisions.[2]

---

1. For a clear and concise overview of this topic, readers may also wish to explore JOSEPH F. MORRISSEY & JACK M. GRAVES, INTERNATIONAL SALES LAW AND ARBITRATION: PROBLEMS, CASES AND COMMENTARY 51–58 (2008).

2. U.C.C. § 1–103(b) (2001). Section 1–103(b) cannot be read in isolation, but must be considered in connection with § 1–103(a), which provides as follows:

28

CISG Article 7 serves a similar purpose and provides as follows:

CISG Article 7

(1) In the interpretation of this Convention, regard is to be had to its international character and to the need to promote uniformity in its application and the observance of good faith in international trade.

(2) Questions concerning matters governed by this Convention which are not expressly settled in it are to be settled in conformity with the general principles on which it is based or, in the absence of such principles, in conformity with the law applicable by virtue of the rules of private international law.[3]

The "general principles on which [the CISG] is based" are discussed in Part II of this chapter, and the role of private international law is examined in Part V. Insofar as UCC § 1–103(b) is concerned, note the following pertinent language from Official Comment 2:

2. **Applicability of supplemental principles of law.** Subsection (b) states the basic relationship of the Uniform Commercial Code to supplemental bodies of law. The Uniform Commercial Code was drafted against the backdrop of existing bodies of law, including the common law and equity, and relies on those bodies of law to supplement its provisions in many important ways. At the same time, the Uniform Commercial Code is the primary source of commercial law rules in areas that it governs, and its rules represent choices made by its drafters and the enacting legislatures about the appropriate policies to be furthered in the transactions it covers. Therefore, while principles of common law and equity may *supplement* provisions of the Uniform Commercial Code, they may not be used to *supplant* its provisions, or the purposes and policies those provisions reflect, unless a specific provision of the Uniform Commercial Code provides otherwise. In the absence of such a provision, the Uniform Commercial Code preempts principles of common law and equity that are inconsistent with either its provisions or its purposes and policies.

The language of subsection (b) is intended to reflect both the concept of supplementation and the concept of preemption.

(a) [The Uniform Commercial Code] must be liberally construed and applied to promote its underlying purposes and policies, which are: (1) to simplify, clarify, and modernize the law governing commercial transactions; (2) to permit the continued expansion of commercial practices through custom, usage, and agreement of the parties; and (3) to make uniform the law among the various jurisdictions.

U.C.C. § 1–103(a) (2001).

3. United Nations Convention on Contracts for the International Sale of Goods, Article 7 (1980).

Some courts, however, had difficulty in applying the identical language of former Section 1–103 to determine when other law appropriately may be applied to supplement the Uniform Commercial Code, and when that law has been displaced by the Code. Some decisions applied other law in situations in which that application, while not inconsistent with the text of any particular provision of the Uniform Commercial Code, clearly was inconsistent with the underlying purposes and policies reflected in the relevant provisions of the Code. *See, e.g., Sheerbonnet, Ltd. v. American Express Bank, Ltd.*, 951 F. Supp. 403 (S.D.N.Y. 1995). In part, this difficulty arose from Comment 1 to former Section 1–103, which stated that "this section indicates the continued applicability to commercial contracts of all supplemental bodies of law except insofar as they are explicitly displaced by this Act." The "explicitly displaced" language of that Comment did not accurately reflect the proper scope of Uniform Commercial Code preemption, which extends to displacement of other law that is inconsistent with the purposes and policies of the Uniform Commercial Code, as well as with its text.[4]

The CISG does not include an official commentary, unlike the UCC. To assist with interpretation, scholarly literature has addressed how and when supplemental bodies of law are to be used in conjunction with the CISG, and especially to fill gaps in the CISG. This chapter considers only what are called *praeter legem* gaps in the CISG, rather than *intra legem* gaps, which are matters that are not dealt with by the CISG at all. A *praeter legem* gap involves an issue that is within the scope of the CISG, but for which the text does not provide a precise answer. CISG Article 7(2) provides guidance with respect to such gaps. As author Lucia Sica has noted, although the CISG's party-autonomy principle permits parties to specify what body of rules or principles will be used to fill any gaps that remain in their contract after the CISG is applied, parties seldom do so.[5]

The UNIDROIT Principles are a particularly useful resource for interpreting the CISG. Even so, as the following discussion will show, the proper use of the UNIDROIT Principles vis-à-vis the CISG is not always clear.[6] As Professor Klaus Peter Berger has noted, "the Principles are used to interpret or supplement interna-

---

4. U.C.C. § 1–103(b) cmt. 2 (2001).

5. Lucia Carvalhal Sica, *Gap-Filling in the CISG: May the UNIDROIT Principles Supplement the Gaps in the Convention?* (2006), *available at* http://www.cisg.law.pace.edu/cisg/biblio/sica.html.

6. As Peter Schlechtriem and Ingeborg Schwenzer indicate, others have

raised the same questions regarding the principles of European Contract Law (PECL). PETER SCHLECHTRIEM & INGEBORG SCHWENZER, COMMENTARY ON THE UN CONVENTION ON THE INTERNATIONAL SALE OF GOODS (CISG) 109–110 (2d (Eng.) Ed. 2005).

tional uniform law instruments and more particularly the ... CISG."[7] This usage makes sense, in that, as Professor Alejandro Garro has noted, "[t]he rules set forth in the UNIDROIT Principles are self-described as 'general,' not because of their abstract nature, but rather because they cover a broad area of contract law. Unless they are displaced by a rule of law that applies as lex specialis[8] to a particular contract, the UNIDROIT Principles are meant to apply to every kind of international contract."[9] Consistent with Professor Garro's assertion, the Principles' Preamble expressly contemplates that they be used to supplement and international instruments such as the CISG:

> These Principles set forth general rules for international commercial contracts.
>
> They shall be applied when the parties have agreed that their contract be governed by them.
>
> They may be applied when the parties have agreed that their contract be governed by general principles of law, the *lex mercatoria*[10] or the like.
>
> They may be applied when the parties have not chosen any law to govern their contract.
>
> *They may be used to interpret or supplement international uniform law instruments.*
>
> They may be used to interpret or supplement domestic law.
>
> They may serve as a model for national and international legislators.[11]

7. Klaus Peter Berger, *International Arbitral Practice and the UNIDROIT Principles of International Commercial Contracts*, 46 Am. J. Comp. L. 129, 133 (1998). *See also* Magnus, *infra* note 27 (advocating for the UNIDROIT principles to be "considered as additional general principles in the context of the CISG," primarily because "they vastly correspond both to the respective provisions of the CISG as well as to the general provisions which have been derived from the CISG").

8. "A specific rule that overrides a general principle of law. It also refers to a specific law within a more general field of law." H. Victor Condé, A Handbook of International Human Rights Terminology 150 (2d ed. 2004).

9. Alejandro M. Garro, *The Gap-Filling Role of the UNIDROIT Principles in International Sales Law: Some Com-*

ments on the Interplay Between the Principles and the CISG, 69 Tul. L. Rev. 1149, 1152 (1995).

10. Another term for "lex mercatoria" is "law merchant," which is "[a] system of customary law that developed in Europe during the Middle Ages and regulated the dealings of mariners and merchants in all the commercial countries of the world until the 17th century" Black's Law Dictionary 903 (8th ed. 2004). "Many of the law merchant's principles came to be incorporated into the common law, which in turn formed the basis of the Uniform Commercial Code." *Id.*

11. International Institute for the Unification of Private Law, UNIDROIT Principles of International Commercial Contracts, Preamble (2004) (emphasis added).

One reason to use the UNIDROIT Principles to interpret or supplement the CISG is to avoid overuse of domestic law through what is sometimes called a "homeward trend"[12] in the application of the CISG. In the General Introduction to his landmark book, *Documentary History of the Uniform Law for International Sales*, Professor John Honnold explains the "homeward trend" as follows:

> The half century of work that culminated in the 1980 Convention was sustained by the need to free international commerce from a Babel of diverse domestic legal systems. ... [T]he Convention's ultimate goal [is] uniform *application* of the uniform rules.

> The Convention, *faute de mieux*,[13] will often be applied by tribunals (judges or arbitrators) who will be intimately familiar only with their own domestic law. These tribunals, regardless of their merit, will be subject to a natural tendency to read the international rules in light of the legal ideas that have been imbedded at the core of their intellectual formation. The mind sees what the mind has means of seeing.[14]

Professor Honnold goes on to express his hope and expectation that several developments would correct this "homeward trend" over time: (1) "comparative law study [would] include the legal culture of international unification," (2) the CISG's legislative history would "disabuse[its readers] of the view that the statutory language is simply an awkward attempt to restate one's familiar domestic law," and (3) international legislation would continue to develop as its own "science," with its own "distinctive procedures and methods."[15]

Due to their international perspective and pedigree, the UNIDROIT Principles are more likely to be appropriate for the international context than domestic law is.[16] In addition, the practice of applying the Principles instead of domestic law to fill gaps in the CISG tends to promote both consistency and fairness.[17] This ap-

---

12. For an introduction to the problem of homeward trend, *see* JOHN O. HONNOLD, A DOCUMENTARY HISTORY OF THE UNIFORM LAW FOR INTERNATIONAL SALES 1 (1989). *See also* DiMATTEO et al., *infra* note 62, at 174–177 (discussing the persistence of the problem).

13. "Adopted or undertaken for lack of something better." WEBSTER'S THIRD NEW INTERNATIONAL DICTIONARY UNABRIDGED 830 (2002).

14. HONNOLD, *supra* note 12, at 1.

15. *Id.*

16. Garro, *supra* note 9, at 1152–1153 ("The main idea is to preclude an easy resort to the domestic law indicated by the conflict of law rule of the forum, thus keeping the settlement of the dispute within its international legal habitat. Rather than undertake a comparative survey of the law of contracts, the UNIDROIT Principles offer the judge or the arbitrator a rule that is likely to be more suitable to an international commercial contract than a domestic rule of contract law.").

17. *Id.* at 1153–1154 ("Consistency is likely to be advanced every time a judge or arbitrator relies on rules that are consonant with the purposes of in-

proach is also consistent with the notion that the CISG should be interpreted in light of other principles and usages that exist in the international context.[18]

Some of the UNIDROIT Principles are quite specific, while others are very general. Using the more general UNIDROIT Principles to supplement the CISG can be very effective. For example, UNIDROIT Article 7.4.1 is less specific than CISG Article 74, although both address an aggrieved party's right to damages.

UNIDROIT Article 7.4.1

Right to Damages

Any non-performance gives the aggrieved party a right to damages either exclusively or in conjunction with any other remedies except where the non-performance is excused under these Principles.[19]

CISG Article 74

Damages for breach of contract by one party consist of a sum equal to the loss, including loss of profit, suffered by the other party as a consequence of the breach. Such damages may not exceed the loss which the party in breach foresaw or ought to have foreseen at the time of the conclusion of the contract, in the light of the facts and matters of which he then knew or ought to have known, as a possible consequence of the breach of contract.[20]

Thus, UNIDROIT Article 7.4.1 may be useful in interpreting and applying CISG Article 74.[21]

Conflict can arise, however, when the Principles are specific enough to create inconsistencies with the CISG.[22] One example is

ternational trade, rather than filling the gaps left by the CISG with the rules and criteria provided by the domestic law, be it the substantive law of the forum or the one determined by its rules of private international law. Resorting to the UNIDROIT Principles ... also advances fairness, because by avoiding the application of the law of the forum or the law indicated by the forum's conflict rules, the dispute will be settled by rules other than those that are likely to be more accessible or familiar to one party than the other."). *See also* Mather, *infra* note 45, at 187 ("If the UNIDROIT Principles contain a relevant rule, that rule should be preferred. The UNIDROIT rules are easy to find, and their applica-

tion will reduce legal research costs and enhance predictability of outcomes.").

18. Garro, *supra* note 9, at 1189. At the same time, it is important to remember that the UNIDROIT Principles are not limited to transactions that implicate the CISG. *Id.*

19. *See supra* note 11, Article 7.4.1.

20. *See supra* note 3, Article 74.

21. Sieg Eiselen, *Remarks on the Manner in which the UNIDROIT Principles of International Commercial Contracts May be Used to Interpret or Supplement CISG Article 74, in* Review of the Convention on Contracts for the International Sale of Goods (CISG) 2002–2003 93, 94 (2004).

22. Sica, *supra* note 5.

the Principles' treatment of interest which, as discussed in Chapter 4, is considerably more precise than the CISG's rules governing the same subject. Even so, some sources have claimed that it would be appropriate to use the UNIDROIT Principles to give specificity to the CISG's treatment of interest, although most commentators would counsel otherwise.[23]

Questions

1. In your own words, what was the problem with the language of former Comment 1 to UCC § 1–103?

2. Does the CISG apply only when it displaces other law?[24]

3. Does CISG Article 7 reflect the same dichotomy between supplementation and supplantation as UCC § 1–103 Comment 2?

4. To what development in the interpretation of the UCC does § 1–103 Comment 2 allude?

5. According to the UNIDROIT Principles' Preamble, for what audience or audiences were the Principles drafted? How do you know?

PROBLEM 1

Both UNIDROIT Article 1.9, which appears below, and CISG Article 9, which can be found on page 55, address usages and practices. The language of each is similar, but not identical. Is it appropriate to interpret CISG Article 9 as implicitly incorporating UNIDROIT Article 1.9's exception for an "unreasonable" application of a usage or practice? Why or why not?

UNIDROIT Article 1.9

Usages and Practices

(1) The parties are bound by any usage to which they have agreed and by any practices which they have established between themselves.

(2) The parties are bound by a usage that is widely known to and regularly observed in international trade by parties in the particular trade concerned except where the application of such a usage would be unreasonable.[25]

---

23. *See, e.g.,* Garro, *supra* note 9, at 1156–1157.

24. *See supra* pages 29–32.

25. *See supra* note 11, Article 1.9.

II. USING GENERAL PRINCIPLES TO DETERMINE HOW (OR WHETHER) THE CISG ADDRESSES AN ISSUE

CISG Article 7(2)'s reference to "the general principles on which [the CISG] is based" raises an important issue: How is one to discern what these "general principles" are? With this question in mind, consider the following excerpt from Professor Ulrich Magnus' article, *General Principles of UN–Sales Law*.

General principles can regularly be derived from the CISG— and other Uniform Law Conventions—in four ways: First, some provisions explicitly claim their applicability to the entire Convention, for example in CISG Art. 6 (principle of party autonomy), Art. 7(1) (principle of good faith) or Art. 11 (principle of lack of form requirements). Their character as a general provision results both from their wording and their position in the Convention's system. In the CISG, they are incorporated in the part "General Provisions." Strictly speaking, they might not be included in the general principles contemplated by Art. 7(2) CISG, since they expressly indicate their general applicability and thus do not constitute principles "hidden in the law [...] without having been directly expressed." However, due to their fundamental importance, which occasionally goes beyond their wording, it appears justified to regard them as part of the Convention's general principles.

Further, a separate comprehensive thought can be derived from several provisions. For example, Art. 67(2) and 69(2) CISG provide that passing of risk requires identification of the goods to the respective contract. This rule can be extended to those cases in which the question—as in Art. 68—is not expressly regulated.

In addition, single provisions might include legal thoughts which are subject to generalization and are to be applied in similar situations. Art. 20(2) CISG can serve as an example. According to this provision, holidays generally do not extend the period for making a declaration, except if the respective notice could not be delivered due to the holiday. This thought can be generalized to the effect that holidays are included in all time limits (e.g., also for delivery), except if the respective action (e.g., delivery) could not have been taken due to the holiday. In this case the time limit is extended accordingly.

Finally, the overall context can show that a certain basic rule is implicitly assumed. An example in the CISG is the rule "pacta sunt servanda."[26] The sentence is not expressed anywhere, but apparently constitutes the basis for the exemption provision of

---

26. "The rule that agreements and stipulations, especially those contained in treaties, must always be kept." BLACK'S LAW DICTIONARY 1140 (8th ed. 2004).

Art. 79 which determines the cases in which an obligor is discharged from his obligation.[27]

In addition to identifying the origins of various CISG general principles, it is useful to categorize them by what they do. Professor Robert Hillman has identified four major categories of general principles: "One set of principles ensures the enforcement of the parties' intentions. Another set helps the parties to realize the fruits of their exchange by avoiding disputes. A third group of principles works to 'keep the deal together' even after a problem surfaces. The final set of principles seeks to make aggrieved parties whole when an agreement ultimately breaks down."[28]

Consistent with the earlier discussion regarding the appropriate use of the UNIDROIT Principles, some scholars have suggested that the Principles are among the "general principles" on which the CISG is based. This approach, while not universally accepted, is popular.[29] As Professor Alejandro Garro states, "[a]s long as the UNIDROIT Principles provide a solution to issues that may conceivably fall under the scope of application of the CISG, they should be used to supplement all questions regarding the formation, interpretation, content, performance, and termination of contracts for the international sale of goods. This suggestion, of course, assumes that the parties have not chosen any other supplementing source of law, and that the application of the UNIDROIT Principles is not otherwise in conflict with mandatory rules of law, the intention of the parties, and applicable trade usages."[30]

Now that these materials have discussed several means by which general principles may be discerned, it is important to examine how they might be applied. The following case, which may be referred to as the "Gran Canaria Tomatoes" case, was decided by the Netherlands' Hoge Raad Tribunal on January 28, 2005, and shows how a tribunal's application of general principles may affect the outcome of the case. Like many CISG cases from other jurisdictions, only an abstract is available in English, because the original opinion was delivered in Dutch. The following is the official abstract as provided on the UNILEX database.[31]

27. Ulrich Magnus, *General Principles of UN–Sales Law* (1995), *available at* http://cisg.law.pace.edu/cisg/text.magnus.html.

28. Hillman, *infra* note 51.

29. *See* Bruno Zeller, Damages Under the Convention on Contracts for the International Sale of Goods 219–221 (2d ed. 2009) (noting the various viewpoints on this usage of the Principles and citing, among other reasons to support this practice, the common parentage of the CISG and UNIDROIT Principles).

30. Garro, *supra* note 9, at 1157.

31. "UNILEX is based on a research project started in 1992 by the Centre for Comparative and Foreign Law Studies— a joint venture of the Italian National Research Council, the University of Rome I 'La Sapienza,' and the International Institute for the Unification of Private Law (UNIDROIT). The project has been financed by the Italian Nation-

A Dutch seller and a Belgian buyer concluded a contract for the delivery of tomato plants. The buyer received and signed an order form referring on the front side to the application of the seller's standard terms which were printed on the back. Among other clauses, the standard terms contained a limitation of the seller's liability in case of non-conformity of the plants, according to which the seller would be liable only if it had been grossly negligent in ignoring the lack of conformity, and anyway only up to a sum corresponding to the price. After receipt of the order form, the seller confirmed the order, again referring to the application of its standard terms printed on the back. The contract was concluded on the basis of the buyer's order and the confirmation of the order by the seller. The plants were delivered and the price paid. An expert examination conducted the following year on the grown tomato plants in Belgium ascertained that a part of them was affected by a disease which infected other plants. The buyer asked the seller for damages and the seller brought an action to obtain a judicial declaration against such a claim. The first instance courts denied any liability of the seller and the buyer appealed.

The Supreme Court confirmed the first instance rulings that the contract was governed by CISG and that the inclusion of the standard terms in the contract was a matter governed but not expressly settled by the Convention (Arts. 4 and 8 CISG), to be settled first of all by recourse to the general principles underlying the Convention (Art. 7(2) CISG). The Court held that the seller's standard terms, including the exoneration clause, had become part of the contract, thereby implicitly applying the general rules on formation of contract and interpretation of parties' statements under CISG and therefore denying recourse to the relevant conflict of law rules (1980 Rome Convention). As a result the Court confirmed that under the circumstances of the case there was no evidence of gross negligence on the part of the seller and therefore rejected the buyer's claim for damages for lack of conformity of the plants.[32]

Questions

1. How would you describe in your own words the role of the CISG's "general principles"?

2. How might you describe in your own words each of the four sources of general principles that Professor Magnus identifies?

al Research Council." http://www.unilex. info/dynasite.cfm?dsmid=13087.

32. From the UNILEX main menu, select "CISG," then select "Cases by

Date," then select "2005." The abstract for this case is hyperlinked by date "28.01.2005" and court "Hoge Raad."

Should some sources be deemed more important or more reliable than others? Why or why not?

3. Professor Magnus has identified 26 general principles of the CISG, including the following:

    a. "[T]he parties' agreements prevail over the provisions of the CISG."[33]

    b. "[A] party who has created a situation of reliance, upon which the other party has acted, has to bear the consequences of such situation."[34]

    c. The parties are obligated "to avoid damages to the other party as far as reasonable."[35]

    How would you characterize each of these principles, by applying the categories Professor Hillman has suggested?

4. How did the tribunal in the "Gran Canaria Tomatoes" case apply CISG general principles, and what effect did this decision have on the outcome of the case?

PROBLEM 2

Professor Magnus has asserted that "concurrent performance" is a general principle of the CISG.[36] If true, this would mean that, as under UCC Article 2, the buyer and seller must stand ready to perform under the contract concurrently, rather than the buyer being required to tender payment in advance of the seller's delivery of conforming goods, or vice versa. The parties, of course, could agree otherwise under the CISG, just as they could under the UCC. Consider the following CISG provisions:

CISG Article 58

(1) If the buyer is not bound to pay the price at any other specific time, he must pay it when the seller places either the goods or documents controlling their disposition at the buyer's disposal in accordance with the contract and this Convention. The seller may make such payment a condition for handing over the goods or documents.

(2) If the contract involves carriage of the goods, the seller may dispatch the goods on terms whereby the goods, or documents controlling their disposition, will not be handed over to the buyer except against payment of the price.

(3) The buyer is not bound to pay the price until he has had an opportunity to examine the goods, unless the procedures for

---

33. Magnus, *supra* note 27.   **35.** *Id.*

34. *Id.*   **36.** *Id.*

delivery or payment agreed upon by the parties are inconsistent with his having such an opportunity.[37]

CISG Article 81

(1) Avoidance of the contract releases both parties from their obligations under it, subject to any damages which may be due. Avoidance does not affect any provision of the contract for the settlement of disputes or any other provision of the contract governing the rights and obligations of the parties consequent upon the avoidance of the contract.

(2) A party who has performed the contract either wholly or in part may claim restitution from the other party of whatever the first party has supplied or paid under the contract. If both parties are bound to make restitution, they must do so concurrently.[38]

How could you use these provisions to argue that "concurrent performance" is a general principle of the CISG? Using Professor Hillman's classifications,[39] what kind of principle would this be? Using Professor Magnus'[40] list of methods for discerning CISG general principles, what technique did you use?

PROBLEM 3

Building on the general principle of "concurrent performance" as discussed in Problem 2, consider the following CISG provision:

CISG Article 52

(1) If the seller delivers the goods before the date fixed, the buyer may take delivery or refuse to take delivery.

(2) If the seller delivers a quantity of goods greater than that provided for in the contract, the buyer may take delivery or refuse to take delivery of the excess quantity. If the buyer takes delivery of all or part of the excess quantity, he must pay for it at the contract rate.[41]

How might the principle of "concurrent performance" be applied if a seller delivered goods before the date fixed by contract or delivered a larger quantity of goods than specified in the contract?

---

37. *See supra* note 3, Article 58.

38. *See supra* note 3, Article 81.

39. *See supra* text accompanying note 28.

40. *See supra* text accompanying note 27.

41. *See supra* note 3, Article 52.

III. INTERPRETING THE CISG AS A "TRUE CODE" AND CONSISTENT WITH ITS INTERNATIONAL CHARACTER

As the prior discussion has suggested, the first task in applying CISG Article 7(2) is to determine whether the CISG contains a provision expressly addressing the question at hand. If not, the second step is to see whether a "general principle" may be discerned to address the matter. Only once the first two steps have been taken is a party to consider the application of "private international law," as described in Part V later in this chapter.

The extent to which the CISG should be considered a comprehensive code is seriously debated in the scholarly literature. On the one hand are those who contend the comprehensive nature of the CISG is overplayed and that the Code drafters purposefully left a fair amount of room for domestic law.[42] As Professor Franco Ferrari has pointed out, "the CISG neither governs all international sales transactions nor, despite some statements to the contrary in case law, does it deal with all issues that may arise in connection with these transactions."[43] One scholar calls this an "eclectic" approach, to distinguish it from a model in which the CISG would "claim a monopoly over international sales law."[44] Others claim that a fair and appropriately generous reading of the CISG would leave little room for application of domestic law.[45] As Peter Winship has acknowledged, an expansive reading of the CISG may come more naturally to an attorney who has been trained in the civil law tradition than one accustomed to applying the common law.[46] This

42. *See, e.g.,* Steven Walt, *The CISG's Expansion Bias: A Comment on Franco Ferrari,* 25 INT'L REV. L. & ECON. 342, 343 (2005) ("[T]he CISG does not have the systematic and comprehensive character of a civil code."). Walt's article goes on to provide a catalog of circumstances in which the CISG does not control an international sale of goods transaction.

43. Franco Ferrari, *What Sources of Law for Contracts for the International Sale of Goods? Why One Has to Look Beyond the CISG,* 25 INT'L REV. L. & ECON. 314, 315 (2005).

44. Filip de Ly, *Sources of International Sales Law: An Eclectic Model,* 25 J.L. & COM. 1, 3 (2005).

45. Henry Mather, *Choice of Law for International Sales Issues Not Resolved by the CISG,* 20 J.L. & COM. 155, 158 (2001) ("In light of the broad and pregnant principles [found in the CISG], most interstitial gaps in the CISG can be filled by using general principles.... Only rarely should tribunals have to use choice of law and apply rules external to

the CISG regime in order to fill CISG gaps.").

46. Winship, *infra* note 76, at 529. *See also* INTERNATIONAL SALES: THE UNITED NATIONS CONVENTION ON CONTRACTS FOR THE INTERNATIONAL SALE OF GOODS 2-10–2-12 (Nina M. Galson & Hans Smit eds. 1984) ("Common law tribunals find more gaps than civil law judges who are accustomed to the traditions of systematic codification."). To respond to the common misconception that civil-law courts interpret codes wholly without consulting cases, it may be useful to add a brief examination of this point. Joseph Lookofsky describes how civil-law courts use case law as follows:

[T]he case law conception is no longer strictly confined to Common law systems. For although judges in jurisdictions like Denmark, France, and Germany are not formally required to follow the decisions of higher (Danish, French, and German) courts, the Scandinavian or Civilian judge who "distinguishes" herself as a maverick, ignorant or disrespectful of relevant

is because, as Winship states, "[a] literal reading of the text will find many matters not *expressly* stated."[47] Even so, as he continues, "[i]f the reader is generous in his approach to the convention text there should be little need to consult conflicts rules and then prove the applicable law—especially as the reader is also under the injunction in Article 7(1) to promote uniformity in interpretation."[48]

A lawyer applying the CISG should expect to rely more on the treaty's own text than on any external sources, including cases interpreting the text. This requires a "true code" methodology that "limits the interpreter to the text of the Convention itself, considering that the legal document is comprehensive enough."[49] The concept of a "true code" is associated with Grant Gilmore, who defined a code as "a legislative enactment which entirely preempts the field and which is assumed to carry within the answers to all possible questions: thus when a court comes to a gap or an unforeseen situation, its duty is to find, by extrapolation and analogy, a solution consistent with the policy of the codifying law."[50] Stated another way, "There are no gaps in a 'true code' because principles and policies supply answers when the text gives out."[51] The UCC, by contrast, while described by some scholars as a "true code,"[52] incorporates aspects of both a "true code" and a "meta code"[53] methodology, through which courts may consider legal principles that are external to the code.[54] Consistent with a "true code" methodology, then, courts applying the CISG should consider domestic law only as a last resort, when no CISG principles apply.[55]

---

precedents, can hardly expect promotion to any higher court bench. For this and other reasons, judges in all national systems tend to follow the decisions of their superior courts, thus indicating broad-based support for the basic *stare decisis* idea.

Lookofsky, *infra* note 57, at 184–185.

47. Winship, *infra* note 76, at 520 (emphasis in original).

48. *Id.*

49. Sica, *supra* note 5.

50. Grant Gilmore, *Legal Realism: Its Cause and Cure*, 70 YALE L.J. 1037, 1043 (1961), *cited in* Sica, *supra* note 5.

51. Robert Hillman, *Applying the United Nations Convention on Contracts for the International Sale of Goods: The Elusive Goal of Uniformity* (1995), *available at* http://www.cisg.law.pace.edu/cisg/biblio/hillman1.html.

52. As Professor Fred Miller has explained, the UCC is to be seen as "the

general commercial law, to be supplemented by other statutory and common law rules." 1 HAWKLAND UCC SERIES § 1–103:5 [Rev]. As proof, he cites UCC § 1–103(b) as "the preempting provision making the Code superior to the principles of law and equity which it has displaced," and § 1–104's description of the Code as "a general act intended as unified coverage of its subject matter." *Id.*

53. Adapting language from Professor William Young, a "meta code" approach "responds to the necessities of the code in question but [is] not dictated by it." William Young, *Book Review*, 66 COLUM. L. REV. 1571, 1576 (1966) (reviewing GRANT GILMORE, SECURITY INTERESTS IN PERSONAL PROPERTY (1965).

54. Sica, *supra* note 5; Hillman, *supra* note 51 ("Although the UCC is considered by many to be successful, its record is a disappointment if measured by the extent to which courts treat it as a 'true code' and by the degree of uniformity achieved.").

To determine whether a gap in the CISG exists, such that it is appropriate to consider domestic law, one must examine how both domestic and foreign tribunals have interpreted the CISG. Joseph Lookofsky and Harry Flechtner suggest that the following factors should be considered in determining the level of deference to be given to a foreign CISG decision:

1) "The stature of the tribunal rendering the decision."

2) "The extent to which the decision is in accord with other decisions."

3) "[T]he persuasive force of the reasoning in the decision—in particular, the extent to which the decision itself comports with the mandate of CISG Article 7(1) to have regard for the international character of the Convention and the need to promote uniformity in its application and the observance of good faith in international trade."

4) "[T]he apparent soundness of the result of the decision."[56]

These factors are particularly useful because, although scholars seem to agree that Article 7(1)'s requirement that "regard ... be had to [the CISG's] international character and ... the need to promote uniformity in its application" requires consideration of foreign case law, the CISG provides no guidance regarding how foreign case law is to be used. For this reason, as Joseph Lookofsky notes, "those who seek to clarify the meaning of other Convention provisions by resort to foreign case law need to deal with a peculiarly slippery CISG source: 'a process or methodology involving awareness of and respect for, but not necessarily blind obedience to, interpretations of the CISG from outside one's own legal culture.' "[57]

At the same time, practical problems with language and availability make it difficult for an attorney to use decisions from foreign tribunals in some instances.[58] Although the UNILEX and Pace Law School Institute of International Commercial Law online databases provide information about a large number of cases, sometimes only the abstracts are available in English. In addition, even those decisions that are translated into English are sometimes awkwardly phrased and thus difficult to apply. Even if it were easier and more convenient to examine the CISG decisions of other tribunals, Robert Hillman has suggested that focusing too much on

55. Hillman, *supra* note 51.

56. Lookofsky & Flechtner, *infra* note 65, at 201.

57. Joseph Lookofsky, *Digesting CISG Case Law: How Much Regard*

Should We Have?, 8 VIND. J. INT'L COM. L. & ARB. 181, 184 (2004).

58. Ferrari, *infra* note 63, at 254.

case law would tend to downplay the "true code" nature of the CISG.[59]

Questions

1. What is a "true code," in your own words? Based on what you have read, do you believe the CISG is a true code? Why or why not? What about the UCC?

2. How would you describe in your own words how common-law courts and civil-law courts use cases differently from one another?

3. Based on what you have read, how would you describe the appropriate weight to be given CISG case law, as compared with case law interpreting the UCC?

PROBLEM 4

Whether the UCC is a "true code" is an open question. Assuming for the purposes of this problem that it is, this fact would affect how US courts apply the UCC. Compare and contrast Professor Miller's guidance on this point with respect to the UCC, as set forth below, with what you have learned in this section about how the CISG is to be interpreted.

> Because the Uniform Commercial Code is a true code and states its own aims, courts construing it should make three changes in their standard legal method. They should: (1) use analogy rather than "outside" law to fill Code gaps; (2) rely somewhat more heavily on the decisions of other Code states in making their own decisions; and (3) give their own decisions somewhat less permanent precedential value.[60]
>
> * * *
>
> Whether resort should be made to the common law or the decision hammered out under the Code through the use of analogy or extrapolation seemed to depend on three factors in most cases under former § 1–103.
>
> The first factor was the extent to which Code rules must be extrapolated to cover the issue. If the matter at hand clearly fell within the scope of a particular Code article, but was seemingly not covered by a particular rule, generally speaking the courts would use Code rules to resolve the matter, if they could do so without excessively extending or projecting them to

---

59. Hillman, *supra* note 51 ("I fear that the current clamor for compiling cases helps create the impression that case law is the primary source of international sales law and that the Convention's principles are inadequate.").

60. 1 Hawkland UCC Series § 1–103:6 [Rev]. Sections 1–103:7 [Rev] and 1–103:8 [Rev] go on to explain these recommendations more fully.

cover that matter. The degree to which they were willing to extend or project stated rules to get coverage depended to a considerable extent upon how thoroughly the common law covered the same issue and upon the strength of the competing common law or extraneous statutory policy as compared to the Code policy. This factor should still be relevant even under the different balancing mandated by current § 1–103.

The second factor was the extent to which the common law covered the issue. While many aspects of commercial law have been thoroughly developed at common law, the absence of such development would usually result in decisions by courts to stay inside the Code, even when a rather substantial extrapolation was necessary to bring Code rules into force. In a sense, the courts had no other place to go but the Code. If, on the other hand, the common law on the point is extensively developed and no Code rule covering it was readily identifiable or could be reached through a modest extension of a stated rule, the courts would usually resort to the outside law and justify this reference by former § 1–103. This latter observation should be less influential under current 1–103, at least to the extent a relevant Code purpose or policy can be identified.

The third factor was the strength of the competing common law or statutory policy as compared to the Code policy. When the common law, to which resort would be made in the absence of Code coverage, reflected a particularly strong social policy, some courts had a tendency to use that policy by making the outside law the basis for their decision, even though applicable Code rules were readily identifiable. This result could be accomplished by reading the common law into the Code, that is to say, by finding that the Code rule was simply a declaration of the common law. When the common law policy differed from that of the UCC, this technique involved an unwarranted abandonment of newly stated legislative policy in favor of a policy which had been discredited and discarded by the legislature. Correctly, therefore, most courts did not employ this manipulation, even when their real preference on the particular point was the common law and not the Code, and this observation will have much greater relevance under current § 1–103. If, however, the common law reflects a strong social policy and no Code rule on the question is readily apparent, courts, justifying their action by reference to former § 1–103, were disinclined to extend the Code at all to gain coverage and instead quickly turned to the common law for decision, and this is unlikely to significantly change under current § 1–103.[61]

61. *Id.* at § 1–103:12 [Rev] (internal
citations omitted).

IV. INTERPRETING THE CISG AS AN INTERNATIONAL INSTRUMENT: AVOIDING HOMEWARD TREND

As the foregoing discussion suggests, interpreting the CISG requires careful attention to its international character.[62] It is not appropriate to read its text through the lens of domestic law by applying domestic meaning to a term that is also used in the CISG, or even using domestic interpretive techniques.[63] In the following excerpt from his article *The Relationship Between the UCC and the CISG and the Construction of Uniform Law*, Professor Franco Ferrari explains the problems with such an approach:

> Even if the CISG's text were identical to that of UCC Article 2, CISG and UCC concepts could not be considered the same—unless interpreters from the other contracting states would reciprocate. One should not see similarities where there are necessarily significant differences.
>
> It might be helpful to illustrate the issue with a practical example. Various legal writers have argued that the CISG concept of trade usages corresponds to—or at least resembles—the UCC's. This view might gain support from the fact that both the CISG and the UCC (a) depart from the requirement that in order to be relevant the usage be obligatory; (b) require a subjective standard to be met; (c) consider only usages of the particular trade the parties are involved in; and (d) set forth the rule, either expressly or implicitly, that express terms control contrary trade usages.
>
> Nevertheless, the concepts cannot be analogized to each other for several reasons. First, the CISG considers relevant only those usages of trade which "in international trade [are] widely known" to the parties. This precludes the applicability of all domestic as well as local usages, except those which are known as rules also governing international trade. Second, unlike the UCC concept of "relevant" trade usages, the CISG concept is not limited by the parol evidence rule which, as many legal writers and a recent court decision have pointed out, has been rejected by the CISG. Third—and for purposes of this [discussion] most importantly—the views on trade usages and their importance differ from system to system. This is a fact which

---

62. For a discussion of what it means to interpret the CISG as an international convention rather than uniform or model law, *see* LARRY A. DiMATTEO ET AL., INTERNATIONAL SALES LAW: A CRITICAL ANALYSIS OF CISG JURISPRUDENCE 8–10 (2005).

63. Franco Ferrari, *CISG Case Law: A New Challenge for Interpreters?*, 17 J.L. & COM. 245, 246, 248 (1998).

the US interpreter must, because of Article 7(1), take into account when construing the CISG concept of trade usages, and which ultimately makes it impossible for the CISG's concept to correspond to the UCC's.

In former socialist countries, for instance, even though trade usages play a certain role, they have only limited application. Indeed, they are considered the source of unforeseeable court decisions and uncertainty in law, consequences which contrast with the requirements of a planned economy. Trade usages do not play an important role in developing countries either, at least in terms of international relations, due to the conviction that they originated mainly in the industrialized world and therefore reflect mainly the interests of developed countries.

Under Article 7(1) and in interpreting the CISG concept of trade usages—as any other concept—Americans must acknowledge these diverging views which consistently differ from their own. Therefore, it is simply wrong to state that the concepts of trade usages under the CISG and the UCC are similar in content.[64]

Because it is impermissible to construe a CISG provision as if it were analogous to a domestic law provision that seems similar, it is more appropriate to assume the term as used domestically is wholly separate from the term as used in the CISG. With this in mind, consider the following excerpt from *Raw Materials, Inc. v. Manfred Forberich, GmbH*, a case that Joseph Lookofsky and Harry Flechtner have suggested may be the "Worst CISG Decision to Date" for the way in which it impermissibly uses domestic law to interpret and apply the CISG.[65]

RAW MATERIALS, INC. V. MANFRED FORBERICH, GmbH

United States District Court for the Northern District of Illinois (2004)
2004 WL 1535839

FILIP, J.

Plaintiff Raw Materials, Inc., an Illinois corporation that deals in used railroad rail, has brought suit against Defendant Manfred Forberich GMBH & Co., KG, a German limited partnership that sells such rail, alleging breach of contract and fraud relating to Defendant's undisputed failure to meet its contractual obligation to

64. Franco Ferrari, *The Relationship Between the UCC and the CISG and the Construction of Uniform Law*, 29 Loy. L. Rev. 1021, 1028–1031 (1996).

65. *See generally* Joseph Lookofsky & Harry Flechtner, *Nominating* Manfred Forberich: *The Worst CISG Decision in 25 Years?*, 9 Vind. J. Int'l Com. L. & Arb. 199 (2005).

deliver 15,000–18,000 metric tons of used railroad rail to Plaintiff. Plaintiff has moved for summary judgment on its breach of contract claim. Defendant has defended on *force majeure*[66] grounds. For the reasons stated below, Plaintiff's motion is denied.

RELEVANT FACTS

RMI is located in Chicago Heights, Illinois. Its primary business is purchasing, processing, and selling used railroad rail which is eventually reheated and rerolled into new products, such as fence posts or sign posts. Forberich is located in Germany and is in the business of selling used railroad rail. Forberich generally obtains its rail from the former Soviet Union.

On February 7, 2002, RMI entered into a written contract with Forberich in which Forberich agreed to supply RMI with 15,000–18,000 metric tons of used Russian rail. The rail was to be shipped from the port in St. Petersburg, Russia. It takes approximately three to four weeks for ships loaded with rail to travel from St. Petersburg, Russia to the United States. The contract provides for "Delivery by: 6–30–2002," "F.O.B.[67] Delivered Our Plant, Chicago Heights, IL," and "Shipping Instructions: RMI, INC. c/c Chicago Heights Steel, Chicago Heights, IL 60411."

The parties agree that in June 2002, Forberich sought an extension of its time for performance under the contract. However, the circumstances surrounding the extension request are disputed. Forberich maintains that, pursuant to its normal practice, it had "earmarked" a particular supplier, Imperio Trading, to provide it with rails that it would use to fulfill its contract with RMI. In late June 2002, Imperio defaulted on its contractual obligation to provide rail to Forberich. Forberich claims that it requested an extension from RMI because of this breach. RMI disputes that Forberich intended to use rail from Imperio to fulfill Forberich's contract with RMI. RMI also asserts, without citing any record evidence, that Forberich's request for an extension was based on a false representation that Forberich was unable to obtain a supply of rail from any source sufficient to meet its obligations to RMI by June 30, 2002.

Whatever the reasons Forberich may have given in seeking its extension, the parties do not dispute that RMI agreed (apparently in a telephone conversation between Mr. Forberich and RMI Vice President Ron Owczarzak), to extend in some manner the time for Forberich to perform the contract. However, the parties dispute the

---

66. Editor's Note: "An event or effect that can be neither anticipated nor controlled." BLACK'S LAW DICTIONARY 673 (8th ed. 2004).

67. Editor's Note: F.O.B. stands for "Free on Board," which means "[t]he seller's delivery is complete (and the risk of loss passes to the buyer) when the goods pass the transporter's rail. The buyer is responsible for all costs of carriage." *Id.* at 690.

terms of the extension. RMI contends that it agreed to extend the delivery date (meaning delivery at RMI's place of business) to a date "later in the calendar year," but that the delivery date was never fixed due to Forberich's failure to attend a planned meeting in Chicago to discuss the extension. For purposes of its motion for summary judgment, "RMI has assumed that had Forberich delivered the contracted goods to RMI's plant by December 31, 2002, the Contract would have been satisfied." Mr. Owczarzak testified that he "would have been satisfied had the 15,000 to 18,000 tons, metric tons of rail, been delivered to a port in the United States as of December 31st, 2002," and that he conveyed this to Mr. Forberich, though he did not specify when or how (orally or by letter). Mr. Forberich's declaration states that he understood that Forberich "had until December 31, 2002, to load the rails and execute the bill of lading to be in compliance with the contract."

Although it is undisputed that Forberich "has never delivered the contracted goods to RMI," the question of whether Forberich was required to deliver the rails to RMI's place of business by December 31, 2002, or merely was obligated to load the rails on a ship by that date is nevertheless significant because it bears on the viability of Forberich's contention that its failure to perform should be excused. Forberich asserts that its failure to perform should be excused because it was prevented from shipping the rail by the fact that the St. Petersburg port unexpectedly froze over on approximately December 1, 2002. According to RMI, on the other hand, the port did not freeze over until mid-December 2002, and, since it takes 3–4 weeks for a ship carrying rail to travel from St. Petersburg to the United States, Forberich would have had to have shipped out the rail before the port froze in order for the shipment to arrive by the December 31, 2002, deadline. Thus, RMI contends that Forberich's failure to perform under the contract could not have been due to the freezing of the port.[5] In other words, according to RMI, regardless of whether the port froze in mid-December 2002, Forberich would have breached the contract in any event because it did not load its ships early enough so that they would arrive by the December 31, 2002, deadline. If, however, Forberich was merely required to load the rail by December 31, 2002, then the freezing over of the port could have prevented Forberich from shipping the rail regardless of whether the port froze on December 1 or in mid-December.

The parties do not dispute that, in a typical winter, the St. Petersburg port does not freeze over until late January, and such

---

5. RMI asserts that Forberich chose not to ship the rail to RMI so that Forberich could, by subsequently entering into more lucrative contracts with other purchasers, take advantage of a rise in rail prices that occurred after RMI and Forberich entered their contract.

freezing does not prevent the vessels from entering and exiting the port. Mr. Forberich testified that ice breakers are normally used to allow for shipping. He further testified that the winter of 2002 was the worst winter in St. Petersburg in almost sixty years and that ice interfered with shipping at the end of November and that even the ice breakers were stuck in the ice. He also testified that these were "unexpected weather conditions." In relation to issues concerning the freezing of the port, Forberich also submitted the declaration of Mikahil Nikolaev, who works at the St. Petersburg port. Mr. Nikolaev's declaration essentially states the same facts that Mr. Forberich testified to regarding the freezing of the port, except that the declaration states that the port was frozen over on December 1, 2002, that such early freezing had not occurred since 1955, and contains the conclusion that no one could have predicted the early freezing of the port. Without citation to the record, RMI's counsel states in RMI's brief in support of summary judgment that "it hardly could come as a surprise to any experienced shipping merchant (or any grammar school geography student) that the port in St. Petersburg might become icy and frozen in the Russian winter months." One of Forberich's ships left the St. Petersburg port on approximately November 20, 2002. No evidence has been presented that any ships left the St. Petersburg port until months after November 20, 2002. On January 10, 2003, Mr. Forberich sent Mr. Owczarzak a letter stating that Forberich could not ship the rails because "[s]ince the last 3 weeks the port is as well as frozen and nothing is possible."

* * *

DISCUSSION

As set forth above, it is undisputed that Forberich was contractually obligated to ship 15,000 to 18,000 metric tons of rail to RMI and that it failed to do so. Thus, Forberich's ability to avoid summary judgment is dependant on whether it has presented sufficient evidence to support its affirmative defense of *force majeure* based on the theory that it was prevented from performing by the freezing over of the St. Petersburg port.[8] For the reasons explained below, the Court denies Plaintiff's motion for summary judgment.

A. Applicable Law

The parties agree that their contract is governed by the Convention on Contracts for the International Sale of Goods. Although the

---

8. In its memorandum in support of its motion for summary judgment, RMI appears to anticipate that Forberich would base its *force majeure* defense on the default of Forberich's supplier, Imperio. However, Forberich has not made such a contention.

contract does not contain an express *force majeure* provision, the CISG provides that:

> A party is not liable for failure to perform any of his obligations if he proves that failure was due to an impediment beyond his control and that he could not reasonably be expected to have taken the impediment into account at the time of the conclusion of the contract or to have avoided or overcome its consequences.

CISG Art. 79. RMI asserts that, "[w]hile no American court has specifically interpreted or applied Article 79 of the CISG, case law interpreting the Uniform Commercial Code's provision on excuse provides guidance for interpreting the CISG's excuse provision since it contains similar requirements as those set forth in Article 79." (D.E. 18 at 8 n. 5.) This approach of looking to case law interpreting analogous provisions of the UCC has been used by other federal courts. *See, e.g., Delchi Carrier SpA v. Rotorex Corp.,* 71 F.3d 1024, 1028 (2d Cir. 1995) ("case law interpreting analogous provisions of Article 2 of the Uniform Commercial Code may also inform a court where the language of the relevant CISG provisions track that of the UCC"); *Chicago Prime Packers, Inc. v. Northam Food Trading Co.,* No. 01–4447, 2004 WL 1166628, at *4 (N.D. Ill. May 21, 2004) (same). Furthermore, Forberich does not dispute that this is proper and, in fact, also points to case law interpreting the UCC. Accordingly, in applying Article 79 of the CISG, the Court will use as a guide case law interpreting a similar provision of § 2–615 of the UCC.

Under § 2–615 of the UCC, "three conditions must be satisfied before performance is excused: (1) a contingency has occurred; (2) the contingency has made performance impracticable; and (3) the nonoccurrence of that contingency was a basic assumption upon which the contract was made." *Waldinger Corp. v. CRS Group Engineers, Inc.,* 775 F.2d 781, 786 (7th Cir. 1985). The third condition turns upon whether the contingency was foreseeable; "[i]f the risk of the occurrence of the contingency was unforeseeable, the seller cannot be said to have assumed the risk. If the risk of the occurrence of the contingency was foreseeable, that risk is tacitly assigned to the seller." *Id.* RMI does not dispute that the freezing over of the port in St. Petersburg was a contingency. Rather, RMI essentially argues that it is entitled to summary judgment because the second and third conditions do not apply inasmuch as the undisputed facts show that the frozen port did not prevent Forberich from performing the contract and that the freezing of the port was foreseeable. Based on the record material cited by the parties, the Court respectfully disagrees.

B. Whether the Frozen Port Could Have Prevented Performance

As mentioned above, RMI contends that the frozen port could not have prevented Forberich from performing because the port did not freeze over until mid-December 2002, and, since it takes 3–4 weeks for a ship carrying rail to travel from St. Petersburg to the United States, Forberich would have had to have shipped out the rail before the port froze in order for the shipment to arrive by the December 31, 2002, deadline. RMI's argument is premised on its contention that it has established beyond genuine dispute that Forberich was obligated to ship the materials so that they would arrive by December 31, 2002 (rather than just load the ships by that date, as Forberich contends). In this regard, RMI asserts that Forberich's admission in its answer that it "promised to deliver the aforementioned goods at RMI's place of business on or before June 30, 2002," is a judicial admission. While the Court agrees that this statement in RMI's answer is a judicial admission that establishes beyond contention the fact that Forberich initially promised to deliver the rail at RMI's place of business on or before June 30, 2002, *see Solon v. Gary Community School Corp.,* 180 F.3d 844, 858 (7th Cir. 1999) ("That Gary Schools admitted the length of Bohney's service in its answer was not simply evidence as to this eligibility criterion, but a judicial admission which removed this point from the realm of contested issues"), this does not establish the inapplicability of the *force majeure* defense for at least two independent reasons.

First, even assuming that Forberich was obligated to deliver the rails by December 31, 2002, Forberich has nonetheless presented evidence (which the Court must construe in the light most favorable to Forberich) that the frozen port prevented it from meeting this obligation. In particular, Mr. Forberich testified that ice interfered with shipping not just in mid-December, but as early as the end of November. The fact that a Forberich ship left the port on approximately November 20, 2002, is not inconsistent with the port freezing in the remaining ten days or so of that month. Furthermore, as noted above, no conclusive evidence has been presented that any ships left the St. Petersburg port until months after November 20, 2002. In light of the undisputed fact that delivery to a port in the US from St. Petersburg takes at least 3–4 weeks and Mr. Owczarzak's testimony that he "would have been satisfied had the 15,000 to 18,000 tons, metric tons of rail, been delivered to a port in the United States as of December 31st, 2002," Forberich has presented evidence that it would have been in a position to meet a December 31, 2002, deadline for delivery to the US by shipping out rail in the last week or so of November or the first few days of December but was prevented from doing so by the frozen port. Thus, for this reason alone, there is a disputed question of fact as to whether the frozen port prevented Forberich from performing its contractual obligations.

The second reason RMI has failed to demonstrate that the frozen port did not prevent Forberich's performance is that although it is established beyond contention that Forberich promised in the February 7, 2002, written agreement that Forberich would deliver the rail at RMI's place of business on or before June 30, 2002, an issue of fact exists regarding the nature of the extension Mr. Owczarzak orally agreed to for the time for performance of the contract.[9] Neither side has presented evidence of what exactly was said by Mr. Owczarzak and Mr. Forberich during the initial telephone conversation in which Mr. Owczarzak agreed to an extension. On June 27, 2002, Mr. Owczarzak sent Mr. Forberich a letter stating "[w]ith reference to our telephone conversation of Wednesday, [sic] Jun 26, 2002, RAW MATERIALS, INC. has agreed to extend the delivery date from June 30, 2002, until a later date during this calendar year on CONTRACT FORB 3464/02. This later date will be confirmed sometime during your visit to Chicago in July of this year." However, this letter contemplates further discussions and, although the parties apparently did not meet in Chicago in July, Mr. Owczarzak testified that they did have further discussions, though he did not testify to the content of these discussions in detail. Mr. Owczarzak also testified that he conveyed to Mr. Forberich that delivery to any port in the US by December 31, 2002, would be satisfactory but he did not specify when or how (orally or by letter) he made this communication. In his declaration, Mr. Forberich stated that his understanding was that Forberich was given an extension "until December 31, 2002, to load the rails and execute a bill of lading to be in compliance with the contract."

Given that the original contract obligated delivery to RMI's place of business in Chicago Heights by June 30, 2002, it appears unlikely that Mr. Owczarzak would have done more than agree to extend the delivery date to December 31, 2002, and change the delivery location to any US port, but the evidence is unclear and contradictory and it is not the Court's role in deciding a summary judgment motion to weigh evidence. *See, e.g., Anderson v. Liberty Lobby, Inc.,* 477 U.S. 242 (1986); *see also David Copperfield's Disappearing, Inc. v. Haddon Advertising Agency, Inc.,* 897 F.2d 288, 292 (7th Cir. 1990) (stating that "the intent of the parties to an oral contract is generally a question of fact."). Thus, a question of fact exists as to whether Forberich was obligated to deliver the rail to the US by

---

9. As indicated by the fact that the parties agreed to the extension, there is no requirement in the contract that any modification be in writing. Furthermore, under the CISG, "[a] contract may be modified or terminated by the mere agreement of the parties." CISG Art. 29.

December 31, 2002, or whether Forberich was merely required to load the rail by that date. Consequently, since it cannot yet be determined whether Forberich would have met its contractual obligations by shipping rail from the port at the end of December, a question of fact exists as to whether the port's freezing prevented Forberich from performing its obligation, even assuming the port froze in mid-December.

C. Foreseeability

RMI's sole basis for its contention that the early freezing of the port was foreseeable is the assertion, without citation to the record, in its brief in support of summary judgment, that "it hardly could come as a surprise to any experienced shipping merchant (or any grammar school geography student) that the port in St. Petersburg might become icy and frozen in the Russian winter months." However, Forberich presented evidence that the severity of the winter in 2002 and the early onset of the freezing of the port and its consequences were far from ordinary occurrences. It is undisputed that although the St. Petersburg port does usually freeze over in the winter months, this typically does not happen until late January, and such freezing does not prevent the vessels from entering and exiting the port. More to the point, Mr. Forberich testified that although ice breakers are normally used to allow for shipping, the winter of 2002 was the worst winter in St. Petersburg in almost sixty years and that ice interfered with shipping at the end of November and that even the ice breakers were stuck in the ice. He also testified that these were "unexpected weather conditions." Whether it was foreseeable that such severe weather would occur and would stop even the ice breakers from working is a question of fact for the jury. In so holding, the Court notes that the freezing over of the upper Mississippi River has been the basis of a successful *force majeure* defense. *See Louis Dreyfus Corp. v. Continental Grain Co.*, 395 So. 2d 442, 450 (La. Ct. App. 1981). In sum, because questions of fact exist as to whether the early freezing of the port prevented Forberich's performance and was foreseeable, Forberich's *force majeure* affirmative defense may be viable and summary judgment would be inappropriate.

CONCLUSION

For the foregoing reasons, Plaintiff's motion for summary judgment is denied.

Questions

1. Is it accurate to say that the *Raw Materials, Inc.* court used case law interpreting UCC § 2–615 "as a guide" in applying CISG

Article 79, as the court states?[68] In answering this question, it might be useful to examine how the court used the CISG in the balance of its opinion, after the first time UCC § 2–615 was mentioned.

2. Note that the court cited precedent in support of its decision to use case law interpreting the UCC as guidance with respect to the analogous CISG provision. Do some quick research on each of the cases cited in this section of the court's decision, looking particularly at law review articles discussing them. From what you have read, are these cases on which you would feel comfortable relying? Why or why not? In crafting your answer, apply Lookofsky and Flechtner's criteria as discussed above.[69]

PROBLEM 5

The relevant UCC and CISG provisions on trade usage are set forth below. What differences do you notice that support Professor Ferrari's assertion earlier in this section[70] that the two should not be interpreted the same way?

UCC § 1–205

Course of Dealing and Usage of Trade.

(1) A course of dealing is a sequence of previous conduct between the parties to a particular transaction which is fairly to be regarded as establishing a common basis of understanding for interpreting their expressions and other conduct.

(2) A usage of trade is any practice or method of dealing having such regularity of observance in a place, vocation or trade as to justify an expectation that it will be observed with respect to the transaction in question. The existence and scope of such a usage are to be proved as facts. If it is established that such a usage is embodied in a written trade code or similar writing the interpretation of the writing is for the court.

(3) A course of dealing between parties and any usage of trade in the vocation or trade in which they are engaged or of which they are or should be aware give particular meaning to and supplement or qualify terms of an agreement.

(4) The express terms of an agreement and an applicable course of dealing or usage of trade shall be construed wherever reasonable as consistent with each other; but when such construction is unreasonable express terms control both course of

---

68. *See supra* page 50.

69. *See supra* text accompanying note 56.

70. *See supra* pages 45–46.

dealing and usage of trade and course of dealing controls usage of trade.

(5) An applicable usage of trade in the place where any part of performance is to occur shall be used in interpreting the agreement as to that part of the performance.

(6) Evidence of a relevant usage of trade offered by one party is not admissible unless and until he has given the other party such notice as the court finds sufficient to prevent unfair surprise to the latter.[71]

CISG Article 9

(1) The parties are bound by any usage to which they have agreed and by any practices which they have established between themselves.

(2) The parties are considered, unless otherwise agreed, to have impliedly made applicable to their contract or its formation a usage of which the parties knew or ought to have known and which in international trade is widely known to, and regularly observed by, parties to contracts of the type involved in the particular trade concerned.[72]

PROBLEM 6

In the *Raw Materials, Inc.* case, the court used UCC § 2–615 to interpret CISG Article 79. The text of each is set forth below. What textual differences exist between UCC § 2–615 and CISG Article 79? What familiar terms are used in the CISG provision that a US-trained attorney might be tempted to interpret in accordance with the UCC? How would you determine an appropriate meaning for such terms? Using Professor Ferrari's analysis of trade usage as a guide, build an argument to explain why it is impermissible to use UCC § 2–615 to interpret CISG Article 79. Imagine that you are crafting your appeal to the United States Court of Appeals for the Seventh Circuit on behalf of the plaintiff, Raw Materials, Inc.

UCC § 2–615

Excuse by Failure of Presupposed Conditions.

Except so far as a seller may have assumed a greater obligation and subject to the preceding section on substituted performance:

(a) Delay in delivery or non-delivery in whole or in part by a seller who complies with paragraphs (b) and (c) is not a breach

---

71. U.C.C. § 1–205 (2001).   **72.** *See supra* note 3, Article 9.

of his duty under a contract for sale if performance as agreed has been made impracticable by the occurrence of a contingency the non-occurrence of which was a basic assumption on which the contract was made or by compliance in good faith with any applicable foreign or domestic governmental regulation or order whether or not it later proves to be invalid.

(b) Where the causes mentioned in paragraph (a) affect only a part of the seller's capacity to perform, he must allocate production and deliveries among his customers but may at his option include regular customers not then under contract as well as his own requirements for further manufacture. He may so allocate in any manner which is fair and reasonable.

(c) The seller must notify the buyer seasonably that there will be delay or non-delivery and, when allocation is required under paragraph (b), of the estimated quota thus made available for the buyer.[73]

CISG Article 79

(1) A party is not liable for a failure to perform any of his obligations if he proves that the failure was due to an impediment beyond his control and that he could not reasonably be expected to have taken the impediment into account at the time of the conclusion of the contract or to have avoided or overcome it or its consequences.

(2) If the party's failure is due to the failure by a third person whom he has engaged to perform the whole or a part of the contract, that party is exempt from liability only if:

(a) he is exempt under the preceding paragraph; and

(b) the person whom he has so engaged would be so exempt if the provisions of that paragraph were applied to him.

(3) The exemption provided by this article has effect for the period during which the impediment exists.

(4) The party who fails to perform must give notice to the other party of the impediment and its effect on his ability to perform. If the notice is not received by the other party within a reasonable time after the party who fails to perform knew or ought to have known of the impediment, he is liable for damages resulting from such non-receipt.

(5) Nothing in this article prevents either party from exercising any right other than to claim damages under this Convention.[74]

---

73. U.C.C. § 2–615 (1992).   **74.** *See supra* note 3, Article 79.

V. THE ROLE OF PRIVATE INTERNATIONAL LAW

Prior sections of this chapter have addressed how one (1) determines whether a gap exists in the CISG and (2) once a gap is found, seeks to apply international sources to minimize the usage of domestic law and avoid the phenomenon of homeward trend. Even so, there remains some role for domestic law. When domestic law is to be applied is determined by application of the rules of private international law, which is another way of talking about the forum's application of its own choice-of-law rules. "The rules of private international law are those of the forum state. They play a secondary role, since they come into play only if relevant general principles cannot be inferred to deal with CISG matters that are not the subject of an express provision."[75]

According to Professor Peter Winship, the 1964 Convention Relating to a Uniform Law on the International Sale of Goods (ULIS), which pre-dated the CISG, made no reference to private international law.[76] The CISG, by contrast, uses private international law to fill substantive gaps and to determine when the CISG applies.[77] At least one commentator has wondered, given the concern about homeward trend, "whether the CISG would have been a better instrument had it not expressly acknowledged the role of private international law."[78] There are also concerns regarding the performance of courts in applying foreign law.[79] For that reason, contracting parties may wish to exclude the application of private international law to supplement the CISG, perhaps in favor of the UNIDROIT principles.[80]

The following unreported case applies the rules of private international law. Note particularly how the court determines (1) that the CISG applies, and (2) that Ontario law, rather than the CISG, governs the question of waiver.

---

75. Michael Bridges, *Choice of Law and the CISG: Opting In and Opting Out, in* DRAFTING CONTRACTS UNDER THE CISG 65, 79 (Harry M. Flechtner et al. eds. 2008).

76. Peter Winship, *Private International Law and the U.N. Sales Convention*, 21 CORNELL INT'L L.J. 487, 491 (1988).

77. *Id.* at 491, 517 ("The 1964 Convention explicitly rejected all reference to private international law rules, while the 1980 Convention expressly incorporates such rules to determine the convention's sphere of application and to fill gaps in the text.").

78. Bridges, *supra* note 75, at 79.

79. *Id.* (noting "rueful observations that courts get foreign law wrong at least as often as they get it right").

80. *Id.* at 79–81.

AJAX TOOL WORKS, INC., PLAINTIFF, v. CAN-ENG MANUFACTURING LTD., DEFENDANT

United States District Court for the Northern District of Illinois, Eastern Division
January 29, 2003, Decided
No. 01 C 5938

MEMORANDUM OPINION AND ORDER. James F. Holderman, United States District Judge:

On March 15, 2002, plaintiff Ajax Tool Works, Inc., buyer, filed a four-count first amended complaint against Can-Eng Manufacturing Ltd., seller, alleging breach of express and implied warranties and breach of contract. On December 23, 2002, seller moved, pursuant to Federal Rule of Civil Procedure 56, for summary judgment. Having considered this matter fully, for the reasons stated herein, seller's motion for summary judgment is denied in part and granted in part.

Statement of Facts

Plaintiff buyer, an Illinois corporation, is a manufacturer of chisels, hammers, and other tools. Defendant seller, an Ontario, Canada corporation, manufactures industrial furnaces, including a fluidized bed furnace, which is at issue in this case. In January 1996, at the request of Lindberg Technical and Management Services, a consulting firm retained by buyer, seller submitted a proposal in which it offered to supply a fluidized bed furnace to buyer. Buyer did not accept this offer. Over the course of 1996, seller submitted two follow-up proposals to buyer, neither of which was accepted. On January 27, 1997, seller sent buyer a fourth proposal to sell a fluidized bed furnace to buyer for $90,000. After issuance of the proposal, the parties entered into an agreement whereby buyer purchased the furnace from seller. The terms of the January 27, 1997, proposal formed the parties' contract.

Page 4 of seller's fourteen-page proposal contained the following relevant terms and conditions:

> "WARRANTY—Seller in connection with apparatus sold will repair or replace, at the option of seller, f.o.b.[81] our factory, any defects in workmanship or material which may develop under proper and normal use during a period of ninety days from date of shipment or completion of installation if installation is undertaken by seller. Such repair or replacement shall constitute a fulfillment of all seller liabilities with respect to such apparatus. Seller shall not be liable for consequential damages. This warranty shall not apply if alterations or modifications of any nature are made by the Purchaser or if erection, installation or starting up is not performed under seller supervision or under seller approved methods."

---

81. *See supra* note 67.

"Seller's liability for the service of any refractories, alloy or other component parts manufactured by other than seller but incorporated in the equipment furnished to Purchaser, shall be limited to the guarantee or liability to seller of the manufacturer or supplier of such components. Seller is not responsible in any manner for operation of the equipment in Purchaser's plant."

"Seller's warranties or guarantees do not cover the process of manufacture or the quality of the product on which this equipment may be used."

* * *

"OTHER UNDERSTANDINGS—All previous oral or written agreements between the parties hereto which are contrary to or inconsistent with this proposal are hereby abrogated, it being understood that there are no agreements, guarantees or understandings which are in conflict with or inconsistent with this proposal. A purchase order covering the materials, apparatus or equipment specified herein shall be considered by both the Purchaser and Seller to be merely an acceptance of this Proposal and the Terms and Conditions set forth herein, and any other terms or conditions which may be printed or contained on such purchase order which are in conflict with or inconsistent with this proposal shall be not applicable. This agreement shall be governed by the laws of the Province of Ontario, Canada. Any terms and conditions herein, which may be in conflict with Ontario Law, shall be deleted, however, all other terms and conditions shall remain in force and effect."

Seller shipped the furnace to buyer on June 26, 1997, and it arrived at buyer's plant on June 27, 1997. Buyer installed and started the furnace itself. Over the course of the next four years, buyer experienced problems with the furnace, particularly that the furnace would not attain and hold the selected temperature, used an excessive amount of sand, and did not function properly with compressed air as the atmosphere. The parties dispute exactly when and how often buyer reported these problems to seller, but viewing the evidence in the light most favorable to buyer, the non-moving party, as this court must, this court finds that buyer lodged a considerable number of complaints with seller. It appears that all of these complaints were made more than ninety days after installation. In response to many of these complaints, seller attempted to repair or in some way remedy the problem, some, at least, at no cost to buyer.

This court now considers seller's motion for summary judgment.

* * *

ANALYSIS

I. Governing Law

As a preliminary matter, this court must determine what law governs the parties' contract. In order to provide for the orderly conduct of international commerce, the United States, Canada, and the province of Ontario have adopted the United Nations Convention on the International Sale of Goods. As Judge Lindberg pointed out, "federal case law interpreting and applying the CISG is scant." *Usinor Industeel v. Leeco Steel Prods., Inc.*, 209 F. Supp. 2d 880, 884 (N.D. Ill. 2002). The CISG "applies to contracts of sale [of] goods between parties whose places of business are in different States when the States are Contracting States." CISG Art. 1 § 1 (a). By agreement, parties may exclude application of the CISG by expressly providing in the contract that the law of a non-CISG jurisdiction applies or that the CISG does not control. CISG Art. 6.

In this case, it is undisputed that buyer, an Illinois corporation, and seller, an Ontario corporation, are parties whose places of business are in different States and that these states are Contracting States. Thus, unless the parties have opted-out, the CISG applies here. The parties' contract states that the "agreement shall be governed by the laws of the Province of Ontario, Canada." Obviously, this clause does not exclude the CISG. Further, although the parties have designated Ontario law as controlling, it is not the provincial law of Ontario that applies; rather, because the CISG is the law of Ontario, the CISG governs the parties' agreement. See *Asante Techs., Inc. v. PMC-Sierra, Inc.*, 164 F. Supp. 2d 1142, 1150 (N.D. Cal. 2001) ("Defendant seller's choice of applicable law adopts the law of British Columbia, and it is undisputed that the CISG *is* the law of British Columbia.") (emphasis in original).

II. Validity of Warranty

Although the CISG applies to the parties' contract, contrary to buyer's argument, the terms and conditions and all limitations contained in the contract are not completely superseded by the provisions of the CISG. The CISG does not preempt a private contract between parties; instead, it provides a statutory authority from which contract provisions are interpreted, fills gaps in contract language, and governs issues not addressed by the contract. In fact, Article 6 states that parties may, by contract, "derogate from or vary the effect of any of [the CISG's] provisions." CISG Art. 6. Accordingly, under the CISG, the terms of the parties' agreement control. In this case, the limited warranty, as part of the contract executed by the parties, lawfully limits buyer's remedies. As will be discussed below, however, there are material facts in dispute as to whether seller has waived this limited warranty.

III. Claims Under the CISG

In counts I and II, buyer alleges that seller breached an express and implied warranty under the Ontario Sale of Goods Act. Seller argues that because buyer cited to the Ontario Sale of Goods Act, instead of the applicable CISG, summary judgment in its favor on these counts is warranted. Under Seventh Circuit precedent, however, a plaintiff "cannot plead herself out of court by citing to the wrong legal theory or failing to cite any theory at all." *Ryan v. Illinois Dep't of Children & Family Servs.*, 185 F.3d 751, 764 (7th Cir. 1999); *see also Bartholet v. Reishauer A.G. (Zurich)*, 953 F.2d 1073, 1078 (7th Cir. 1992) (explaining that "the complaint need not identify a legal theory, and specifying an incorrect theory is not fatal"). In the case at hand, "it is of no moment therefore that buyer's complaint identified the wrong statute as the basis for [its] claim, as long as [its] allegations gave notice of a legally sufficient claim and [it] brought the legal support for [its] claim to the district court's attention in [its] response to seller's summary judgment motion." *Ryan*, 185 F.3d at 764 (citations omitted). It is clear that under the CISG actions for breach of express and implied warranties are actionable. CISG 35(1); CISG 35(2). Thus, summary judgment on the basis that buyer brought its claims under the Ontario Sale of Goods Act rather than the CISG is denied.

IV. Breach of Express Warranty (Count I) and Breach of Contract (Count III)

Page 7 of the January 27, 1997, proposal states that the "constant flow of particles assures tremendously uniform temperatures of +/– 5 [degrees] with in [sic] the work space." Further, the document, also on page 7, states that "the bed maintains excellent temperature uniformity throughout." Finally, page 11 states that one of the atmosphere capabilities is "Air." Buyer alleges that seller breached these express warranties and express provisions of the contract.

Articles 30 and 35 of the CISG require a seller to "deliver goods which are of the quantity, quality and description required by the contract...." CISG Art. 35; *see* Art. 30 ("The seller must deliver the goods, hand over any documents relating to them and transfer the property in the goods, as required by the contract and this Convention."). The issue, therefore, is whether the good delivered, i.e., the furnace, complied with the express warranties of the contract. The parties dispute this point. Buyer asserts, inter alia, that the furnace did not maintain a constant temperature, used an excess amount of sand, and, contrary to the express warranty, did not function properly with air as the atmosphere to fluidize the furnace. Seller disputes these allegations and maintains that the furnace worked as specified. Because there are material facts in dispute as to whether the furnace conformed to the express warranty and specifications in the contract, this court cannot grant summary judgment.

Seller argues that although there may be material facts in dispute as to the condition of the furnace, the limited warranty precludes buyer's recovery. Seller asserts that its only obligation to buyer was to repair or replace any defects in workmanship or material during a period of ninety days from the date of shipment. Because the alleged problems with the furnace occurred after the ninety-day warranty period, seller contends, buyer is prohibited from proceeding on the claims it has asserted against seller.

Seller advances a strong argument, and buyer fails to address this argument under the CISG in its response. Because there are material facts in dispute as to whether seller has waived its right to enforce the limited warranty, however, this court cannot, as a matter of law, enforce the limited warranty. A waiver is the "intentional or voluntary relinquishment of a known right, or such conduct as warrants an inference of the relinquishment of such right. . . ." BLACK'S LAW DICTIONARY 1580 (6th ed. 1990). As this court has explained above, the CISG is the governing law in this case. However, the parties did not present, and this court could not find, any cases under the CISG that address the issue of waiver. Article 7 of the CISG provides that in such a case where "questions concerning matters governed by this Convention which are not expressly settled in it are to be settled in conformity with the general principles on which it is based or, in the absence of such principles, in conformity with the law applicable by virtue of the rules of private international law." Here, under private international law, because of the parties' express choice-of-law provision, Ontario law would apply.

Under Ontario law, a party can waive "by its words and conduct" the right to rely on a limited warranty. *General Refractories Co. of Canada Ltd. v. Venturedyne Ltd.,* 2002 WL 32938 at 157, 2002 Carswell Ont. 36 (Ont. S.C.J. 2002). If seller gave, after the ninety-day period, "repeated assurance that it would support" the furnace, a trier of fact could find that it waived its limited warranty. *Id.* at 159. Further, buyer may be able to rely on the doctrine of promissory estoppel to preclude enforcement of the limited warranty. The *General Refractories* court stated that "[a] promise, whether express or inferred from a course of conduct, is intended to be legally binding if it reasonably leads the promisee to believe that a legal stipulation, such as strict time of performance, will not be insisted upon. . . ." *Id.* at 158 (*quoting Owen Sound Pub. Library v. Mial Devs. Ltd.* (1979), 102 D.L.R. (3d) 685 (Ont. C.A.), at 691).

The record shows that there are material facts in dispute as to whether seller, by providing service and repair, some of which at no charge, after the ninety-day limited warranty period, waived its limited warranty or whether buyer can preclude enforcement under the doctrine of promissory estoppel. Consequently, summary judgment must be denied as to the claims alleged in counts I and III of buyer's complaint.

[Discussion of Breach of Implied Warranty (Count II), Breach of Contract (Count IV), and Buyer's Recovery have been omitted.]

CONCLUSION

For the above stated reasons, defendant's motion for summary judgment is denied as to counts I, II, III, and IV of plaintiff buyer's complaint and granted as to buyer's demand of consequential damages, lost productivity damages, and attorneys' fees.

Questions

1. As the court notes, "The parties' contract states that the 'agreement shall be governed by the laws of the Province of Ontario, Canada.' " The court comments on this language, "Obviously, this clause does not exclude the CISG." Why does this clause fail to exclude the CISG?[82] How should the parties have changed this phrasing if they wanted to exclude the CISG?

2. What is the relative role of the terms of the parties' contract and the CISG, vis-à-vis one another?

3. Since the CISG does not explicitly address a cause of action in warranty, how can you explain the court's holding that "[i]t is clear that under the CISG actions for breach of express and implied warranties are actionable?"[83] In formulating your answer, consider CISG Article 35, which states as follows:

CISG Article 35

(1) The seller must deliver goods which are of the quantity, quality and description required by the contract and which are contained or packaged in the manner required by the contract.

(2) Except where the parties have agreed otherwise, the goods do not conform with the contract unless they:

(a) are fit for the purposes for which goods of the same description would ordinarily be used;

(b) are fit for any particular purpose expressly or impliedly made known to the seller at the time of the conclusion of the contract, except where the circumstances show that the buyer did not rely, or that it was unreasonable for him to rely, on the seller's skill and judgment;

(c) possess the qualities of goods which the seller has held out to the buyer as a sample or model;

---

82. *See supra* page 60.   **83.** *See supra* page 61.

(d) are contained or packaged in the manner usual for such goods or, where there is no such manner, in a manner adequate to preserve and protect the goods.

(3) The seller is not liable under subparagraphs (a) to (d) of the preceding paragraph for any lack of conformity of the goods if at the time of the conclusion of the contract the buyer knew or could not have been unaware of such lack of conformity.[84]

4.   How does the court determine that the CISG does not address the issue of waiver? From what you have read earlier in this chapter, are there other avenues the court might have considered, rather than looking to Ontario law to decide this issue?

---

84. *See supra* note 3, Article 35.

Chapter 3

CHOICE OF FORUM

Returning to the hypothetical that was presented in Chapter 1, assume that your Minnesota business client is negotiating for the purchase of a substantial item of used equipment from a Canadian seller in the Province of Ontario. In preparing a draft contract for this transaction you have choices concerning dispute resolution. If no express provision is made in the contract, the forum will be any court of the plaintiff's choice in which jurisdiction can be obtained over the defendant.

A choice of forum clause may be exclusive or nonexclusive. If the parties agree that disputes can be resolved in the courts of State X, this may be open to interpretation as to whether the State X courts are simply one permissible place to sue (sometimes termed a prorogation) or whether State X courts have exclusive jurisdiction, termed a derogation because it derogates from the jurisdiction that the courts of Minnesota or Ontario might otherwise assert. Two questions can arise:

1. Will the courts of State X agree to hear a matter that does not directly affect people or property in or connected with that State? Why devote valuable judicial resources of State X to this matter?

2. Will the courts of Minnesota or Ontario actually decline jurisdiction of a matter that they could otherwise properly hear? Can the parties oust the courts of jurisdiction in this fashion?

In an earlier era, courts all over the world jealously guarded their jurisdiction. In a related matter, for many decades courts refused to enforce agreements to arbitrate because they "ousted courts of their jurisdiction." Exclusive forum clauses were likewise rejected. The following case was thus a great milestone and serves as an introduction to the complications that arise when different national courts get involved with what should be a single item of litigation.

M/S BREMEN AND UNTERWESSER REEDEREI, GmBH, PETITIONERS v. ZAPATA OFF-SHORE COMPANY

U.S. Supreme Court (1972)

407 U.S. 1, 92 S. Ct. 1907

An action for limitation of liability was brought by a tug owner which had contracted to tow a barge from Louisiana to Italy. The United States District Court for the Middle District of Florida, 296 F. Supp. 733, denied a motion to stay the limitation action and to enjoin the tug owner from proceeding further in the London Court of Justice. On appeal by the tug owner, the Court of Appeals affirmed, 428 F.2d 888, and 446 F.2d 907. Certiorari was granted. The Supreme Court, Mr. Chief Justice Burger, held that where an American company with special expertise contracted with a foreign company, pursuant to arm's length negotiations by experienced and sophisticated businessmen, for the towing of a complex machine thousands of miles across seas and oceans, and a clause providing for the treating of any disputes before the London Court of Justice was a part of such contract, the clause was prima facie valid and was to be honored by the parties and enforced by the courts in the absence of some compelling and countervailing reason making enforcement unreasonable.

Vacated and remanded for further proceedings.

MR. JUSTICE WHITE filed a concurring opinion.

MR. JUSTICE DOUGLAS dissented and filed opinion.

Opinion after remand, 464 F.2d 1395.

MR. CHIEF JUSTICE BURGER delivered the opinion of the Court.

We granted certiorari to review a judgment of the United States Court of Appeals for the Fifth Circuit declining to enforce a forum-selection clause governing disputes arising under an international towage contract between petitioners and respondent. The circuits have differed in their approach to such clauses.[1] For the reasons stated hereafter, we vacate the judgment of the Court of Appeals.

In November 1967, respondent Zapata, a Houston-based American corporation, contracted with petitioner Unterweser, a German

---

1. Compare, e.g., Central Contracting Co. v. Maryland Casualty Co., 367 F.2d 341 (CA3 1966), and Wm. H. Muller & Co. v. Swedish American Line Ltd., 224 F.2d 806 (CA2), cert. denied, 350 U.S. 903, 76 S. Ct. 182, 100 L. Ed. 793 (1955), with Carbon Black Export, Inc. v. The Monrosa, 254 F.2d 297 (CA5 1958), cert. dismissed, 359 U.S. 180, 79 S. Ct. 710, 3 L. Ed. 2d 723 (1959).

corporation, to tow Zapata's ocean-going, self-elevating drilling rig Chaparral from Louisiana to a point off Ravenna, Italy, in the Adriatic Sea, where Zapata had agreed to drill certain wells.

Zapata had solicited bids for the towage, and several companies including Unterweser had responded. Unterweser was the low bidder and Zapata requested it to submit a contract, which it did. The contract submitted by Unterweser contained the following provision, which is at issue in this case:

"Any dispute arising must be treated before the London Court of Justice."

In addition the contract contained two clauses purporting to exculpate Unterweser from liability for damages to the towed barge.[2]

In addition, the contract provided that any insurance of the Chaparral was to be "for account of" Zapata. Unterweser's initial telegraphic bid had also offered to "arrange insurance covering towage risk for rig if desired." As Zapata had chosen to be self-insured on all its rigs, the loss in this case was not compensated by insurance.

After reviewing the contract and making several changes, but without any alteration in the forum-selection or exculpatory clauses, a Zapata vice president executed the contract and forwarded it to Unterweser in Germany, where Unterweser accepted the changes, and the contract became effective.

On January 5, 1968, Unterweser's deep sea tug Bremen departed Venice, Louisiana, with the Chaparral in tow bound for Italy. On January 9, while the flotilla was in international waters in the middle of the Gulf of Mexico, a severe storm arose. The sharp roll of the Chaparral in Gulf waters caused its elevator legs, which had been raised for the voyage, to break off and fall into the sea, seriously damaging the Chaparral. In this emergency situation Zapata instructed the Bremen to tow its damaged rig to Tampa, Florida, the nearest port of refuge.

On January 12, Zapata, ignoring its contract promise to litigate any dispute arising in the English courts, commenced a suit in admiralty in the United States District Court at Tampa, seeking $3,500,000 damages against Unterweser in personam and the Bremen in rem, alleging negligent towage and breach of contract.[3]

2. The General Towage Conditions of the contract included the following:

"1.... (Unterweser and its) masters and crews are not responsible for defaults and/or errors in the navigation of the tow.

"2....

"b) Damages suffered by the towed object are in any case for account of its Owners."

3. The Bremen was arrested by a United States marshal acting pursuant to Zapata's complaint immediately upon her arrival in Tampa. The tug was sub-

Unterweser responded by invoking the forum clause of the towage contract, and moved to dismiss for lack of jurisdiction or on forum non conveniens grounds, or in the alternative to stay the action pending submission of the dispute to the "London Court of Justice." Shortly thereafter, in February, before the District Court had ruled on its motion to stay or dismiss the United States action, Unterweser commenced an action against Zapata seeking damages for breach of the towage contract in the High Court of Justice in London, as the contract provided. Zapata appeared in that court to contest jurisdiction, but its challenge was rejected, the English courts holding that the contractual forum provision conferred jurisdiction. [4]

In the meantime, Unterweser was faced with a dilemma in the pending action in the United States court at Tampa. The six-month period for filing action to limit its liability to Zapata and other potential claimants was about to expire, but the United States District Court in Tampa had not yet ruled on Unterweser's motion to dismiss or stay Zapata's action. On July 2, 1968, confronted with difficult alternatives, Unterweser filed an action to limit its liability in the District Court in Tampa. That court entered the customary injunction against proceedings outside the limitation court, and Zapata refiled its initial claim in the limitation action. [6]

sequently released when Unterweser furnished security in the amount of $3,500,000.

4. Zapata appeared specially and moved to set aside service of process outside the country. Justice Karminski of the High Court of Justice denied the motion on the ground the contractual choice-of-forum provision conferred jurisdiction and would be enforced, absent a factual showing it would not be fair and right to do so. He did not believe Zapata had made such a showing, and held that it should be required to stick to (its) bargain. App. 206, 211, 213. The Court of Appeal dismissed an appeal on the ground that Justice Karminski had properly applied the English rule. Lord Justice Willmer stated that rule as follows:

"The law on the subject, I think, is not open to doubt.... It is always open to parties to stipulate ... that a particular Court shall have jurisdiction over any dispute arising out of their contract. Here, the parties chose to stipulate that disputes were to be referred to the 'London Court, which I take as meaning the High Court in this country. Prima facie it is the poli-

cy of the Court to hold parties to the bargain into which they have entered.... But that is not an inflexible rule, as was shown, for instance, by the case of The Fehmarn, (1957) 1 Lloyd's Rep. 511; (C.A.) (1957) 2 Lloyd's Rep. 551....

"I approach the matter, therefore, in this way, that the Court has a discretion, but it is a discretion which, in the ordinary way and in the absence of strong reason to the contrary, will be exercised in favour of holding parties to their bargain. The question is whether sufficient circumstances have been shown to exist in this case to make it desirable, on the grounds of balance of convenience, that proceedings should not take place in this country...." (1968) 2 Lloyd's Rep. 158, 162–163.

6. In its limitation complaint, Unterweser stated it "reserve(d) all rights" under its previous motion to dismiss or stay Zapata's action, and reasserted that the High Court of Justice was the proper forum for determining the entire controversy, including its own right to limited liability, in accord with the contractual forum clause. Unterweser later counter-

It was only at this juncture, on July 29, after the six-month period for filing the limitation action had run, that the District Court denied Unterweser's January motion to dismiss or stay Zapata's initial action. In denying the motion, that court relied on the prior decision of the Court of Appeals in *Carbon Black Export, Inc. v. The Monrosa*, 254 F.2d 297 (CA5 1958), cert. dismissed, 359 U.S. 180, 79 S. Ct. 710, 3 L. Ed. 2d 723 (1959). In that case the Court of Appeals had held a forum-selection clause unenforceable, reiterating the traditional view of many American courts that "agreements in advance of controversy whose object is to oust the jurisdiction of the courts are contrary to public policy and will not be enforced." 254 F.2d, at 300–301. Apparently concluding that it was bound by the *Carbon Black* case, the District Court gave the forum-selection clause little, if any, weight. Instead, the court treated the motion to dismiss under normal forum non conveniens doctrine applicable in the absence of such a clause, citing *Gulf Oil Corp. v. Gilbert*, 330 U.S. 501, 67 S. Ct. 839, 91 L. Ed. 1055 (1947). Under that doctrine unless the balance is strongly in favor of the defendant, the plaintiff's choice of forum should rarely be disturbed. Id., at 508, 67 S. Ct., at 843. The District Court concluded: "the balance of conveniences here is not strongly in favor of (Unterweser) and (Zapata's) choice of forum should not be disturbed."

Thereafter, on January 21, 1969, the District Court denied another motion by Unterweser to stay the limitation action pending determination of the controversy in the High Court of Justice in London and granted Zapata's motion to restrain Unterweser from litigating further in the London court. The District Judge ruled that, having taken jurisdiction in the limitation proceeding, he had jurisdiction to determine all matters relating to the controversy. He ruled that Unterweser should be required to "do equity" by refraining from also litigating the controversy in the London court, not only for the reasons he had previously stated for denying Unterweser's first motion to stay Zapata's action, but also because Unterweser had invoked the United States court's jurisdiction to obtain the benefit of the Limitation Act.

On appeal, a divided panel of the Court of Appeals affirmed, and on rehearing en banc the panel opinion was adopted, with six of the 14 en banc judges dissenting. As had the District Court, the majority rested on the *Carbon Black* decision, concluding that at the very least that case stood for the proposition that a forum-selection clause will not be enforced unless the selected state would

claimed, setting forth the same contractual cause of action as in its English action and a further cause of action for salvage arising out of the Bremen's services following the casualty. In its counterclaim, Unterweser again asserted that the High Court of Justice in London was the proper forum for determining all aspects of the controversy, including its counterclaim.

provide a more convenient forum than the state in which suit is brought. From that premise the Court of Appeals proceeded to conclude that, apart from the forum-selection clause, the District Court did not abuse its discretion in refusing to decline jurisdiction on the basis of forum non conveniens. It noted that (1) the flotilla never "escaped the Fifth Circuit's mare nostrum, and the casualty occurred in close proximity to the district court"; (2) a considerable number of potential witnesses, including Zapata crewmen, resided in the Gulf Coast area; (3) preparation for the voyage and inspection and repair work had been performed in the Gulf area; (4) the testimony of the Bremen crew was available by way of deposition; (5) England had no interest in or contact with the controversy other than the forum-selection clause. The Court of Appeals majority further noted that Zapata was a United States citizen and "(t)he discretion of the district court to remand the case to a foreign forum was consequently limited"—especially since it appeared likely that the English courts would enforce the exculpatory clauses.[8] In the Court of Appeals' view, enforcement of such clauses would be contrary to public policy in American courts under *Bisso v. Inland Waterways Corp.*, 349 U.S. 85, 75 S. Ct. 629, 99 L. Ed. 911 (1955), and *Dixilyn Drilling Corp. v. Crescent Towing & Salvage Co.*, 372 U.S. 697, 83 S. Ct. 967, 10 L. Ed. 2d 78 (1963). Therefore, (t)he district court was entitled to consider that remanding Zapata to a foreign forum, with no practical contact with the controversy, could raise a bar to recovery by a United States citizen which its own convenient courts would not countenance."[9]

In addition, it is not disputed that while the limitation fund in the District Court in Tampa amounts to $1,390,000, the limitation fund in England would be only slightly in excess of $80,000 under English law.

We hold, with the six dissenting members of the Court of Appeals, that far too little weight and effect were given to the forum clause in resolving this controversy. For at least two decades we have witnessed an expansion of overseas commercial activities by business enterprises based in the United States. The barrier of distance that once tended to confine a business concern to a modest territory no longer does so. Here we see an American company with

---

8. The record contains an undisputed affidavit of a British solicitor stating an opinion that the exculpatory clauses of the contract would be held prima facie valid and enforceable against Zapata in any action maintained in England in which Zapata alleged that defaults or errors in Unterweser's tow caused the casualty and damage to the Chaparral.

9. The Court of Appeals also indicated in passing that even if it took the view that choice-of-forum clauses were enforceable unless "unreasonable" it was "doubtful" that enforcement would be proper here because the exculpatory clauses would deny Zapata relief to which it was "entitled" and because England was "seriously inconvenient" for trial of the action.

special expertise contracting with a foreign company to tow a complex machine thousands of miles across seas and oceans. The expansion of American business and industry will hardly be encouraged if, notwithstanding solemn contracts, we insist on a parochial concept that all disputes must be resolved under our laws and in our courts. Absent a contract forum, the considerations relied on by the Court of Appeals would be persuasive reasons for holding an American forum convenient in the traditional sense, but in an era of expanding world trade and commerce, the absolute aspects of the doctrine of the *Carbon Black* case have little place and would be a heavy hand indeed on the future development of international commercial dealings by Americans. We cannot have trade and commerce in world markets and international waters exclusively on our terms, governed by our laws, and resolved in our courts.

Forum-selection clauses have historically not been favored by American courts. Many courts, federal and state, have declined to enforce such clauses on the ground that they were "contrary to public policy," or that their effect was to "oust the jurisdiction" of the court. Although this view apparently still has considerable acceptance, other courts are tending to adopt a more hospitable attitude toward forum-selection clauses. This view, advanced in the well-reasoned dissenting opinion in the instant case, is that such clauses are prima facie valid and should be enforced unless enforcement is shown by the resisting party to be "unreasonable" under the circumstances. We believe this is the correct doctrine to be followed by federal district courts sitting in admiralty. It is merely the other side of the proposition recognized by this Court in *National Equipment Rental, Ltd. v. Szukhent*, 375 U.S. 311, 84 S. Ct. 411, 11 L. Ed. 2d 354 (1964), holding that in federal courts a party may validly consent to be sued in a jurisdiction where he cannot be found for service of process through contractual designation of an "agent" for receipt of process in that jurisdiction. In so holding, the Court stated:

> "(I)t is settled ... that parties to a contract may agree in advance to submit to the jurisdiction of a given court to permit notice to be served by the opposing party, or even to waive notice altogether." *Id.*, at 315–316, 84 S. Ct., at 414.

This approach is substantially that followed in other common-law countries including England. It is the view advanced by noted scholars and that adopted by the Restatement of the Conflict of Laws.[13] It accords with ancient concepts of freedom of contract and

---

13. Restatement (Second) of the Conflict of Laws § 80 (1971); Reese, The Contractual Forum: Situation in the United States, 13 Am. J. Comp. Law 187 (1964); A. Ehrenzweig, Conflict of Laws § 41 (1962). See also Model Choice of Forum Act (National Conference of

reflects an appreciation of the expanding horizons of American contractors who seek business in all parts of the world. Not surprisingly, foreign businessmen prefer, as do we, to have disputes resolved in their own courts, but if that choice is not available, then in a neutral forum with expertise in the subject matter. Plainly, the courts of England meet the standards of neutrality and long experience in admiralty litigation. The choice of that forum was made in an arm's-length negotiation by experienced and sophisticated businessmen, and absent some compelling and countervailing reason it should be honored by the parties and enforced by the courts.

The argument that such clauses are improper because they tend to "oust" a court of jurisdiction is hardly more than a vestigial legal fiction. It appears to rest at core on historical judicial resistance to any attempt to reduce the power and business of a particular court and has little place in an era when all courts are overloaded and when businesses once essentially local now operate in world markets. It reflects something of a provincial attitude regarding the fairness of other tribunals. No one seriously contends in this case that the forum selection clause "ousted" the District Court of jurisdiction over Zapata's action. The threshold question is whether that court should have exercised its jurisdiction to do more than give effect to the legitimate expectations of the parties, manifested in their freely negotiated agreement, by specifically enforcing the forum clause.

There are compelling reasons why a freely negotiated private international agreement, unaffected by fraud, undue influence, or overweening bargaining power,[14] such as that involved here, should be given full effect. In this case, for example, we are concerned with a far from routine transaction between companies of two different nations contemplating the tow of a extremely costly piece of equipment from Louisiana across the Gulf of Mexico and the Atlantic Ocean, through the Mediterranean Sea to its final destination in the Adriatic Sea. In the course of its voyage, it was to traverse the

Commissioners on Uniform State Laws 1968).

14. The record here refutes any notion of overweening bargaining power. Judge Wisdom, dissenting, in the Court of Appeals noted:

Zapata has neither presented evidence of nor alleged fraud or undue bargaining power in the agreement. Unterweser was only one of several companies bidding on the project. No evidence contradicts its Managing Director's affidavit that it specified English courts in an effort to meet Zapata Off-Shore Company half way.

Zapata's Vice President has declared by affidavit that no specific negotiations concerning the forum clause took place. But this was not simply a form contract with boilerplate language that Zapata had no power to alter. The towing of an oil rig across the Atlantic was a new business. Zapata did make alterations to the contract submitted by Unterweser. The forum clause could hardly be ignored. It is the final sentence of the agreement, immediately preceding the date and the parties' signatures....' 428 F.2d 888, 907.

waters of many jurisdictions. The Chaparral could have been damaged at any point along the route, and there were countless possible ports of refuge. That the accident occurred in the Gulf of Mexico and the barge was towed to Tampa in an emergency were mere fortuities. It cannot be doubted for a moment that the parties sought to provide for a neutral forum for the resolution of any disputes arising during the tow. Manifestly much uncertainty and possibly great inconvenience to both parties could arise if a suit could be maintained in any jurisdiction in which an accident might occur or if jurisdiction were left to any place where the Bremen or Unterweser might happen to be found.[15] The elimination of all such uncertainties by agreeing in advance on a forum acceptable to both parties is an indispensable element in international trade, commerce, and contracting. There is strong evidence that the forum clause was a vital part of the agreement,[16] and it would be unrealistic to think that the parties did not conduct their negotiations, including fixing the monetary terms, with the consequences of the forum clause figuring prominently in their calculations. Under these circumstances, as Justice Karminski reasoned in sustaining jurisdiction over Zapata in the High Court of Justice, "(t)he force of

15. At the very least, the clause was an effort to eliminate all uncertainty as to the nature, location, and outlook of the forum in which these companies of differing nationalities might find themselves. Moreover, while the contract here did not specifically provide that the substantive law of England should be applied, it is the general rule in English courts that the parties are assumed, absent contrary indication, to have designated the forum with the view that it should apply its own law. *See, e.g., Tzortzis v. Monark Line A/B*, (1968) 1 W.L.R. 406 (CA); *see generally* 1 T. Carver, Carriage by Sea 496–497 (12th ed. 1971); G. Cheshire, Private International Law 193 (7th ed. 1965); A. Dicey & J. Morris, The Conflict of Laws 705, 1046 (8th ed. 1967); Collins, Arbitration Clauses and Forum Selecting Clauses in the Conflict of Laws: Some Recent Developments in England, 2 J.Mar.L. & Comm. 363, 365–370 and n. 7 (1971). It is therefore reasonable to conclude that the forum clause was also an effort to obtain certainty as to the applicable substantive law.

The record contains an affidavit of a Managing Director of Unterweser stating that Unterweser considered the choice-of-forum provision to be of "overriding importance" to the transaction.

He stated that Unterweser towage contracts ordinarily provide for exclusive German jurisdiction and application of German law, but that "(i)n this instance, in an effort to meet (Zapata) half way, (Unterweser) proposed the London Court of Justice. Had this provision not been accepted by (Zapata), (Unterweser) would not have entered into the towage contract...." He also stated that the parties intended, by designating the London forum, that English law would be applied. A responsive affidavit by Hoyt Taylor, a vice president of Zapata, denied that there were any discussions between Zapata and Unterweser concerning the forum clause or the question of the applicable law.

16. See nn. 14–15, supra. Zapata has denied specifically discussing the forum clause with Unterweser, but, as Judge Wisdom pointed out, Zapata made numerous changes in the contract without altering the forum clause, which could hardly have escaped its attention. Zapata is clearly not unsophisticated in such matters. The contract of its wholly owned subsidiary with an Italian corporation covering the contemplated drilling operations in the Adriatic Sea provided that all disputes were to be settled by arbitration in London under English law, and contained broad exculpatory clauses. App. 306–311.

an agreement for litigation in this country, freely entered into between two competent parties, seems to me to be very powerful."

Thus, in the light of present-day commercial realities and expanding international trade we conclude that the forum clause should control absent a strong showing that it should be set aside. Although their opinions are not altogether explicit, it seems reasonably clear that the District Court and the Court of Appeals placed the burden on Unterweser to show that London would be a more convenient forum than Tampa, although the contract expressly resolved that issue. The correct approach would have been to enforce the forum clause specifically unless Zapata could clearly show that enforcement would be unreasonable and unjust, or that the clause was invalid for such reasons as fraud or overreaching. Accordingly, the case must be remanded for reconsideration.

We note, however, that there is nothing in the record presently before us that would support a refusal to enforce the forum clause. The Court of Appeals suggested that enforcement would be contrary to the public policy of the forum under *Bisso v. Inland Waterways Corp.*, 349 U.S. 85, 75 S. Ct. 629, 99 L. Ed. 911 (1955), because of the prospect that the English courts would enforce the clauses of the towage contract purporting to exculpate Unterweser from liability for damages to the Chaparral. A contractual choice-of-forum clause should be held unenforceable if enforcement would contravene a strong public policy of the forum in which suit is brought, whether declared by statute or by judicial decision. *See, e.g., Boyd v. Grand Trunk W.R. Co.*, 338 U.S. 263, 70 S. Ct. 26, 94 L. Ed. 55 (1949). It is clear, however, that whatever the proper scope of the policy expressed in *Bisso*, it does not reach this case. *Bisso* rested on considerations with respect to the towage business strictly in American waters, and those considerations are not controlling in an international commercial agreement. Speaking for the dissenting judges in the Court of Appeals, Judge Wisdom pointed out:

> (W)e should be careful not to overemphasize the strength of the (*Bisso*) policy.... (T)wo concerns underlie the rejection of exculpatory agreements: that they may be produced by over-weening bargaining power; and that they do not sufficiently discourage negligence.... Here the conduct in question is that of a foreign party occurring in international waters outside our jurisdiction. The evidence disputes any notion of overreaching in the contractual agreement. And for all we know, the uncertainties and dangers in the new field of transoceanic towage of oil rigs were so great that the tower was unwilling to take financial responsibility for the risks, and the parties thus allocated responsibility for the voyage to the tow. It is equally possible that the contract price took this factor into account. I

conclude that we should not invalidate the forum selection clause here unless we are firmly convinced that we would thereby significantly encourage negligent conduct within the boundaries of the United States.

428 F.2d at 907–908. (Footnotes omitted.)

Courts have also suggested that a forum clause, even though it is freely bargained for and contravenes no important public policy of the forum, may nevertheless be "unreasonable" and unenforceable if the chosen forum is seriously inconvenient for the trial of the action. Of course, where it can be said with reasonable assurance that at the time they entered the contract, the parties to a freely negotiated private international commercial agreement contemplated the claimed inconvenience, it is difficult to see why any such claim of inconvenience should be heard to render the forum clause unenforceable. We are not here dealing with an agreement between two Americans to resolve their essentially local disputes in a remote alien forum. In such a case, the serious inconvenience of the contractual forum to one or both of the parties might carry greater weight in determining the reasonableness of the forum clause. The remoteness of the forum might suggest that the agreement was an adhesive one, or that the parties did not have the particular controversy in mind when they made their agreement; yet even there the party claiming should bear a heavy burden of proof. Similarly, selection of a remote forum to apply differing foreign law to an essentially American controversy might contravene an important public policy of the forum. For example, so long as *Bisso* governs American courts with respect to the towage business in American waters, it would quite arguably be improper to permit an American tower to avoid that policy by providing a foreign forum for resolution of his disputes with an American towee.

This case, however, involves a freely negotiated international commercial transaction between a German and an American corporation for towage of a vessel from the Gulf of Mexico to the Adriatic Sea. As noted, selection of a London forum was clearly a reasonable effort to bring vital certainty to this international transaction and to provide a neutral forum experienced and capable in the resolution of admiralty litigation. Whatever "inconvenience" Zapata would suffer by being forced to litigate in the contractual forum as it agreed to do was clearly foreseeable at the time of contracting. In such circumstances it should be incumbent on the party seeking to escape his contract to show that trial in the contractual forum will be so gravely difficult and inconvenient that he will for all practical purposes be deprived of his day in court. Absent that, there is no basis for concluding that it would be unfair, unjust, or unreasonable to hold that party to his bargain.

In the course of its ruling on Unterweser's second motion to stay the proceedings in Tampa, the District Court did make a conclusory finding that the balance of convenience was strongly in favor of litigation in Tampa. However, as previously noted, in making that finding the court erroneously placed the burden of proof on Unterweser to show that the balance of convenience was strongly in its favor.[19] Moreover, the finding falls far short of a conclusion that Zapata would be effectively deprived of its day in court should it be forced to litigate in London. Indeed, it cannot even be assumed that it would be placed to the expense of transporting its witnesses to London. It is not unusual for important issues in international admiralty cases to be dealt with by deposition. Both the District Court and the Court of Appeals majority appeared satisfied that Unterweser could receive a fair hearing in Tampa by using deposition testimony of its witnesses from distant places, and there is no reason to conclude that Zapata could not use deposition testimony to equal advantage if forced to litigate in London as it bound itself to do. Nevertheless, to allow Zapata opportunity to carry its heavy burden of showing not only that the balance of convenience is strongly in favor of trial in Tampa (that is, that it will be far more inconvenient for Zapata to litigate in London than it will be for Unterweser to litigate in Tampa), but also that a London trial will be so manifestly and gravely inconvenient to Zapata that it will be effectively deprived of a meaningful day in court, we remand for further proceedings.

Zapata's remaining contentions do not require extended treatment. It is clear that Unterweser's action in filing its limitation complaint in the District Court in Tampa was, so far as Zapata was concerned, solely a defensive measure made necessary as a response to Zapata's breach of the forum clause of the contract. When the six-month statutory period for filing an action to limit its liability had almost run without the District Court's having ruled on

19. Applying the proper burden of proof, Justice Karminski in the High Court of Justice at London made the following findings, which appear to have substantial support in the record:

(Zapata) pointed out that in this case the balance of convenience so far as witnesses were concerned pointed in the direction of having the case heard and tried in the United States District Court at Tampa in Florida because the probability is that most, but not necessarily all, of the witnesses will be American. The answer, as it seems to me, is that a substantial minority at least of witnesses are likely to be German. The tug was a German vessel and was, as far as I know, manned by

a German crew . . . Where they all are now or are likely to be when this matter is litigated I do not know, because the experience of the Admiralty Court here strongly points out that maritime witnesses in the course of their duties move about freely. The homes of the German crew presumably are in Germany. There is probably a balance of numbers in favour of the Americans, but not, as I am inclined to think, a very heavy balance. App. 212. It should also be noted that if the exculpatory clause is enforced in the English courts, many of Zapata's witnesses on the questions of negligence and damage may be completely unnecessary.

Unterweser's initial motion to dismiss or stay Zapata's action pursuant to the forum clause, Unterweser had no other prudent alternative but to protect itself by filing for limitation of its liability. Its action in so doing was a direct consequence of Zapata's failure to abide by the forum clause of the towage contract. There is no basis on which to conclude that this purely necessary defensive action by Unterweser should preclude it from relying on the forum clause it bargained for.

For the first time in this litigation, Zapata has suggested to this Court that the forum clause should not be construed to provide for an exclusive forum or to include in rem actions. However, the language of the clause is clearly mandatory and all-encompassing; the language of the clause in the *Carbon Black* case was far different.[21]

The judgment of the Court of Appeals is vacated and the case is remanded for further proceedings consistent with this opinion.

Vacated and remanded.

Mr. Justice WHITE, concurring.

I concur in the opinion and judgment of the Court except insofar as the opinion comments on the issues which are remanded to the District Court. In my view these issues are best left for consideration by the District Court in the first instance.

Mr. Justice DOUGLAS, dissenting. (Omitted)

Questions and Comments

1. The Court notes that in an exclusively American towage contract, "it would quite arguably be improper to permit an American tower to avoid ... (an important public policy) by providing a foreign forum for resolution of his disputes with an American towee."

Do you assume that a choice of the "High Court of London" as the exclusive forum would be unenforceable in a towage contract between two Americans on the Mississippi River?

Might the answer be different if the towee were a Mexican corporation?

2. Assuming a contractual choice of forum in State X or choice of law in State X, a potential issue is presented when the laws of State X either allow or deny enforcement of a right that is directly contrary to the laws of states that are more closely connected to the transaction. What laws are a reflection of "public policy" or "fundamental public policy?"

---

21. *See* 359 U.S., at 182, 79 S. Ct., at 712.

3. A choice of forum that requires passengers who live in the State of Washington to bring suit in Florida for injuries allegedly sustained on a cruise ship has been upheld despite the apparent inconvenience to the plaintiffs. (*Carnival Cruise Lines v. Shute*, 499 U.S. 585, 111 S.Ct. 1522, 113 L.Ed.2d 622 (1991).)

I. CHOICE OF FORUM—ONTARIO OR MINNESOTA?

It is cumbersome and expensive to try a case in which the court must apply foreign law. Whether it is a Canadian court applying Minnesota law or a US court applying Ontario law, the problems are numerous.

First, the parties will be put to the expense and difficulty of hiring a legal expert to testify as to the substance of that foreign law. This can be a major item.

Second, to explain and argue the client's position effectively, the attorneys must understand both the local and the foreign law. This often means at least two attorneys for each party.

Third, the judge will be required to apply a law with which she or he is not familiar. Both at trial and on appeal, this makes the proceedings cumbersome. Visualize your local judge or judges in Pennsylvania or Texas applying the law of Japan or Egypt for example. It will likely be an experience long remembered. A Canadian judge applying US law or vice versa is not quite so challenging due to the similarities of their legal systems, but there can still be major problems. Think back, for example, to the distinctions regarding such matters as the meaning of "warranty."

When applying foreign law, there can be difficult questions presented as to what issues are procedural (where the court applies its local rules) and what are substantive (in which case the chosen foreign law applies). In addition, some foreign rules of law may be denied application if they violate fundamental principles of the forum nation. There may be difficulties concerning compelled attendance of witnesses from the foreign country or production of documents or physical evidence. Local counsel is necessary (local procedure) and foreign counsel is often necessary to guide the way through application of that foreign substantive law to the facts.

In our hypothetical, the choice of forum may be easy. If the decision is made to apply Ontario law, then the forum should be Ontario, and likewise for Minnesota. In fact, if no choice of law is expressly made in a contract but the parties agree upon a forum, courts will assume that the parties intended to apply the law of that forum, however in this case that would be the CISG.

Another strategic consideration is that judgments can be enforced only where the judgment debtor has property that is subject to execution. If the defendant only has property in Canada, a new action will have to be brought in Canada to enforce a US judgment if the judgment debtor does not pay voluntarily. In matters involving the US and Canada this is not a difficult proceeding. However, in many countries, facts must be proven in the local court establishing a prima facie case for the validity of the foreign judgment before it can be enforced. Most countries refuse to enforce foreign judgments that were obtained in jurisdictions that are viewed as either unfriendly or as lacking an acceptable level of due process.

There is a new Hague Convention on Choice of Court Agreements which has been ratified by Mexico and is under consideration in the US, the EU and elsewhere. Generally, this convention provides that where parties have selected an exclusive forum, then:

First, no other court will exercise jurisdiction over the case, and

Second, with certain exceptions, other courts will enforce the judgment of the chosen court.

Application is limited to cases in which both courts involved are located in a Contracting State.

II. JUDGE OR ARBITRATOR?

The parties may agree that arbitration will be the exclusive method of resolving disputes arising under the contract. Most national laws now require courts to respect and to enforce these provisions and thus this becomes an effective choice of forum. Since the parties can direct the arbitrator to apply any specific law they choose, it can also be used as an effective choice of law.

Compared to actions in court, arbitration is supposed to be relatively fast, inexpensive and final. As arbitration has become a more complex process with such things as more sophisticated discovery, this proceeding can be more extended and therefore more expensive. Arbitration involves no jury. Thus where a jury trial would otherwise be available, an agreement to arbitrate means that the right to a jury is lost along with the right to appeal. This may be viewed as an advantage or disadvantage depending upon one's circumstances.

In our hypothetical, these are the principal considerations dictating whether one would chose to agree to arbitrate disputes. However, agreement on choice of law and forum can be most difficult in transactions involving parties from countries with fundamentally different legal systems or unreliable legal systems.

Selection of the law of a third country with disputes to be resolved in that country could be a solution.

Assume that a Mexican seller and a Chinese buyer agree to a forum in Manila or Tokyo. Will the courts in the chosen jurisdiction accept jurisdiction of the case? The court is being asked to expend local time and resources to resolve a matter that has nothing to do with people or property within its jurisdiction. Assume that these parties agree to apply the law of Singapore. If the matter is litigated in China or Mexico, will the court respect the choice of Singapore law when Singapore has no connection to the transaction? Many jurisdictions will not permit that. For example, the "traditional" rule under the Uniform Commercial Code provides:

> (W)hen a transaction bears a reasonable relation to this state and also another state or nation the parties may agree that the law either of this state or of such other state or nation shall govern their rights and duties. § 1–301(a) (numbered § 1–105 in several states).

Singapore has no "reasonable relation" to the transaction in question. The proposed amendments to Article 1 would have changed this rule to permit a local court to enforce the law of a jurisdiction selected by the parties even though it had no relation to the transaction. Thus the proposed revision of Article 1 provided that:

> (1) ... (A)n agreement by parties to a domestic transaction that any or all of their rights and obligations are to be determined by the law of this State or of another State is effective, whether or not the transaction bears a relation to the State designated, and

> (2) an agreement by parties to an international transaction that any or all of their rights and obligations are to be determined by the laws of this State or of another State or country is effective, whether or not the transaction bears a relation to the State or country designated.

However, the states that adopted the revised Article 1 all rejected this particular provision and the official 2009 version of Article 1 now deletes it.

Providing for arbitration is a method of making certain that your choice of law will be enforced and that the parties will enjoy a neutral forum. If the Mexican seller and the Chinese buyer wish to be bound by the law of a neutral country, they may, for example, provide for arbitration in Singapore under Singapore law. An arbitrator will apply whatever law the parties selected. One must also be concerned whether the country where your defendant's assets are located will enforce arbitration awards. In many countries, all arbitration awards are generally enforceable. The United Nations Convention on the Recognition and Enforcement of Foreign Arbitral Awards, commonly referred to as the New York Convention, has been ratified by 144 nations. Those nations are committed to enforcing awards involving parties from different countries, but surprises may be in store. Vietnam is one of the countries that elected to limit application of the treaty to "commercial" disputes. An Australian company performed construction services in Vietnam and pursuant to the terms of the contract, obtained an arbitration award in Australia for an unpaid balance due. Enforcement in a Vietnamese court was denied because the dispute was not "commercial." In Vietnamese law at that time, "commercial" transactions involved only the sale of goods and activities related to the sale of goods. This case is unreported as it was decided before the Vietnamese adopted a case reporting system.

The cost of arbitrating international disputes can be quite substantial. Some jurisdictions such as the small island of Guernsey have adopted laws to facilitate arbitration of international disputes to entice foreign parties to bring in arbitration business. For the Mexican seller, the prospect of litigation in China is a daunting challenge, however, other than avoiding the "home town court" problem, arbitration in Guernsey Island can be equally expensive and formidable.

There is no appeal permitted from arbitration decisions and thus no review of the result. Enforcement is mandated except upon proof of particularly egregious problems such as bribery although some courts have denied enforcement based upon "manifest disregard of the law." This loss of the right of appeal can be a distinct disadvantage as even the most ardent advocates of arbitration admit that arbitrators can get the law wrong or ignore proper procedural rules. Since arbitration decisions may be rendered without a statement of reasons for the ruling and are almost never reported, it is not easy to assess the magnitude of these problems.

III. COMMERCIAL LAW IN DEVELOPING COUNTRIES

A distinction can be made between countries that are "developing" in an economic sense and those that are "developing" in a legal sense. Some countries with serious economic shortcomings have legal systems that are advanced in many respects supported by judicial systems that are relatively sophisticated and dependable. On the other hand, some countries have serious shortcomings in existing commercial law and/or are lacking a tradition of a respected and independent judiciary.

Countries that had a relatively pure communist economic system had little need for commercial law. Facilities of production are owned by the government and their operation and relationships to each other are the product of government planning and assigned tasks and thus are not based upon contract law. Private citizens might sell personal property to each other, but such transactions do not reach the legal system. The traditional legal background in countries such as the USSR and the People's Republic of China was based upon Germanic law due to adoption of the German codes at the beginning of the twentieth century. (Some scholars in these countries refer to this as "Roman law" but it was copied in the early twentieth century directly from the then-new German codes.)

When China, Vietnam, and the various countries that resulted from the breakup of the USSR began to pursue a market economy, a workable system of commercial law became necessary to make this a smooth operation. These countries, particularly China and Vietnam, have looked to international treaties and international standards to guide them. For example, many Vietnamese drafting committees work under a Government directive that they are to adopt laws that comply with "best international practices" and they strive to achieve this goal. When treating with the subject of transactions in personal property, they give consideration to the provisions of the CISG as representative of a widely accepted international norm despite the fact that Vietnam has not ratified this treaty.

In China, Article 142 of the GPCL, the basic law governing all commercial and civil acts in the PRC, provides:

> If any international treaty concluded or acceded to by the People's Republic of China contains provisions differing from those in the civil law of the People's Republic of China, the provisions of the international treaty shall apply, unless the provisions are ones on which the People's Republic of China has announced reservations.

> International practice may be applied on matters for which neither the law of the People's Republic of China nor any international treaty concluded or acceded to by the People's Republic of China has any provisions.

The notion that the terms of international treaties prevail over domestic law when the two are in conflict is not novel, but not all legal systems expressly provide for this result. The notion that "international practice" should be controlling in legal issues where Chinese law does not provide answers is an unusual provision. While it leaves a great deal of room for interpretation as to when national law fails to make provisions and as to what is in fact "international practice," it manifests an intention to move the laws of China firmly in the direction of "international practice."

IV. A LAWYER'S THOUGHTS ON CONTRACTING WITH A CHINESE COMPANY

The following was written by Dan Harris, attorney at Harris & Moure and lead editor of the Chinese Law Blog (www.chinalawblog. com). It appeared on that Blog on July 5, 2009. The comments that follow develop interesting problems related to obtaining injunctive relief when contracts call for arbitration.

China OEM Agreements. Why Ours Are In Chinese. Flat Out.

Posted by Dan on July 5, 2009 at 11:18 AM

Discussion: Comments (12) : TrackBacks (2) : Linking Blogs : Add to del.icio.us

Had a nice conversation with a potential client last week. Company has a great new product it wants made in China. Like many companies starting out in China, this one is in the process of shopping for its China lawyers and my firm was one of four suggested to it by its regular corporate counsel.

I told this company that we would almost certainly do their OEM contract in Chinese and I quoted them a flat fee for doing that, along with an English language translation. They told me that the other law firms were saying that the contract would be in English and they would "need to" charge by the hour and it would even be impossible to estimate how long it would take due to the negotiations that would take place between this company and its Chinese manufacturer. (Ed. "OEM" means original equipment manufacturing.)

I think one big reason so many US law firms do not write their OEM agreements in Chinese is simply because they do not have any lawyers who can read and write Mandarin fluently. My firm has two lawyers (and various others) who can read and write (and speak) Mandarin fluently and we usually favor putting our clients' OEM contracts in Chinese for the following reasons.

Because international contracts are so often between parties from different countries, they commonly are written in two or more languages. Nearly all of the contracts we draft for our Western clients doing business in China are in English and Chinese (though about ten percent of the time, we also translate them into German,

Spanish, Korean, or French as well). This duality of language can, if not handled properly, pose big problems.

When we do a contract in both English and Chinese, we always call for the contract to specify ONE official language to control if there is a dispute. We do not advise drafting a contract that is silent on the official language nor do we advise drafting contracts that call for both English and Chinese to apply. Having two official languages pretty much doubles the chances for ambiguity and pretty much doubles the attorney time (and fees) that will be incurred in fighting over the meaning of the *two* contracts. It is expensive enough litigating on one contract; there is no benefit to litigating on two. So the question for us comes down to whether English or Chinese should be the official language of the contract and the answer to that question requires we first decide where we would most like to see disputes resolved. If we go for arbitration in English, then we almost certainly will want English as the official language. But if we decide the Chinese courts will be the best place to resolve conflicts, then we want Chinese to be the official language.

Now I know most of you think the obvious answer here is to do anything possible to avoid Chinese courts, but you would be wrong. Let me explain.

In determining where best to resolve conflicts on an OEM contract, the analysis has to begin with first trying to determine the most likely and the potentially most damaging disputes and then analyzing where best to handle each sort of dispute. Disputes between foreign companies and Chinese manufacturers most often involve the following:

1. The Chinese company provides poor quality product. To say this is common would be an understatement. The best way to deal with a dispute involving the Chinese company providing poor product is usually to seek to work it out with the Chinese manufacturer. If that proves impossible AND there is enough at stake to warrant suing, arbitration is likely going to be the best course of action. Not to minimize the importance of these cases, but they usually involve only one shipment and they usually involve a finite amount of money.

Litigation outside China against a China based manufacturer usually does not make sense. Because most Chinese companies do not have any meaningful assets outside China and because China does not enforce foreign judgments, getting a judgment outside China against the Chinese company will likely have virtually no value. Therefore, there is no point in having a contract that calls for jurisdiction in a court outside China. For more on the difficulty/impossibility of enforcing foreign judgments in China, check out "Taking Judgments To China (And Korea), Let's Not Sue Twice."

2. The Chinese company manufactures the foreign company's product without the foreign company's permission and in direct violation of the OEM agreement. You have a great product and you have taken it to China for manufacturing there. You are currently selling in just a few countries, but as your plans call for you to eventually sell into China and India and maybe even Africa some day. All of a sudden, you learn that your Chinese manufacturer is not making just the 100,000 units you ordered, but, in fact, is making 500,000 units and shipping the extra 400,000 to India, Africa and the rest of Asia, where it is selling them for 1/5 of what you are charging.

If your agreement calls for arbitration in Hong Kong or New York, or even Beijing ... good luck. What you need, and what you need fast, in these situations, is a court order (injunctive relief) requiring the Chinese manufacturer to stop making your product and to stop NOW. And guess what, pretty much the only way you are going to get that badly needed court order is from a Chinese court.

If your contract calls for arbitration and you sue in a Chinese court to get an injunction to stop your manufacturer from breaching your contract by manufacturing and selling your product, you almost certainly will not succeed. The Chinese manufacturer will show the court your arbitration clause and request it decline the case in favor of resolving the dispute in arbitration. Once you are in arbitration, you pretty much will not be able to get an injunction.

It is possible to write your OEM contract to call for arbitration with a Chinese court "carve out" for injunctive relief, but many/ most Chinese courts do not enforce these sorts of provisions.

For these reasons, we usually favor our OEM contracts calling for dispute resolution in the Chinese courts. And if you are going to be in a Chinese court, you do want your contract to be in Chinese. The reason for this is simple. If your contract is in English, the Chinese courts will use their own translator to translate it. Translations can be easily manipulated and it is virtually always better to have your contract translated by *your own* law firm in advance so you know exactly what it says before you sign it, than to have it translated into Chinese by an unknown translator only *after* you have sued on it.

3. The Chinese manufacturer refuses to return the foreign company's molds after the foreign company seeks to terminate its relationship with the Chinese manufacturer. This often happens when the foreign company terminates its relationship with the Chinese supplier. Not surprisingly, the key here is to have a contract in Chinese that makes clear that the mold belongs to you and that there will be hell to pay (in legal terms) if the Chinese manufacturer does not return these to you pronto. But what if the manufacturer does not return your molds? Damages are usually not what is needed. You need the molds immediately because without them you cannot manufacture your products. Again, the best positioned foreign company is the one with a contract in Chinese who can go to a Chinese court for an injunction mandating the manufacturer return the molds.

Comments

Most do not realize there is a big difference between being able to simply translate into Mandarin and being able to translate legal terms into Mandarin. Same can be said for Japanese.

Posted by: Tim / July 6, 2009 1:39 AM

And also people don't realize how easy it is to get wrong. Even simple terms like "should" can cause huge problems. When you say that someone "should" do something, are you saying that it is a good idea or that it is mandatory that they do it?

Both English and Chinese legal writing deal with this problem by using specific terms with precise meanings and avoiding terms that have ambiguous meanings, but you have to be pretty specialized to know what those terms are.

Also, there are concepts that don't carry across well. "Consideration" is a concept in common law that doesn't exist in Chinese law. Also there are terms that mean completely different things. My favorite is "unilateral contract."

Posted by: Twofish / July 6, 2009 11:23 AM

Why are Chinese courts reluctant to enforce injunctive relief carve outs? Simply because they don't want to bother with litigating the merits of a case that may need to be litigated in parallel elsewhere as well? If so, why not simply provide that for any case invoking injunctive relief, the whole shebang gets done in the People's court?

The broader question is in what circumstances would you want an arbitration/foreign forum clause in a contract with a Chinese OEM? If the chips hit the fan, you will pretty much always be either be suing for money and/or injunctive relief, which only a Chinese court can meaningfully provide if the OEM is like 99% out there that have no real assets outside of China.

Posted by: ceh / July 6, 2009 1:06 PM

Tim,

So true. . . . So true of translating in every language. There are incredibly few people who can do legal translations well.

Posted by: Dan / July 7, 2009 7:08 AM

I'm guessing here but I think the reason that Chinese courts are reluctant to agree to a carve-out for injunctive relief is that it's very hard to say "injunctive relief" in Chinese.

This illustrates the land mines in legal translation. Even the term "injunctive relief" or even "law" is hard to translate sometimes.

Posted by: Twofish / July 7, 2009 11:09 AM

China's Big Political Picture Writ Small For Business. China Law Blog

I am not generally a fan of extrapolating the way a country conducts its politics to the way its enterprises conduct its businesses even in China where so many businesses are government owned. I am not saying it cannot be done, but I generally find it . . . []

August 23, 2009 10:19 AM

China's First Foreign Nail House. Dude, Where's Your Contract? China Law Blog

Lara Farrar and Xie Yu wrote an excellent article for the China Daily and AsiaOne on the recent controversy swirling around what is being called China's first foreign nail house case. The article is entitled, "1st foreigner 'nail household' in China," . . . []

Questions and Comments

1. What problems does the author Mr. Harris identify when two languages are both designated as the official language of the contract? The CISG is in eight languages ranging from Russian to Arabic and all are "official." In a transaction involving companies based in Egypt and Germany, what result when a term in the Arabic version has a different meaning from the same provision in the German version?

2. A foreign judgment cannot be enforced without some sort of local proceedings. In many countries, the local court will completely review or even retry the case. As Mr. Harris notes in the case of China, if the Chinese courts are to retry the case, then it may not help to have a foreign judgment in the first place.

3. Court injunctions are enforceable by sanctions such as money fines or even imprisonment in some legal systems. An arbitrator has no such power and thus cannot by himself effectively order action or inaction. Thus, if a party to a contract will likely need an injunction to obtain effective relief, arbitration is effective only if the legal system is willing to enforce an arbitrator's orders. How does this problem get

resolved in China? What is an "injunctive relief carve out?" How is it supposed to operate?

4. Completely accurate translation of documents is simply impossible. In Vietnamese legal vocabulary, houses are goods. There is some logic for this as the land under the house belongs to the People, meaning the Government. As noted, until recently in Vietnam "commercial" had a meaning that was limited to the sale of goods and related services. This definition was changed with the adoption of the newly revised Vietnamese Commercial Law, but given problems of this nature, the translator can only produce the comparable word without vouching for the word having a similar meaning. An effective translator must understand both legal systems and the significance of the vocabulary being utilized in each.

Chapter 4

INTEREST AND USURY

I. INTRODUCING INTEREST AND USURY

THE FIRST HYPOTHETICAL—A SECOND-HAND VOLKS-WAGEN GOLF AUTOMOBILE

In 2001, an Italian limited liability company purchased a second-hand Volkswagen Golf TDI automobile from a German seller over the internet. The price of the car was about 13,000 euros[1] and was paid in full by the time it was delivered to the buyer. The buyer then spent approximately 620 euros on a new paint job for the vehicle and approximately that same amount on replacement parts, plus approximately 250 euros on registration expenses. Shortly after the vehicle was delivered, it was confiscated by the Italian Traffic Police Division when it was determined that it had been stolen from its true owner about five months before it was sold to this purchaser. The purchaser sued for reimbursement of the purchase price and all of its expenditures on the vehicle, plus interest.[2]

THE SECOND HYPOTHETICAL—HIGH-FASHION ITALIAN TEXTILES

In 1998, an Italian textile company named Tessile 21 S.r.l agreed to sell a certain quantity of high-fashion textiles to a Greek company, Ixela S.A. The purchase price for the textiles was to be approximately 11,000 euros.[3] The purchaser paid approximately

---

1. The case was decided before the Euro came into existence as the common currency for the European Union. The price of the car and the amount spent by the buyer have therefore been converted from Deutsche Marks and Lire, respectively, to Euros.

2. The facts of this hypothetical are based upon a case that was heard before the District Court of Freiberg, Germany, a translation of which can be found at http://www.cisg.law.pace.edu/cisg/wais/db/cases2/020822g1.html.

3. This case was decided before the Euro came into existence as the common

one-third of this price, but refused to pay the other two thirds, even after repeated requests. The seller sued for the balance due, plus interest.[4]

PROBLEM 1

Assume that you represent the buyer in the first hypothetical. On what grounds does your claim for interest rest? How is your claim for interest different from the claim you would make on behalf of the seller in the second hypothetical? Answer this question first as a matter of instinct, and then consult CISG Article 78, Interest for the Buyer, and Article 84(1), Interest for the Seller, which are reproduced later in this chapter, on page 99.

Before exploring the concept of interest insofar as it relates to buyers and sellers under the CISG, these materials will begin by examining US law governing a more familiar kind of interest: interest that is charged to borrowers of money.

The concept of interest is said to date back to ancient times.[5] In the US, charging interest is common and generally uncontroversial, becoming unlawful only when it reaches the level of usury. The meaning of the word "usury" has evolved over time and has not always had a negative connotation. "Originally, the word 'usury' meant only the charging of a fee for the *use* of money, a practice that was recognized even in the earliest of times as legitimate."[6] In modern times, by contrast, usury has been defined as "the exaction of a greater sum for the use of money than the highest rate of interest allowed by law."[7] Although some courts have described usury as "malum prohibitum,"[8] suggesting that there is no moral implication of violating usury laws,[9] others characterize usury as morally wrong.[10]

currency for the European Union. The price of the textiles has therefore been converted from Lire into Euros.

4. The facts of this hypothetical are based upon a case that was heard before the Tribunale (or District Court) of Pavia. A translation of this case can be found at http://www.cisg.law.pace.edu/cisg/wais/db/cases2/991229i3.html.

5. "The lending of money or commodities such as grain in return for interest has been documented as early as 3000 B.C. and no doubt, predates that." RENUART & KEEST, *infra* note 20, at 14.

6. LAUREN KROHN, CONSUMER PROTECTION AND THE LAW: A DICTIONARY 322 (1995).

7. *Foreign Commerce v. Tonn*, 789 F.2d 221, 223 (3d Cir. 1986), *citing Evans v. Nat'l Bank of Savannah*, 251 U.S. 108, 114 (1919).

8. "An act that is a crime merely because it is prohibited by statute, although the act itself is not necessarily immoral." BLACK'S LAW DICTIONARY 978 (8th ed. 2004).

9. *Schneider v. Wilmington Trust Co.*, 310 A.2d 897 (Del. Ch. 1973), *rev'd in part on other grounds*, 320 A.2d 709 (Del. 1974); *Lloyd v. Scott*, 29 U.S. 205, 222 (1830) ("The act of usury has long since lost that deep moral stain which was formerly attached to it; and it is now considered only as an illegal or immoral act, because it is prohibited by law.").

The following are the generally accepted elements of a usury cause of action:

1. A loan of money;

2. An absolute obligation to repay the principal;[11]

3. The exaction of greater compensation than allowed by law for the use of the money by the borrower; and

4. An intent to violate the law.[12]

Note that this test, by its own terms, does not apply to a sales transaction such as those described in the hypotheticals that opened this chapter. The question of whether, or how, usury laws affect sales transactions is an important theme that will be revisited later in this section.

Returning to the elements of usury, not all jurisdictions impose an "intent" requirement.[13] In addition, even those jurisdictions requiring intent have varying interpretations of the kind of intent required.[14] In some jurisdictions, intent to violate the law is not required; instead, intent to charge the interest rate that is deemed usurious will suffice.[15] Others require "a knowing and corrupt intent."[16] Regardless of how a given jurisdiction chooses to deal with the matter of intent, because a usury action is considered penal in nature, the test is to be strictly construed.[17] Construing the test narrowly makes particular sense when the penalty for usury is

10. *First Fed. Sav. & Loan Ass'n v. Norwood Realty Co.*, 212 Ga. 524, 526, 93 S.E.2d 763, 766 (1956) ("'[E]xaction of usury is odious, illegal, and immoral.'").

11. *See infra* notes 25–29 and accompanying text.

12. *See, e.g., In re Donnay*, 184 B.R. 767, 778 (D. Minn. 1995).

13. Some cases seem to omit the "intent" element. *See, e.g., Dopp v. Yari*, 927 F. Supp. 814, 820 (D.N.J. 1996) (listing only the first three elements); *Thrift v. Hubbard*, 44 F.3d 348, 359 (5th Cir. 1995) (same). Others expressly state that intent is not an element of the cause of action for usury. *See, e.g., Gillivan v. Austin*, 640 F. Supp. 1325, 1328 (D.V.I. 1986). Under federal law, however, intent is an element of a usury cause of action. 12 U.S.C. § 86 (2006) ("The taking, receiving, reserving, or charging a rate of interest greater than is allowed by section 85 of this title, *when knowingly done*, shall be deemed a forfeiture of the entire interest which the note,

bill, or other evidence of debt carries with it, or which has been agreed to be paid thereon....") (emphasis added).

14. *Gillivan, supra* note 13, at 1328–1329.

15. *In re Donnay, supra* note 12, at 781. *See also Gillivan, supra* note 13, at 1328; Krohn, *supra* note 6, at 323 ("For example, a creditor who intends to charge 10 percent interest but does not know that the legal rate is 8 percent is guilty of usury, because the intent was to charge an amount that turned out to be over the legal rate. On the other hand, a creditor who intends to charge 8 percent but accidentally miscalculates in setting payments so that the actual rate paid by the consumer is 10 percent will not be guilty of usury, because he or she intended to charge an amount that would have been legal but for the miscalculation.").

16. *Gillivan, supra* note 13, at 1328.

17. *First Bank v. Tony's Tortilla Factory, Inc.*, 877 S.W.2d 285, 287 (Tex. 1994).

harsh, costing the creditor in some jurisdictions not only the unlawful interest it has sought to charge, but also any outstanding principal and lawful interest.[18] More commonly, however, the remedy for usury is more modest—a refund of interest above the legal limit.[19] Other limitations also exist to prevent usury laws from being overbroad or unduly punitive. For example, because the purpose of usury laws has been described as "to protect desperately poor people from the consequences of their own desperation,"[20] corporations may not be able to assert a usury defense.[21] Furthermore, whether a transaction is usurious is generally decided based on the facts as they existed at the time of contract formation, not as they developed afterward. For example, if a contract called for a variable interest rate that was lawful when the parties entered the contract and later rose to an unanticipated extent, the contract should not be deemed usurious.[22]

Usury under US law is governed by both federal and state law.[23] Even so, the spectrum of cases governed by state usury laws is quite narrow.

> Banks and lending institutions chartered by the federal government are allowed by federal law to charge the maximum rate allowed to state lenders in the state in which they are doing business. States, in turn, have laws allowing state lending institutions to charge the same rates as federal institutions. The result of all of these various rates is a crazy-quilt of laws governing interest rates. The consumer generally finds that a state's basic usury law rarely applies to the particular loan for which he or she is applying.[24]

18. *Seidel, infra* note 20, at 740. In other jurisdictions, the penalty may be less severe. *See, e.g., Gillivan, supra* note 13, at 1327 (providing that the borrower recovers twice the amount of interest already paid and escapes any obligation to pay further interest).

19. KROHN, *supra* note 6, at 323.

20. *Seidel v. 18 E. 17th St. Owners, Inc.*, 79 N.Y.2d 735, 740, 598 N.E.2d 7, 9 (1992), *quoting Schneider v. Phelps*, 41 N.Y.2d 238, 243, 359 N.E.2d 1361, 1365 (1977). *See also* ELIZABETH RENUART & KATHLEEN E. KEEST, THE COST OF CREDIT: REGULATION, PREEMPTION, AND INDUSTRY ABUSES 3 (2005).

21. *Seidel, supra* note 20, at 740.

22. *In re Donnay, supra* note 12, at 780 ("'[A] contract that is valid when made cannot then become void for usury because it subsequently develops that the lender will receive a greater return

for the use of the money than the highest lawful rate.").

23. *Evans, supra* note 7, at 111 ("The National Bank Act establishes a system of general regulations. It adopts usury laws of the states only in so far as they severally fix the rate of interest."). 12 U.S.C. § 85 (2006) ("When no rate is fixed by the laws of the State, or Territory, or District, the bank may take, receive, reserve, or charge a rate not exceeding 7 per centum, or 1 per centum in excess of the discount rate on ninety day commercial paper in effect at the Federal Reserve Bank in the Federal Reserve District where the bank is located, whichever may be the greater, and such interest may be taken in advance, reckoning the days for which the note, bill, or other evidence of debt has to run.").

24. KROHN, *supra* note 6, at 324. *See also* RENUART & KEEST, *supra* note 20, at

In the United States, usury law applies only to loans or agreements to forbear collecting a debt. Thus, when interest is paid on an investment, usury laws do not apply. In addition, usury laws do not apply when "the collection of the entire interest is at risk and depends upon a contingency," so long as "the parties contracted in good faith without the intent to evade the usury laws."[25] As James Avery Webb's *Treatise on the Law of Usury, and Incidentally, of Interest* states, "There is no usury where the principal is placed in jeopardy by the terms of the agreement. To carry the case beyond the usury statute, however, the hazard or contingency must be *bona fide* and not a mere color of a risk or such possibilities of unexpected loss as might occur in the ordinary course of the borrowing and lending of money."[26] Comment *a* to the Restatement (First) of Contracts § 527 makes the point clearly:

> Usury laws do not prohibit the taking of business chances in the employment of money. A creditor who takes the chance of losing all or part of the sum to which he would be entitled if he bargained for the return of his money with the highest permissible rate of interest is allowed to contract for greater profit. On the other hand, it is not permissible to use this form of contract as a device for obtaining usurious profit. If the probability of the occurrence of the contingency on which diminished payment is promised is remote, or if the diminution should the contingency occur is slight as compared with the possible profit to be obtained if the contingency does not occur, the transaction is presumably usurious.[27]

Illustration 1 to § 527 shows how this principle might be applied:

Ill. 1. A borrows $5000 from B to use in A's business, promising that if the business makes a profit of a stated amount during

41 ("[T]he National Bank Act (NBA) sets the ceiling for interest rates that may be charged by federally-chartered banks. Under this Act, federal banks are treated as 'most favored lenders" and may charge the higher of: (1) the interest rate allowed lenders in the state where the bank is located; or (2) one percent above the discount rate on ninety-day commercial paper in effect at the Federal Reserve Bank in the district where the bank is located."). The authors go on to describe a total of eight different federal statutes that pre-empt state usury and lending laws, at least in part: in addition to the NBA, the Home Owners' Loan Act (HOLA), the National Credit Union Administration (NCUA), the National Housing Act (NHA), the Depository Institutions Deregulation and Monetary Control Act of 1980 (DIDA), the 1982 Depository Institutions Act (DIA), the Interstate Banking and Branching Efficiency Act of 1994 (IBBEA), and the Gramm-Leach-Bliley Act (GLB Act). *Id.* at 41–43.

25. *Dopp, supra* note 13, at 822 (citing several additional authorities for the same proposition); *see also* KROHN, *supra* note 6, at 323.

26. JAMES AVERY WEBB, A TREATISE ON THE LAW OF USURY AND, INCIDENTALLY, OF INTEREST 44 (1899) (emphasis in original).

27. RESTATEMENT (FIRST) OF CONTRACTS § 527 (1932). This section does not appear in the Second Restatement, but is still cited with approval by courts and commentators alike.

the ensuing year, to repay B $6000, but if the business suffers a loss during that year to repay B $4000 in full satisfaction; and in case the business fails to earn the stated profit but suffers no loss, to repay the amount of the loan without interest. The bargain is not usurious unless the probability that the business will earn the stated sums as profit is so great as to make the agreement a colorable device for usury.[28]

One justification for the Restatement's rule is that the "usurious" interest rate in such a case can fairly be considered to be "a bonus ... for participating in an uncertain transaction."[29]

Having established that usury laws do not normally apply to investments, this discussion will now return to another area of law that, as mentioned earlier, has not historically been regulated by usury law: sales of goods. Most authorities hold that usury laws do not apply to a sale of goods or property on credit.[30] Furthermore, usury laws generally do not apply to contingent interest charges that arise only upon default of the buyer,[31] at least so long as the creditor docs not encourage late payments to generate the additional interest revenue.[32]

Under US law up until World War II, sales on credit were generally unregulated by state legislatures, falling instead under ordinary contract law.[33] And even now, interest that a seller charges to a buyer who has failed to pay for goods may or may not be governed by laws prohibiting usury. Instead, such charges may be regulated as what is sometimes called "convenience credit" and thus fall within the purview of Retail Installment Sales Acts (RISAs) or separate laws dealing with sales on an open account.[34]

---

28. *Id.*

29. *Dopp*, note 13, at 823.

30. *Foreign Commerce, supra* note 7, at 223, *citing State ex rel. Turner v. Younker Brothers. Inc.*, 210 N.W.2d 550, 559 (Iowa 1973) (in turn, according to the *Foreign Commerce* court, citing "overwhelming state and federal precedent").

31. *Dopp, supra* note 13, at 823 (noting that such transactions are acceptable because "the borrower ... may discharge himself from [the ostensibly usurious interest rate] by punctual payment of the principal").

32. *In re Donnay, supra* note 12, at 779 (noting that the creditor in question not only did not encourage the debtor to make late payments, but actually "terminated its relationship with [the debtor] partially because of late payment").

Thus, the court held that the transaction was not usurious. *Id.*

33. RENUART & KEEST, *supra* note 20, at 16–17. *See also* WEBB, *supra* note 26, at 52 (stating the then-contemporary rule that "ordinary contracts for rents, sales, transfers of stocks and bonds, compensation for services, guarantees of liability and so on, when entered into in good faith do not come within the pale of usury"). Webb goes on to demonstrate that, even at that time, courts and commentators were concerned that parties could use a lawful form to mask an unlawful transaction: "[T]hese *forms* of contract are quite frequently resorted to for the purpose of concealing usury and thereby evading the law." *Id.* (emphasis in original).

34. RENUART & KEEST, *supra* note 20, at 21.

Convenience creditors are sellers who forbear the collection of existing debts in return for installment payments with interest. Such creditors include doctors, lawyers, hospitals, utilities, oil companies, farm supply companies, and other businesses which have no formal charge account plan but which are willing to finance debts either to increase their volume of business or in order to avoid the collection process as long as their customers are making payments. These credit agreements are often evidenced merely by a sales receipt which states that a monthly charge will be imposed if the debt is not paid within thirty days.[35]

Such "convenience" interest is similar to the kind of interest that CISG Article 78 allows a creditor to recover as a matter of course, even without the parties having negotiated such an agreement.

Having briefly discussed how US law deals with the matter of interest in several different contexts, this section now turns to the international marketplace, in which perspectives on interest vary considerably. Some countries are more permissive than the United States with respect to interest,[36] while others outlaw it entirely, regardless of whether the interest is charged on a debt or paid on an investment.

The following excerpt from Kristen David Adams, *Promise Enforcement in Mortgage Lending: How U.S. Borrowers and Lenders Can See Themselves as Part of a Shared Goal*, 28 Rev. Banking & Fin. L. 507, 522–525 (2009), provides an overview of how Islamic law, or *Shari'a*, and Jewish law, approach the concept of interest.

The *Shari'a*'s well-known prohibition against *riba*, or interest, is part of the broader prohibition against unlawful benefits in commercial transactions. In addition, the prohibition against *riba* is broader than the common prohibition against usury; instead, *riba* normally includes all interest, regardless of its rate. Usury, by contrast, can be defined as either excessive interest or, in some contexts, interest exceeding the amount of principal loaned. . . .

One author's definition of *riba* reveals an important core theme: "*Riba* means . . . unearned profits that are not reflective of business risk." Thus, one overarching concern with *riba* is that it does not represent a morally justifiable means of earning money. As a better alternative to *riba*, Islamic law encourages business models in which a borrower and lender act as partners in the business enterprise, both bearing some risk and potentially earning some profit as well.

---

35. *Id.*

36. Brazil is probably the most commonly cited example.

Jewish law, likewise, includes strong prohibitions on interest, or *ribbis*. Notably, the Jewish legal tradition distinguishes between Biblical and Rabbinical prohibitions, with the latter being stricter than the former and also stricter than the *Shari'a* prohibition on *riba*. When taken as a whole, the prohibitions on *ribbis* share a common theme: lending is never to be a means of gaining dominance over a borrower. Instead, all persons in the Jewish community are to share in conditions of equality at a fundamental level. Similarly, and as part of the prohibition against *ribbis*, the lender should not accept blessings, praise, or gifts for making the loan. In fact, some interpretations of the prohibition on *Ribbis Devarim*, or "[r]*ibbis* involving words," prohibit the borrower even from thanking the lender for the loan. While Jewish law connects these prohibitions on blessings, praise, gifts, and perhaps even thanks with the law of *ribbis*, these rules can also be seen as logically consistent with a sense of fundamental equality between debtors and creditors. Jewish law also recognizes a community responsibility for upholding this prohibition that goes beyond the borrower and the creditor. An attorney who facilitates a proscribed transaction may find himself or herself not only "in breach of the secondary prohibition against enabling wrongdoing," but also in violation of "the primary substantive prohibition against active participation in a transaction involving interest."[37]

Building on the prior excerpt, Professors Frank Vogel and Samuel Hayes, III have identified five potential rationales for the *Shari'a's* prohibition on *riba*:

1. "Mathematical equivalency," which can be defined as "the goal of exalting fairness of exchange, advanced by insisting on exact mathematical equality of exchange whenever that equality is possible and appropriate."[38]

2. "Avoiding commercial exploitation," which is associated with "the fear of the strong exploiting the weak."[39]

3. "Minimizing commerce in currency and foodstuffs," which can be explained as follows: "If money is to remain a neutral measure of value, it must not be dealt with as a commodity. Because foodstuffs are often used in lieu of money and because they are basic needs of mankind, they

---

37. Kristen David Adams, *Promise Enforcement in Mortgage Lending: How U.S. Borrowers and Lenders Can See Themselves as Part of a Shared Goal*, 28 Rev. Banking & Fin. L. 507, 522–525 (2009).

38. Frank E. Vogel & Samuel L. Hayes, III, Islamic Law and Finance: Religion, Risk, and Return 78 (2006).

39. *Id.* at 82.

should be treated as much as possible as if they also were neutral and stable values, withdrawn from commerce."[40]

4. "Linking lawfulness of gain to risk-taking," which is consistent with the belief that "gain is morally justified only when one faces risk to secure it, while riskless gain is unjust."[41]

5. "Using money and markets to allocate and moderate risk," which is associated with the position that interest should be paid only in situations of moderate risk—not where the risk is too high, thus constituting gambling, or too low, such that interest is not morally justified.[42]

Insofar as Jewish law is concerned, this discussion has alluded to two different kinds of prohibitions on *ribbis*—Biblically prohibited *ribbis* and rabbinically prohibited *ribbis*, which is also called *Ribbis DeRabbanan*.[43] "Biblically prohibited [r]*ibbis* is called Ribbis Ketzutzah (lit. pre-arranged [r]*ibbis*). This is because the Torah prohibits [r]*ibbis* only when arrangements for the payments were made at the time that the loan was extended."[44] If the contract, when made, calls for *ribbis* to be paid, the contract violates the Biblical proscription on *ribbis*, even if payment is to be made at some point in the future.[45] If, however, the debtor decides of his or her own accord to give the lender a gift, the Rabbinical prohibition on *ribbis* is implicated, but the Biblical prohibition is not.[46] This is because, "[b]y Rabbinic law, the borrower is prohibited from paying interest or offering a gift to the lender even if he had not previously committed himself to do so."[47] In fact, Rabbinic law prohibits the borrower from giving any gift to the lender during the life of the loan, "even if he does not mention the gift in connection with the loan."[48]

Questions

1. At a fundamental level, how are Islamic law's treatment of *riba* and Jewish law's treatment of *ribbis* different from the United States' approach to usury? How are they different from one another?

2. Although there are obvious differences between the US approach to interest, on the one hand, and the Islamic and Jewish traditions, on the other, there are also some similarities

---

40. *Id.* at 83.
41. *Id.*
42. *Id.* at 85–86.
43. RABBI YISROEL REISMAN, THE LAWS OF RIBBIS 51, 58 (1995).
44. *Id.* at 51.

45. *Id.*
46. *Id.*
47. *Id.* at 58.
48. *Id.* at 59.

to be considered. What common concerns do both share, insofar as unlawful interest is concerned?

3. What does it mean for a creditor to "encourage late payments to generate additional interest revenue?"[49]

PROBLEM 2

Building upon Illustration 1 to the Restatement (First) of Contracts § 527, how would you change the facts of that Illustration to create a situation in which either "the probability of the occurrence of the contingency on which diminished payment is promised is remote, or the diminution should the contingency occur is slight compared with the possible profit to be obtained if the contingency does not occur"?[50] What difference would this change in facts make?

PROBLEM 3

Return to the first hypothetical on page 88 (the Second-Hand Volkswagen Golf) and now assume that the vehicle was sold to a purchaser in Syria. Syria participates in the CISG but also prohibits *riba*. What policy considerations would militate in favor of—and against—allowing the purchaser to recover interest on the purchase price?

II. THE CISG'S APPROACH TO INTEREST

Because of the significant international variation in the extent to which interest is permitted, the drafters of the CISG faced a considerable challenge in seeking to determine whether and how to address the topic. The CISG's legislative history reflects vigorous debate on the topic. In fact, according to one source, when the topic was discussed at the Drafting Conference phase, "the meeting almost failed."[51] Ultimately, as a compromise, the CISG drafters decided to include a right to interest, but not to define how it would be calculated.

The following excerpt from Professor Franco Ferrari provides some additional background on the debate and the drafters' decision to take the approach they chose:

49. See *supra* text accompanying note 32.

50. See *supra* text accompanying note 27.

51. INTERNATIONAL SALES LAW 557 (Ingeborg Schwenzer & Christiana Fountoulakis eds. 2007) ("Islamic countries were against a general duty to pay interest based on legal cultural reasons; other contracting states objected to the application of the interest rate existing at the creditor's place of business. Whereas in the lead-up to the Drafting Committee, an agreement was reached on the inclusion of Art. 84 CISG, the general duty to pay interest on sums in arrear stated by Art. 78 CISG was not inserted until the last minute.").

The ... issue of interests on sums in arrears, was one of the most debated issues during the 1980 Vienna Conference [at which the CISG was adopted]. And although this issue has been examined very often not only in legal writing, but in many court decisions and several arbitral awards as well, it still creates difficulties, for the reasons that will be pointed out *infra.*

This issue did not, on the contrary, cause any difficulties under the [Convention Relating to a Uniform Law on the International Sale of Goods, or "ULIS," which preceded the CISG], since Article 83 ULIS provided for "a rule for interest in arrears in the event of payment in arrears of the price which provided for one percent above the official discount rate in the creditor's country." This formula has not been retained by the drafters of the Vienna Sales Convention, although there were various attempts to do so. Apart from these attempts to fix the rate of interest in the same way as the ULIS, other attempts were made to precisely determine the rate of interests, but they were not successful either. The German view in favour of a fixed interest rate was rejected, as was the view of the Czechoslovakian Delegation, according to which the applicable rate of interest should be the discount rate prevailing in the country of the debtor. The same is true with the viewpoint held jointly by Denmark, Finland, Greece and Sweden, according to which interest should be calculated on the basis of the customary rate for commercial credits at the creditor's place of business.

The different political, economic and religious views made it impossible to agree upon a formula to calculate the rate of interest. Thus, the Vienna Sales Convention contains a provision considered to work as a compromise among the different views presented during the Vienna Conference Article 78, which limits itself to merely providing for "the general entitlement to interest" in case of payments in arrears. In other words, Article 78 only sets forth the obligation to pay interest as a general rule, and it does so independently from the damage caused by the payment in arrears, as pointed out by several court decisions, which expressly stated that the entitlement to interests does not exclude the possibility to claim damages ex Article 74. And since Article 78 does not set forth a time starting from which interests may be calculated either, it has been said that "Art. 78 is more conspicuous for the questions it fails to answer than the questions it answers. In particular, it does not stipulate the rate of interest or how the rate is to be determined by a tribunal in the absence of explicit guidance in the Convention."[52]

The good news resulting from the compromise on which the CISG drafters finally settled, as Professor Michael Van Alstine has pointed out, "is that the matter remains almost entirely within the parties' control."[53] Wise contracting parties, thus, will specify the rate of interest to govern their transaction rather than leaving the matter to chance and a variety of possible interpretations. The drafters also declined to provide a means of reconciling the religious and cultural objections to interest with the CISG provisions awarding interest.[54] These decisions have caused interpretive difficulties for tribunals and scholars alike. Even so, Peter Schlechtriem and Ingeborg Schwenzer describe the "finally adopted compromise rules in Articles 78 and 84(1) . . . [as] a substantial progress compared to the United Kingdom's proposal that interest should be governed exclusively by domestic law."[55]

With this background in mind, it becomes easier to understand why Articles 78 and 84(1), which provide in relevant part as follows, were phrased in such general terms:

CISG Article 78

If a party fails to pay the price or any other sum that is in arrears, the other party is entitled to interest on it, without prejudice to any claim for damages recoverable under Article 7.[56]

CISG Article 84(1)

If the seller is bound to refund the price, he must also pay interest on it, from the date on which the price was paid.[57]

For those who may wonder why the CISG includes two provisions on interest rather than just one, the following perspective may be useful: "The parallel existence of Art. 78 and Art. 84 CISG can only be explained historically: the ULIS provided for a duty to pay

52. Ferrari, *infra* note 66, at 116–119.

53. Michael P. Van Alstine, *The UNCITRAL Digest, the Right to Interest, and the Interest Rate Controversy in* DRAFTING CONTRACTS UNDER THE CISG 505, 523 (Harry M. Flechtner et al., eds. 2008).

54. Professors Morrissey and Graves provide some useful advice with respect to such a conflict: "In cases where enforcement [of an arbitral award] is likely to be in an Islamic country,... a tribunal should be careful to indicate that the award consists of a certain amount where interest is not included, and a

different amount if interest is allowed. In that case, perhaps, the award (not including interest) might indeed be enforced." JOSEPH F. MORRISSEY ,& JACK M. GRAVES, INTERNATIONAL SALES LAW & ARBITRATION: PROBLEMS, CASES AND COMMENTARY 290 (2008).

55. PETER SCHLECHTRIEM & INGEBORG SCHWENZER, COMMENTARY ON THE UN CONVENTION ON THE INTERNATIONAL SALE OF GOODS (CISG) 881 (2005).

56. United Nations Convention on Contracts for the International Sale of Goods, Article 78 (1980).

57. *Id.* at Article 84(1).

interest only where the price was to be refunded, but not for a general duty to pay interest as laid down in Art. 78 CISG; Art. 84 CISG had already been agreed on when, at the last minute, Art. 78 CISG was included in the convention."[58]

Article 78 was applied in the 2002 Swiss case denominated *X.GmbH v. Y. e.V.* Read the following excerpt from the court's opinion and consider the questions that follow:

COMMERCIAL COURT (*HANDELSGERICHT*) AARGAU

5 November 2002 [OR.2001.00029]
Translation by Martin F. Koehler

* * *

A. [The background facts]

1. The Plaintiff seller is a limited liability corporation based in the Canton of Aargau. The object of its business operation is all types advertisement, especially during sports events by using fixed balloons.

The Defendant buyer is an incorporated association based in Wiesbaden, Germany, and the possessor of the right of commercialization of the German Touring Car Masters (DTM).

2. In June 1999, P. contacted the seller as the agent for the buyer, asking if the seller would be in the position to manufacture inflatable triumphal arches, to be used as advertising media during car racing events. On 9 June 1999, the seller presented a cost estimate. He offered the manufacturing and labeling of one triumphal arch, the appropriate supercharger as well as the so-called "service expenditure" for the positioning, maintenance and taking down of one triumphal arch.

On 6 April 2000, the buyer confirmed the order for the manufacturing of three triumphal arches for the total price of *Sf* [Swiss francs] 127,157.50.... On Friday, 26 May 2000, the seller delivered the three triumphal arches to the ... site, where the seller set up the arches and briefed the employees of one of the companies called in by the buyer to position the arches and handle the supercharger. One triumphal arch was set up above the access road of the pit stop area; the other arches were set up on the green space next to the racing circuit. On Saturday, 27 May 2000, one of the arches next to the circuit collapsed. As a result, the race management center insisted that all arches be removed. In a fax of that same day, the [buyer] complained of the defects that had occurred. The buyer also responded by letter dated 29 May 2000, whereupon on 14 June

---

58. Schwenzer & Fountoulakis, *supra* note 51, at 595.

2000, by authorized proxy, the [seller] declared the contract suspended.

B. [The legal proceedings]

1. In a complaint dated 3 May 2001, the seller claimed:

"1. The [buyer] should be obliged to pay to the seller the amount of *Sf* 127,157.50 with 5% interest as of 20 June 2000.

2. The follow-up and compensation cost should be at expense of the buyer."

2. In his answer to the seller dated 19 December 2001, the buyer applied for dismissal of the seller's complaint.

* * *

CONSIDERATIONS

1. a) As the buyer is based in Wiesbaden, Germany, [and the seller in Switzerland] the facts of the case are international.... As the parties did not stipulate a place of delivery or payment of the purchase price, according to Art. 57(1)(a) CISG the purchase price needs to be paid at the place of the seller's establishment. The place of fulfillment in terms of Art. 5 No. 1 of the Lugano Convention is the registered office of the seller. This means that the Commercial Court of the Canton of Aargau has jurisdiction.

* * *

2. Switzerland and Germany are both Contracting States of the United Nations Convention on Contracts for the International Sale of Goods of 11 April 1980. The provisions of the CISG apply to contracts for the sale of goods between parties whose places of business are in different Contracting States (Art. 1(1)(a) CISG). Contracts for the supply of goods to be manufactured or produced are on a par with sales contracts. (Art. 3(1) CISG). Such a contract for the supply of goods has been concluded by the parties, as the manufacture of three inflatable triumphal arches is the primary subject of the contract. The contractual relationship is therefore subject to the CISG.

3. The buyer asserts the defectiveness of the work delivery. The seller denies this; seller alleges perfect performance of the contract.

a) According to Art. 35(1) CISG, the seller must deliver goods of the quantity, quality and description required by the contract. Unless the parties have agreed otherwise, the goods provided for a certain purpose are only considered in conformity to the contract if they are suitable for the certain purpose of which the seller has been made aware at the conclusion of the contract explicitly or otherwise, except where the circumstances show that the buyer did not rely, or that it was unreasonable for the buyer to rely, on the seller's skill and judgment (Art. 35(2)(b) CISG).

b) In the case under consideration, it is clear that the purpose of the use of the goods to be manufactured or produced was known to the seller; namely, use as advertising media next to and across the racing track. As safety is of vital importance in this enterprise, a test was carried out at the site ... on 2 May 2002. As a result, it became evident that that additional safety measures needed to be taken; it was generally agreed to install a safety wire in order to avoid a breakdown of the arch that was to be set up across the racing track in case of a failure of the supercharger, as well as to raise the so-called site stamps in order to prevent sagging....

* * *

c) [One of the] ... arch[es], delivered by the [seller] and set up on 26 May 2002, on a lawn next to the Hockenheimring, collapsed on the morning of 27 May 2002.... This occurred after the race (training and preliminary heat) had started. The arch lost air and drifted with the wind towards the racing track. [Another] arch, which was mounted above the access road of the pit started to vibrate because of the racing cars going through with a reduced speed of 60 km/h. As a result, the concrete elements used for the fixation of [this] arch began to falter. For this reason, the race organizers demanded that all three arches be removed. Thus both a quality or manufacturing flaw as well as an insufficient stability of the arch set up above the pit access [existed].... Consequently, it was a case of non-compliance with the contract (defects), for which the seller was liable according to Art. 35(2)(b) in connection with Art. 36(1) CISG.

4. a) In case of a seller's non-compliance with a contract or CISG obligation, in principle the following five legal remedies (defects rights) are at the buyer's disposal:

- Right to performance (Art. 46(1) CISG);
- Right to cure (Art. 48 CISG);
- Right to avoid the contract because of a fundamental breach of contract (Art. 49(1)(a) CISG);
- Right of price reduction (Art. 50 sentence 1 CISG);
- Right to damages (Art. 45(1)(b) in connection with Arts. 74–77 CISG).

In the present case, the buyer declared the contract's avoidance, due to the existence of a fundamental breach of contract, analogously already in his notification of defects dated 27 May 2000, and unmistakably, in the letter of his legal representative dated 14 June 2000. As, according to Art. 48(1) CISG, the seller "subject to Art. 49" may remedy any failure even after the date for delivery, the question arises concerning the relationship between the seller's right to cure (according to Art. 48(1) CISG) and the buyer's right to avoid the contract (according to Art. 49(1)(a) CISG). About this the following may be stated.

b) The term fundamental breach of contract according to Art. 49(1)(a) CISG is defined in Art. 25 CISG. According to this Article, the condition for a fundamental breach of contract is an especially weighty impairment of the buyer's interest in the performance. Yet, besides the objective weight or importance of a defect, it is decisive of the substantiality of a breach of contract, whether the defect can be removed by subsequent repair or substitute delivery. The UN Sales Law proceeds from the fundamental precedence of preservation of the contract, even in case of an objective fundamental defect. When in doubt, the contract is to be maintained even in case of fundamental defects, and an immediate contract avoidance should stay exceptional. Because, as long as and so far as (even) a fundamental defect can still be removed by remedy or replacement, the fulfillment of the contract by the seller is still possible and the buyer's essential interest in the performance is not yet definitively at risk. According to doctrine as well as jurisdiction of the UN Sales Law, an objective fundamental defect does not mean a fundamental breach of contract when the defect is removable and the seller agrees to remedy this defect without creating unreasonable delay or burden on the buyer. That the buyer is obliged to accept a remedy (subsequent cure of the defect) offered by the seller results from Art. 48(2) CISG. According to this provision, when the seller notifies the buyer of his readiness for performance, the buyer may not within a reasonable period of time "resort to any remedy which is inconsistent with performance by the seller." For this reason, the buyer does not have the right to avoid the contract even in case of an objective fundamental defect as long as and as far as the seller comes up with a remedy (subsequent cure of the defect) and such is still possible.

c) In the present case, both the quality problem or manufacturing defect ... and the lack [of] stability could have been remedied. And it is certain that the seller reacted immediately to the notice of defects dated 27 May 2000, and made different proposals ... through which ... subsequent performance, could be reached. The buyer reacted to the seller's readiness to remedy on 14 June 2000, by declaring the contract avoided.

Buyer was not entitled to do so ..., even in the case of an objective fundamental defect.

d) aa) According to UN Sales Law doctrine, a buyer's right of immediate contract avoidance is conceded by way of exception, without having to wait for the seller's readiness to remedy or the remedy itself. Yet, these exceptional facts of the case require that a remedy not be possible, is refused by the seller, or is not reasonable for the buyer.

* * *

bb) ... The arches were supposed to be used as advertising media in several races during the entire season. If a remedy would have been carried out after the first use on 27 May 2003, within a useful period of time, the arches could have been used during further races.... It was not a case of complete impossibility, but only a partial impossibility. As far as the still possible part of the owed performance is concerned, the seller can rely on his entitlement to remedy....

5. a) For this reason, the buyer was not able to declare the contract avoided in a legally binding way in his writing of 14 June 2000. In this case, the legal consequences depend on the reaction of the seller. Only if the seller consents to the avoidance of the contract will the contract get avoided. If, however, the seller disagrees with the avoidance of the contract or does not declare the contract avoided himself, the contract consequently will continue.

In this proceeding, the seller asks the buyer for performance: payment of the purchase price. Thus, seller holds on to the continued existence of the contract, and consequently the primary duty of the buyer: to pay the seller for the goods. Based on the contract concluded by the parties and according to Art. 53 CISG, the buyer is bound to pay the purchase price and to receive the goods. The fact, that—with the exception of the right to avoid the contract—the buyer is entitled to certain rights in the event of defects, does not alter the situation.

b) The seller submitted claims for damages, but he did not substantiate them nor did he reserve the assertion of these claims "in further proceedings." Claims against the buyer for damages, as defined by Art. 45(2)(b) in connection with Art. 74–77 CISG, consequently are not to be judged in the present lawsuit.

6. a) The purchase price must be paid according to Art. 58(1) and (3) in connection with Art. 59 CISG without specific summons or adherence to formalities, as soon as the seller has made the goods available to the buyer and the buyer has had the opportunity to examine the goods. In the present case, the maturity of the charge would have arisen on 26 May 2000, when the three arches were delivered and ready to be examined by the buyer. However, the seller billed the purchase price of *Sf* 127,157.20 on 31 May 2000, on terms "20 days netto" (KB 10), which must be seen as a deferment of payment and reprieve of the maturity. The payment claim therefore did not mature until 20 June 2000.

b) If the buyer fails to pay the purchase price when due, the seller is entitled to interest on it "without prejudice to any claim for damages recoverable under Art. 74." (Art. 78 CISG). The amount of interest is not laid down in the UN Sales Law. It is controversial, whether one must aim for autonomous contract gap-filling and a uniform solution or if recourse must be made to national law. In regard to national law, the mainly recommended recourse, it is again uncertain how the determination of that law within the scope of the conflicts of law is supposed to take place. The doctrine convincingly postulates that to determine the relevant national law, it is the connection to the currency that is decisive for the primary claim. Decisive in this connection is the rule of the amount of the interest on arrears that is reached by the concerned system of laws.

c) In the present case, the primary claim is owed in Swiss francs. Thus, Swiss law is the applicable law for the determination of the amount of interest owed on arrears. Since the seller did not prove or demand a discount rate that would exceed the usual 5% percent, the statutory interest on arrears of 5% is owed.

d) In the CISG's sphere of application, even the default of payment on the date of maturity creates a dereliction of duty, so that the need of payment of interest sets in immediately with the maturity. As the maturity started off on 20 June 2000 (see 6a, *supra*), the [seller] is entitled to interest to the amount of 5% from this date on.

7.   Proceeding on that assumption, the buyer is fully liable to pay the cost.

Aargau, 5 November 2002

Commercial Court of the Canton of Aargau

Questions

1.   In your own words, what is the rationale for recovery of interest under CISG Article 78, and how is this different from the reasoning supporting Article 84(1)?

2.   Why must the buyer in the Swiss case excerpted above pay interest on the contract price even though the seller delivered defective goods?

3. What distinction does the Swiss court draw between "funda-mental defect" and "fundamental breach," and how does this distinction affect the outcome of this case?

4. Why does interest in this case accrue from June 20, 2000, rather than May 26, 2000?

5. Why does the court apply Swiss domestic law to determine the appropriate amount of interest? What other law might the court have applied? (The materials in Part III will assist you in answering this question if you find it difficult to form an instinctive response.)

6. The court indicated that the seller would receive only the statutory interest rate of 5% since it failed to prove (or even demand) a higher rate of interest. Under what circumstances might a seller demand a higher rate of interest? What evidence do you suppose might have been persuasive to the court, if presented?

PROBLEM 4

Return to the second hypothetical on page 89 (the high-fashion textiles) and now assume the seller delivered textiles that were stained and badly faded, but, upon the buyer's notification of the problem, offered to replace the goods at no cost to the buyer, with a 10% price adjustment to account for the buyer's inconvenience. Assuming that the buyer refuses to accept delivery of the replace-ment goods, must the buyer pay the contract price? If so, must the buyer also pay interest on the contract price? Explain your answer.

III. CHOICE OF LAW CHALLENGES

As the preceding case demonstrates, some tribunals have as-sumed that the CISG does not govern the interest rate and have instead applied domestic law. As Bruno Zeller has noted, most courts and some commentators have taken this approach.[59] Others have assumed that the general principles underlying the CISG govern, even though the CISG does not address the matter direct-ly.[60] In advocating for the latter perspective in the specific context of Article 78, Professor Michael Bridge states as follows: "As for whether the various questions concerning interest are governed by the Convention, it is hard to agree with those courts who see them as excluded. Why is there an Article 78 at all if the practical

59. BRUNO ZELLER, DAMAGES UNDER THE CONVENTION ON CONTRACTS FOR THE INTERNA-TIONAL SALE OF GOODS 133 (2d ed. 2009).

60. *See infra* note 66 and accompa-nying text.

questions that follow on from its provision do not fall within the CISG?''[61]

The following excerpt from Professor Franco Ferrari's survey article, *Specific Topics of the CISG in Light of Judicial Application and Scholarly Writing*, 15 J.L. & Com. 1, 117–125 (1995), provides a concise statement of the problem created by divergent interpretations of the CISG provisions on point.

> The lack of a specific formula to calculate the rate of interest on sums in arrears has led some courts as well as several legal writers to consider this issue as being a gap *praeter legem i.e.*, as being governed by, but not expressly settled in, the CISG, whereas other courts and legal scholars consider the issue ... as falling outside the scope of application of the CISG, *i.e.*, as being a gap *intra legem*.[62] This had necessarily to lead to diverging solutions, since under the CISG, the aforementioned kinds of gaps have to be dealt with differently. According to Article 7(2) CISG, the gaps *praeter legem* (or internal gaps) have to be filled by resorting to the general principles on which the Convention is based or, in the absence of such principles, by having recourse to the law applicable by virtue of the rules of private international law. On the contrary, if an issue is considered as falling outside the Convention's scope of application, *i.e.*, if it is an external gap, it must be solved in conformity with the law applicable by virtue of the rules of private international law, *i.e.*, without any tentative recourse to the "general principles" of the CISG.

> Unfortunately, the CISG does not set forth any useful criterion to determine ... when a gap is to be considered as being a lacuna *praeter legem* as opposed to a lacuna *intra legem*, although this distinction appears to be quite important for the consequences in which it results. Undoubtedly, the setting forth of a criterion to be used to decide whether a gap must be considered a lacuna *intra legem* or one *praeter legem* would have favored the uniform application of the Vienna Sales Convention.

> * * *

> .... Although many scholars hold th[e] view [that the rate of interest is governed by domestic law], they appear not to agree on how to determine the applicable domestic law. Indeed, some scholars favor the view according to which the applicable

---

61. Michael Bridge, *A Commentary on Articles 1–13 and 78*, in The Draft UNCITRAL Digest and Beyond: Cases, Analysis and Unresolved Issues in the U.N. Sales Convention 235, 258 (Franco Ferrari et al. eds. 2004).

62. Gaps *intra legem* and *prater legem* are discussed in Chapter 2 at page 30 et seq.

domestic law is to be determined by virtue of the rules of private international law, thus, making applicable, "in general, the subsidiary law applicable to the sales contract since no special connecting points seem to have developed for the entitlement to interest." Other scholars, however, argue in favor of either the application of the law of the creditor, independently from whether this is the *lex contractus*, or the application of the law of the debtor.

On the other hand, there are a few authors holding the contrasting view according to which the issue *de quo*[63] has to be dealt with as a lacuna *praeter legem*, on the grounds that "[t]he mandate of Article 7(1) to construe the Convention to promote 'uniformity in its application' requires us to seek a principle governing the scope of Article 78 that can be considered as a basis for uniform application of the Convention." Indeed, the "deference to domestic law ... seems inconsistent with the policy underlying Article 78." Thus, it has been suggested that "the interest to be paid is defined by the function of the assessment of damages, *i.e.*, to put the seller in the same position he would have been had the sum been paid in time," a formula which, however, must be criticized for leading to a confusion of the line between damages and interest which Article 78 has expressly drawn.

* * *

.... As has been rightly pointed out by one commentator, the arbitral awards do not lay down a uniform substantive law rule derived from the general principles of the CISG. They merely lay down a conflict of laws rule, since this rule refers to the law of the State where the creditor has his place of business, an approach which, in the end, does not offer anything new but a uniform rule of private international law which, for the reason mentioned above, is to be rejected.

As far as the court decisions are concerned, where the issue *de quo* is solved by resorting to domestic law, a distinction must be made: there are, on the one hand, cases applying the domestic law by virtue of the rules of private international law, on the other hand, cases where the domestic law of the creditor is applied without, however, it being the law made applicable by the rules of private international law.

Even though many solutions which differ greatly from each other can be found both in scholarly writing and judicial practice, there seems to be the tendency to apply the *lex contractus*, *i.e.*, the law which would be applicable to the sales

63. "Of which." BLACK'S LAW DICTIONARY 474 (8th ed. 2004).

contract if it were not subject to the Vienna Sales Convention. Thus, in respect of the formula to calculate the rate of interest, the interest rate of the country of the seller generally applies, at least where the rules of private international law of the forum are based upon criteria comparable to those set forth by the 1980 EEC Convention on the Law Applicable to Contractual Obligations.[64] Absent a choice of law, this Convention makes applicable the law with which the contract has the closest connection, as already mentioned above. This is presumed to be the law where the party who is to effect the "characteristic performance" has its habitual residence, and since the characteristic performance has to be effected by the seller, it is the interest rate of the country where the seller has its place of business which generally is applicable.

Quid juris,[65] however, where the seller's law does prohibit the payment of interest? In this line of cases, the claim does not become unenforceable as suggested by several authors. It is here suggested, that Article 78 remains enforceable even in this line of cases, but that in order to calculate the rate of interest recourse should be had to the level of interest generally applied in international commerce in the particular trade concerned.[66]

* * *

Questions

1. Based on what you have read, did the court in *X.GmbH v. Y. e.V* find that the gap in the CISG was a gap *praeter legem* or a gap *intra legem*? Which approach would be most consistent with the notion of the CISG as "true code," as that term was used in Chapter 2?[67]

2. Building on the prior question, why must domestic law ultimately be applied in this particular case, regardless of the interpretive methodology the tribunal chooses?

3. The concept of "general principles" underlying the CISG was presented in Chapter 2 at pages 34–39. Some scholars have argued that (1) "full compensation" is an underlying CISG principle and (2) this principle can be used to justify payment of interest.[68] Assuming that these are appropriate assertions,

64. The text of the convention is available at http://www.jus.uio.no/lm/ec. applicable.law.contracts.1980/.

65. "What is the law?" BLACK'S LAW DICTIONARY 1282 (8th ed. 2004).

66. Franco Ferrari, *Specific Topics of the CISG in Light of Judicial Applica-* *tion and Scholarly Writing*, 15 J.L. & COM. 1, 117–125 (1995).

67. *See supra* pages 39–44.

68. *See, e.g.,* Klaus Peter Berger, *International Arbitral Practice and the UNIDROIT Principles of International Commercial Contracts*, 46 AM. J. COMP. L. 129, 136–138 (1998) (arguing in favor of

how can "full compensation" be used to justify an award of interest even when applicable domestic law forbids it?

4. Building on the prior question and assuming that the CISG provisions awarding interest are motivated by the principle of "full compensation," should interest be awarded in all cases in which money is owed, or only when the interest creditor can show that it had to pay interest—for example, if it was forced to borrow money because of the interest debtor's delay in making payment?

5. Francesco Mazzotta has called CISG Article 78 a "headless corpse."[69] Based on what you have read, why might this be a fair description?

6. As Professor Ferrari notes in the excerpt that appeared in the prior section, the drafters of the CISG emphasized that an award of interest is distinguishable from an award of damages. Stated another way, the CISG does not require a culpable delay in payment for interest to be due. When is delayed payment not culpable?

7. As Professor Ferrari notes, courts may determine the applicable law by making reference to "the rules of private international law." What does this mean?

8. According to Professor Ferrari, why does the law of the seller's home country often determine the interest rate to be applied?

9. One alternative to applying the law of the seller's home country would be to apply the law of the currency in which the sales price is to be paid. What problems could this approach create when the currency in question is the Euro, as in the two hypotheticals that begin this chapter?

10. Building on the prior question, as one source has noted, "Differing interest rates in the [buyer's and seller's] ... places of business ... may give rise to unjust enrichment or its opposite when one party has its place of business in a country with high inflation."[70] How could the parties craft their contract to avoid this risk?

the notion of a "general principle" of "full compensation"). But see Francesco G. Mazzotta, *CISG Article 78: Endless Disagreement Among Commentators, Much Less Among the Courts*, PACE REV. OF CISG 123 (2004), *available at* http://www.cisg.law.pace.edu/cisg/biblio/mazzotta78.html (arguing that "full compensation" produces a result that is at odds with the CISG's text). "[G]ener-

al principles on which the [CISG] is based" is language that comes from CISG Article 7. *See supra* note 56, Article 7.

69. Mazzotta, *supra* note 68.

70. André Corterier, *A New Approach to solving the Problem of the Interest Rate Problem of Article 78 CISG*, 5 INT'L TRADE & BUS. L. ANN. 33, 37 (2000).

PROBLEM 5

Return to the first hypothetical on page 89. André Corterier has suggested that CISG Article 76 may be applied by analogy to create a means of calculating interest under CISG Article 78.[71] Article 76 provides as follows:

CISG Article 76

(1) If the contract is avoided and there is a current price for the goods, the party claiming damages may, if he has not made a purchase or resale under Article 75, recover the difference between the price fixed by the contract and the current price at the time of avoidance as well as any further damages recoverable under Article 74. If, however, the party claiming damages has avoided the contract after taking over the goods, the current price at the time of such taking over shall be applied instead of the current price at the time of avoidance.

(2) For the purposes of the preceding paragraph, the current price is the price prevailing at the place where delivery of the goods should have been made or, if there is no current price at that place, the price at such other place as serves as a reasonable substitute, making due allowance for differences in the cost of transporting the goods.

Corterier has suggested that, based on Article 76, the interest rate to be applied under Article 78 is "the market rate for the sum and currency owed at the time and place the payment should have been made."[72] One of the reasons he urges adoption of this method is its apparent consistency with both the UNIDROIT Principles and PECL (The Principles of European Contract Law).[73] Based on the first hypothetical, what would be the result if this approach were applied? On what policy basis could one argue in favor of—and also against—this approach?

IV. THE UNIDROIT AND PECL APPROACHES

The drafters of the UNIDROIT Principles and PECL created much more specific rules than the CISG regarding how interest is calculated. Although the UNIDROIT Principles are used to interpret many provisions of the CISG, most commentators have rejected this idea in the context of CISG Articles 78 and 84 because the CISG's history shows that the parties not only could come to no

71. *Id.* at 40–41.
72. *Id.*
73. The PECL project was completed in 2003. The full text of PECL, together with some information on the project's history, can be found at http://www.frontpage.cbs.dk/law/commission_on_european_contract_law/.

agreement regarding how interest should be calculated, but affirmatively decided against continuing to try to do so.[74]

The relevant provisions of each are set forth below:

UNIDROIT Article 7.4.9

Interest for Failure to Pay Money

(1) If a party does not pay a sum of money when it falls due the aggrieved party is entitled to interest upon that sum from the time when payment is due to the time of payment whether or not the non-payment is excused.

(2) The rate of interest shall be the average bank short-term lending rate to prime borrowers prevailing for the currency of payment at the place for payment, or where no such rate exists at that place, then the same rate in the State of the currency of payment. In the absence of such a rate at either place the rate of interest shall be the appropriate rate fixed by the law of the State of the currency of payment.

(3) The aggrieved party is entitled to additional damages if the non-payment caused it a greater harm.[75]

PECL Article 9–508

(1) If payment of a sum of money is delayed, the aggrieved party is entitled to interest on that sum from the time when payment is due to the time of payment at the average commercial bank short-term lending rate to prime borrowers prevailing for the contractual currency of payment at the place where payment is due.

(2) The aggrieved party may in addition recover damages for any further loss so far as these are recoverable under this Section.[76]

Questions

1. What are some advantages and disadvantages of the CISG approach, on the one hand, and the PECL and UNIDROIT approaches, on the other?

2. Both the UNIDROIT Principles and PECL focus on the "short-term lending rate to prime borrowers" at the place where payment

74. *See, e.g.,* Francesco G. Mazzotta, *CISG Articles 78 and 84(1) and their PECL Counterparts* (2004), *available at* http://cisgw3.law.pace.edu/text/peclcomp78.html#er.

75. International Institute for the Unification of Private Law, UNIDROIT

Principles of International Commercial Contracts, Article 7.4.9 (2004).

76. Commission on European Contract Law, The Principles of European Contract Law, Article 9–508 (1999).

is due. What policy reasons support using this means of determining interest?

3. What objections might some of the signatory countries have raised, or what problems might have arisen, had the CISG adopted an approach similar to that employed in the PECL and UNIDROIT provisions?

4. Do the PECL and UNIDROIT approaches favor either interest creditors or interest debtors? If so, how?

Chapter 5

COMMERCIAL AGENTS—
FRANCHISES

I. DURATION AND TERMINATION
IN THE UNITED STATES

In American jurisdictions, the legal relationship between principals and agents as well as that between franchisors and franchisees was exclusively controlled by the contractual agreement between the parties and was therefore governed by common law. Contracts entered with new franchisees tend to be one-sided agreements written by the franchisor who ordinarily holds the dominant bargaining power. The various states also developed differing approaches to the impact of the law of consideration, the finding of implied terms regarding duration, and the calculation of damages.

Various state statutes have been enacted in recent years in an effort to provide franchisees with greater rights. Some apply to only a single industry such as car dealers. Most are aimed at limiting the franchisor's right to terminate, to discriminate among franchisees or to add additional franchisees in the same territory. Federal legislation has been ineffective.

When distribution agreements are first entered between two parties, the usual situation is that no one knows how long this arrangement will last. The usual result is that duration is either not mentioned or the agreement is expressly stated to be terminable at will. As with employment contracts, the traditional common law approach was to find contracts of indefinite duration to be terminable at will by either party. Even when a party has sustained substantial expense relying upon, preparing to perform, or actually performing a contract of indefinite duration, courts were unwilling to imply a promise that the contract would be continued for a reasonable period of time. This rule of interpretation was so deeply ingrained that in most jurisdictions, a promise by the principal or franchisor to continue the contract for some defined or definable period was found to be unenforceable on the grounds of lack of mutuality of obligation. An obligation to perform the promise relating to duration was permitted only where the agent or franchisee was also obligated to continue the relationship or had given some "additional" or "special" consideration in exchange for this "additional" promise.

The next case demonstrates the traditional contract law view of this issue.

E.I. DU PONT DE NEMOURS & CO. v. CLAIBORNE-RENO CO.

United States Court of Appeals, Eighth Circuit (1933)
64 F.2d 224

Action by the E.I. Du Pont De Nemours & Co. against the Claiborne-Reno Company, in which defendant set up counterclaim. Judgment for defendant, and plaintiff appeals.

Reversed and remanded.

SANBORN, CIRCUIT JUDGE.

The parties will be referred to in this opinion as the Du Pont Company and the Reno Company.

The Du Pont Company brought suit against the Reno Company for $5,989.88, part of which was for goods sold and delivered, and part for a balance due upon a promissory note. The Reno Company admitted this indebtedness, but set up a counterclaim for $350,000 damages for breach of contract. The case was tried to a jury, which returned a verdict in favor of the Reno Company for $41,588.12. From the judgment entered upon the verdict, the Du Pont Company has appealed.

The Reno Company had been, from the 23d day of October, 1924, until the 1st day of December, 1930, the sole distributor in the state of Iowa of certain products manufactured only by the Du Pont Company, and intended mainly for the finishing, refinishing, and polishing of automobiles. These products were referred to as Duco. The original contract between the parties, which was made in 1924, had been several times renewed, with slight variations, prior to October 1, 1927. On that date a contract substantially similar to those which preceded it was entered into. It was in the form of a letter prepared by the Du Pont Company and accepted by the Reno Company. We set it forth in full:

'September 1, 1927.

'Claiborne-Reno Co., 1023 Locust St., Des Moines, Iowa.

'Gentlemen: This will confirm our agreement whereby you will act as sole distributor of our Spray Duco, Spray Thinner, Blue Diamond Undercoats and Rubbing Compounds to automobile refinishing shops and furniture refinishing shops in the following territory, with the exception of such shops as we may find it necessary to serve direct because of their connection with manufacturing or industrial consumers of Duco materials.

'Entire State of Iowa.

'It is understood and agreed that this contract is entered into upon the following conditions:

'That it is our intention and desire to continue under this agreement so long as your services, in our judgment, prove satisfactory.

'That our object is to secure as rapidly as possible sufficient distribution of our Duco finish process to satisfactorily cover the territory in question among responsible refinishers who are in a position to provide adequate facilities to enable them to turn out first-class work.

'That the sale of our material or process will not be limited by being connected with the sale or use of any other material, apparatus or process in which you are or may become interested, such as air brush equipment, upholstery, materials, hardware, accessories, et cetera.

'That you will endeavor to have your customers refrain from the use of competitive products, and that under no circumstances will such products be used in your shop.

'That you will not use, teach or recommend processes of application and finishing not approved by us.

'That you will not grant exclusive rights for the use of our Duco Finish or process to any refinisher in any given territory without our written approval. In this connection it is understood that we wish to avoid the granting of exclusive rights so far as possible, as our experience has shown that refinishers do more satisfactory work when they know they do not have a monopoly in the district they are serving.

'That you will provide satisfactory-facilities for instruction and demonstration in the use and application of our materials, and process to your customers and furnish them with whatever service may be necessary to enable them to turn out first-class work. In those cases where you consider it necessary to make a charge for demonstration and instruction services it should not exceed the approximate cost to you, and in no cases should charges be made which may appear to be a premium or license fee for the use of our process or materials.

'That you will co-operate with us in formulating sales promotion plans by supplying statistical information that we may need from time to time.

'That we will furnish materials to automobile refinishing shops in your territory only on orders approved by you.

'That freight will be allowed on shipments to your warehouse, but that no freight will be allowed on shipments made by us direct to your customers.

'That all materials will be billed to you at current list prices with freight allowances as specified in preceding paragraph, and in consideration of your services under this agreement we will allow you a discount of 25 per cent.

'That your prices to your customers will not exceed our invoice list prices to you f. o. b. your city, plus an additional 10c per gallon on items sold by the gallon and 1c per pound on materials sold by the pound to cover your own warehouse and handling expense, except the following: On 244 Line Duco, 259 Line Duco, and 235 Line Duco you may add 25 cents per gallon to our invoice list price instead of 10c per gallon.

'That our invoices shall be rendered promptly after shipments are made and shall be payable on the following terms: Invoices dated 1st to 15th inclusive, less 1 per cent discount on last day of current month or net without discount on 15th of following month; invoices dated 16th to 31st inclusive, less 1 per cent discount on 15th of following month or net without discount on last day of following month.

'That no discount is to apply on drums which are charged extra and returnable for corresponding credit F.O.B. Parlin, if returned in good condition within four months from date of shipment.

'That this agreement does not include Duco and Thinner prepared for brush application.

'That this agreement cancels and replaces agreement dated January 1, 1927.

'Please signify your acceptance and approval of these conditions by signing and returning the enclosed duplicate of this letter within five days.

'Yours very truly,

'E.I. Du Pont de Nemours & Company, Chemical Products Division,

'H.E. Lackey, Director of Sales.

'Me:

'Accepted and Approved: Claiborne-Reno Company

'By M.M. Reno Sec. & Tr.

'Date Oct. 1st 27.'

On October 17, 1930, the Du Pont Company gave notice to the Reno Company of the termination of the contract effective the December 1st following, and it was this termination by the Du Pont Company which the Reno Company asserts constituted a breach of the contract.

The Reno Company's cause of action, briefly stated, is this: That it had since 1924 acted as the sole distributor for Duco in the state of Iowa under the agreement in question and similar agreements; that it had developed the territory and created a demand for the Du Pont Company's products, had abandoned the sale of competitive products, had maintained facilities for instruction and demonstration in the use of and application of Duco, had expended large sums of money in furtherance of the Du Pont Company's interests, and had in all things carried out its obligations under the contract; that, under the terms of the contract, the Du Pont Company could not terminate it so long as the services of the Reno Company were, in the judgment of the Du Pont Company, satisfactory; that the termination of the contract was at a time when, in the judgment of the Du Pont Company, the services of the Reno Company were not unsatisfactory; that the Du Pont Company did not exercise good faith in terminating the agreement; and that the result of the refusal of the Du Pont Company to continue was the destruction of the Reno Company's business.

The question whether the termination of the contract by the Du Pont Company was in good faith, as claimed by it, or in bad faith, as claimed by the Reno Company, was submitted to the jury, and determined adversely to the former. There had been a motion by the Du Pont Company for a directed verdict at the close of the evidence, and the failure of the court to direct a verdict in its favor is assigned as error.

The important question in this case is whether the termination of this contract by the Du Pont Company gave to the Reno Company a cause of action for damages. Reduced to its lowest terms, the claim of the Reno Company is that what it bargained for and received from the Du Pont Company was an agreement that it should be the sole distributor of Duco in the state of Iowa so long as the Du Pont Company was satisfied with its services and so long as it (the Reno Company) chose to perform the services; that the consideration for the promise on the part of the Du Pont Company was the promise of the Reno Company to act as sole distributor and to do the things which it was required to do under the agreement, and the performance of that promise. The Du Pont Company, on the other hand, claims that the contract was unenforceable because the Du Pont Company did not promise to continue until dissatisfied, and because of uncertainty of consideration and lack of mutuality of obligation; that it is a bilateral contract, depending for its consideration upon the mutual promises of the parties, and that, being terminable at will by the Reno Company, it was also terminable at will by the Du Pont Company; and that the question whether, in its judgment, the services of the Reno Company were satisfactory, is not a justiciable question.

There is much to be said in favor of requiring men to adhere strictly to their undertakings, whatever they may be, but there are certain established rules with reference to contracts which are not to be disregarded, no matter how great the hardship may be which grows out of an adherence to them. No doubt, the rule which requires mutuality of obligation with respect to contracts to be performed in the future, where the promise of one party constitutes the sole consideration for the promise of the other, arises from what is regarded by the courts as the inherent unfairness of enforcing a contract which requires performance by one of the parties, but leaves the other party free to accept or reject performance.

With some of the contentions of the Du Pont Company we cannot agree. It is urged that the language of the contract does not indicate a promise by the Du Pont Company to remain bound until dissatisfied with the services of the Reno Company; that all that is expressed is a mere desire and intention to continue the contract while satisfied.

The mere expression of an intention or desire is not a promise. An intention is but the purpose a man forms in his own mind; a promise is an express undertaking, or agreement to carry the purpose into effect. *Holt v. Akarman*, 84 N.J. Law 371, 86 A. 408, 409; *Scott v. S.H. Kress & Co.* (Tex. Civ. App.) 191 S.W. 714; 6 Words and Phrases. First Series, 5675; 1 Williston, Contracts (1920) § 26.

No special form of words, however, is necessary to create a promise. All that is necessary is that a fair interpretation of the words used shall make it appear that a promise was intended.

. . .

Contracts are ordinarily to be performed by business men, and should be given the interpretation which would be placed upon them by the business world. Where one corporation presents to another corporation a form of agreement reciting, "It is understood and agreed that this contract is entered into upon the following conditions: That it is our intention and desire to continue under this agreement so long as your services, in our judgment, prove satisfactory," we have no doubt that such language would ordinarily be understood to mean a promise to continue until dissatisfied. *See Horton v. Winbigler*, 175 Cal. 149, 165 P. 423.

We do not agree with the contention of the Du Pont Company that there was such uncertainty with reference to the quantity of its products to be taken by the Reno Company as to make the contract void.

The following language from the opinion of this court in *Marrinan Medical Supply, Inc., v. Ft. Dodge Serum Co.* C.A. 8) 47 F.(2d) 458, 462 is applicable:

> If the contract here in question were a pure contract of sale, the criticism of uncertainty would be formidable. But we have held that the contract is not purely one of sale. It partakes of the character not only of a sales contract, but also of a factorage contract, and perhaps also of a sales agency contract. In the two latter classes of contracts, uncertainty as to amount is inherent in their very nature. Where territory is to be exploited and orders to be solicited by salesmen, the number and amount of such orders cannot, of course be foretold. They can be determined only by the potential demand of the territory and the diligence of the salesmen. Contracts of factorage or sales agency are not invalid for such uncertainty, and we hold that the present contract is not on that account invalid.

If there is uncertainty, lack of mutuality, or lack of consideration in the contract with which we are concerned, it arises out of the fact that the Reno Company was in a position at any time to terminate the contract without incurring any liability therefor. Had the contract been one for a definite term, it might have been sustained upon the authority of *Marrinan Medical Supply, Inc., v. Ft. Dodge Serum Co., supra*. The only substantial difference between the contract involved in that case and this contract was that the former was to continue for a definite period, and both parties were bound by it during that period. It is placing an unnatural construction upon this contract to hold that the promises made by the Reno Company and their performance constituted the consideration for the Du Pont Company remaining bound so long as it was satisfied, and that its promise in that regard was bought and paid for. The contract itself provides that the consideration for the services of the Reno Company is the discount of 25 per cent upon all materials ordered from the Du Pont Company. The agreement was nothing more than a sales agency agreement, terminable at will by the Reno Company, but containing a promise of the Du Pont Company to continue so long as satisfied with the services of its distributor. For that reason, it is not controlled by *Conley Camera Co. v. Multiscope & Film Co.* C.A. 8) 216 F. 892, which involved a contract containing a promise of the Camera Company to sell cameras for an indefinite period to the Multiscope Company in consideration of the payment of $500 and an order for $9,000 worth of photographic wooden ware . . . . .

. . . .

While it is true that in the contract under consideration there is no specific provision that the Reno Company could terminate the contract at will, we regard this fact as immaterial, and we interpret the contract as allowing it so to do. *Moore v. Security Trust & Life Ins. Co.* C.A. 8) 168 F. 496, 499, certiorari denied 219 U.S. 583, 31 S. Ct. 469, 55 L. Ed. 346; *Willcox & Gibbs Sewing-Machine Co. v. Ewing*, 141 U.S. 627, 12 S. Ct. 94, 35 L. Ed. 882; *Victor Talking Machine Co. v. Lucker*, 128 Minn. 171, 150 N.W. 790; 32 A.L.R. 232.

We gather, from the cases in this and other circuits to which we have referred that, where a contract is so lacking in mutuality of obligation or certainty of consideration that it may be canceled, as in the *Woerheide* case, or that specific performance will be denied on that sole ground, as in the *Miami Coca-Cola Bottling Co.* case, its termination by either party creates no liability for damages resulting from a refusal to carry on.

The contract here is such that, because of the uncertainty of continued performance by the Reno Company, a court of equity would, upon that ground alone, refuse specific performance. Had the Du Pont Company brought a suit in equity to cancel the contract, upon the authority of the *Woerheide* case, it would have been canceled for uncertainty of consideration. Our conclusion, therefore, is that, whether the termination by the Du Pont Company was in good faith or bad faith, no action for damages could be based upon it.

We have much sympathy with the theory upon which the case was disposed of in the court below. It seems fair that, after having spent six years in developing the territory assigned to it, the Reno Company should have been permitted to continue or should have been compensated for the injury done it by having its business taken away. However, the injury done to the Reno Company was one against which its contract, rather obviously, did not afford protection. As was said by Judge Stone in the *Woerheide* case (page 204 of 251 F.): The entire trouble is found in the contract itself. It was not at its making strong enough to hold. * * *

The fact that the promisee relies on the promise to his injury, or the promisor gains some advantage therefrom, does not establish consideration without the element of bargain or agreed exchange.

Restatement of the Law of Contracts of the American Law Institute, vol. 1, § 75, Comment c.

It is unnecessary to consider other questions presented.

The judgment is reversed, and the case remanded for further proceedings not inconsistent with this opinion.

Questions

1. What did Reno claim was the promise made by Du Pont as to the duration of the contract? Does the Court assume or find that Du Pont made the promise as claimed? If so, why did it hold this promise to be unenforceable? Assuming adequacy of consideration is not an issue in an action at law, can you find consideration for this promise? (Distinguish this from an action in equity where the concern does relate to adequacy of consideration.)

2. Reno promised to do certain things, thus incurring a bargained for legal detriment which is consideration for the return promises of Du Pont. Why did this bargain not include the promise by Du Pont not to terminate so long as the performance by Reno was satisfactory? Was it necessary for Reno to promise that it would not terminate whenever it chose? How long would Reno be obligated to perform?

3. The court assumes that the promises of a franchisee to do the things that a franchisee would normally be expected to do are given in exchange for a *terminable at will* promise to perform the duties of the franchisor. If one assumes that the things Reno was to do are all given as a bargained exchange for a terminable at will relationship, then there is no consideration to support the additional promise not to terminate without good cause. To enforce this promise relating to duration, the court is insisting that there must be some *additional* consideration. Note that the court cites with approval the enforcement of a duration clause in the *Conley Camera* case because there the franchisee paid $500 and placed a minimum order. Why were the specific promises made by Reno any less valid as consideration than the $500 paid by the *Conley Camera* franchisee?

4. There is no authority for the proposition that consideration requires an equal number of promises by each party. One promise by A can serve as consideration for multiple promises by B. For example, A can promise to pay $10,000 in exchange for which B will replace broken boards, scrape off old paint and apply two coats of new paint to a garage. No one would suggest

that there is not sufficient consideration to support all three of B's promises. Thus a court that refuses to enforce a promise made as one part of what is an otherwise enforceable bargain must be operating on the assumption that it knows what terms "belong" in a franchise contract and what terms are unusual or special, thus requiring special consideration.

5. Is it not sad to read a judge's apology for the fact that contract law, as the court is there interpreting it, results in unfairness due to a failure to enforce a promise that was seriously made in a commercial transaction. Often this is justified by a technical or formalistic requirement such as "lack of consideration" or "lack of mutuality of obligation."

The common law that applies to franchises has been undergoing transition in many states.

JACK'S COOKIE COMPANY v. A.A. BROOKS
United States Court of Appeals, Fourth Circuit (1955)
227 F.2d 935

Action by cookie distributor against cookie manufacturer for breach of agency contract, unjust enrichment, and libel allegedly arising from statements contained in circular letter announcing termination of agency. The United States District Court for the Eastern District of South Carolina, at Columbia, Charles Cecil Wyche, J., at conclusion of distributor's case, dismissed claims of breach of contract and unjust enrichment and thereafter entered judgment upon verdict for distributor on claim of libel, and both parties appealed. The Court of Appeals, Soper, Circuit Judge, held that evidence upon question whether contract had been breached and whether distributor had kept promises he made and had faithfully and efficiently carried out his part of business should have been submitted to jury.

Reversed and remanded for new trial in accordance with opinion.

Soper, Circuit Judge.

This suit grows out of the termination of an agency contract between Jack's Cookie Company, a North Carolina corporation, and A.A. Brooks, a citizen of South Carolina who was engaged in the business of selling and distributing the products of diverse manufacturers in South Carolina and neighboring states. Jack's terminated the contract after it had been in operation for about nineteen months and notified the trade by circular letter that Brooks was no longer its sales representative. Thereupon Brooks sued Jack's claiming damages for breach of contract and unjust enrichment, and also claiming actual and punitive damages for libel on the ground that certain statements in the circular letter imputed to him a lack of business capacity and insinuated that he had been discharged for dishonesty or misconduct. At the conclusion of the plaintiff's case the District Judge, on motion of the defendant, dismissed the claims of breach of contract and unjust enrichment on the grounds that the arrangement between the parties lacked mutuality and was indefinite in duration and terminable at the will of either party.

The case proceeded on the claim of libel and was submitted to the jury at the close of all the evidence on the issue of actual damages, the right to punitive damages being refused. The jury found for the plaintiff on this cause of action in the sum of $17,500, and both parties have appealed.

Jack's had been in the business of manufacturing cookies in Charlotte, North Carolina, since 1947, but had not been very successful and in consequence it was reorganized in 1950 and a new management was installed under a new president, John Barton, who set about changing the methods of operation. The company had previously distributed its product in its own trucks on certain routes in and around Charlotte, and Barton decided to sell to independent distributors rather than from his own trucks in introducing the product in new territory. Brooks had had experience as a manufacturer's representative in handling diversified lines of goods which he sold to wholesalers and distributors. He was on the lookout for new accounts and one of his circulars fell into Barton's hands and led to a meeting between the men and the formation of an oral contract.

It was agreed that Brooks was to set up a sales organization for the sale of Jack's product by wholesale distributors in Virginia and West Virginia, and also in the Carolinas, with the exception of certain cities in the latter states. He agreed to produce a reasonable amount of business and to pay his own expenses and he was to receive as compensation a commission of five per cent on gross sales after a deduction of five per cent for freight charges. He was to have the position so long as he did a good job, but he was free to stop work for Jack's at any time. There is no dispute that these terms formed part of the contract, but as to another element the testimony was in conflict. On behalf of Jack's it was testified that Brooks was not to take on any additional lines of merchandise; but Brooks denied that he made any such agreement.

Entering upon his duties on or about January 1, 1952, Brooks visited jobbers to whom he was already selling other merchandise and divided the territory amongst them giving them exclusive areas for the sale of Jack's cookies upon their agreement that they would not handle competing goods. He had one salesman working for him at the time, but employed additional men to assist him in the work, and paid them four-fifths of his commissions. His efforts were successful and sales were greatly increased in the territory assigned him, so that by September, 1953 the gross sales had risen from approximately $1500 to approximately $50,000 per month, and his net return amounted to $1,000 per month for a number of months in 1953. Upon his advice Jack's increased the minimum purchase by the distributors from $50 to $200, and he selected new distributors in certain localities in place of old ones appointed by Jack's who had proved unsatisfactory. In April, 1953, after he found the line profitable, he asked for a written contract which he had previously refused to sign, but the company declined.

Dissatisfaction arose in certain particulars. Brooks did not keep any record of his sales or of his employees, and he did not make it clear to them that they were his employees and not Jack's, and in some instances the salesmen called on Jack's for services which Brooks should have given. Barton was obliged to call a meeting of salesmen in Charlotte in order to instruct the salesmen on this point. Barton instructed Brooks to open an office in Columbia as headquarters for Brooks' operations and in January Brooks rented an office and engaged a secretary, but it was not opened until July and then it proved to be the headquarters of an employment agency operated by his wife and his secretary. Brooks hired and fired a large number of salesmen during the period and he had only two salesmen at work in September, 1953.

In April, 1953, in order to increase sales and instruct the retailers as to the distribution of the product, it was agreed that one Henry Hall, an experienced man, should be employed to go out with the salesmen on their routes in order to demonstrate how to display the goods, and he was paid for these services by Jack's for seventy-five days, and thereafter one-half of his salary was paid by each of the parties.

While working for Jack's Brooks took on several new lines for distribution, contrary to his agreement with Jack's, if the testimony of Barton is accepted.

On September 1, 1953 Brooks was called into Jack's office and discharged. He was paid in full for goods sold up to that date. Henry Hall, as an employee of Jack's, was put in charge of the distribution of the merchandise on a salary basis.

On or about September 3, 1953 Barton sent out to the trade a letter announcing that Brooks had ceased to be Jack's representative in the following terms:

This is to notify you that effective September 1, 1953, Mr. A.A. Brooks and his organization are no longer the sales representatives of Jack's Cookie Company, Charlotte, N.C.

We are sorry that situations of this nature have to arise, but we have no hesitancy in doing that which in our judgment is best for the company, its distributors, representatives and customers. You will be contacted as soon as possible by an official representative of this company. It is our sincere desire to serve you in an efficient manner with quality products of which you can be proud. Your business is greatly appreciated and we will do everything in our power to continue to be worthy of it.

Should there be any questions whatsoever concerning this situation, please do not hesitate to call Mr. Howard Walters at 3–9033, Charlotte, N.C.

We think it was error to submit the libel charge to the jury because the letter does not convey a defamatory meaning. ...

. . .

We think, however, that the case should have been submitted to the jury on the issue of breach of contract, because in our opinion the evidence, taken in the light most favorable to the agent, indicated something more than a contract in which the agent is appointed merely to sell the goods of a manufacturer on commission, and there is no promise on either side to continue the relationship for a definite period. In such event each sale constitutes the acceptance of an offer in a series of independent transactions and the manufacturer fulfills his agreement by paying the stipulated commission and is ordinarily at liberty to terminate the arrangement at will without breach of contract. *See Willcox & Gibbs Sewing-Machine Co. v. Ewing*, 141 U.S. 627, 12 S. Ct. 94, 35 L. Ed. 882; *Motor Car Supply Co. v. General Household Utilities Co.*, 4 Cir., 80 F.2d 167; *E. I. DuPont de Nemours & Co. v. Claiborne-Reno*, 8 Cir., 64 F.2d 224, 89 A.L.R. 238; *Curtis Candy Co. v. Silberman*, 6 Cir., 45 F.2d 451; *Terre Haute Brewing Co. v. Dugan*, 8 Cir., 102 F.2d 425; *Shealy v. Fowler*, 182 S.C. 81, 188 S.E. 499.

On the other hand, if the manufacturer appoints an agent not merely to sell the goods, but the agent in addition to making sales furnishes additional consideration, as when he sets up a distributive system for the manufacturer's goods and his compensation is measured by the amount of goods sold in the territory assigned to him, the manufacturer is not at liberty to terminate the agreement at will even though it contains no provision for its termination, but must retain the agent in the employment for a reasonable period of time. Williston on Contracts, § 1027(a), p. 2852; *Joy v. City of St. Louis*, 138 U.S. 1, 50, 11 S. Ct. 243, 34 L. Ed. 843; Restatement of

Agency, § 442 Comment c; *Kelly-Springfield Tire Co. v. Bobo*, 9 Cir., 4 F.2d 71; *Bassick Mfg. Co. v. Riley*, D.C. E.D.Pa., 9 F.2d 138; *J. C. Millett Co. v. Park & Tilford Distillers Corp.*, D.C.N.D.Cal. S.D., 123 F. Supp. 484; *Shealy v. Fowler*, 182 S.C. 81, 188 S.E. 499.

There is evidence in this case which tends to show that Brooks' employment falls into the latter category, and hence the question should have been submitted to the determination of the jury; and if they should so find, they should go further and determine the additional question whether the agent was permitted to retain the agency for a reasonable time, and if not, to ascertain the damages, if any, which he suffered thereby.

However, the jury should be instructed first to consider whether Brooks kept the promises which he made. This issue involves in the first place a determination of the disputed question whether Brooks promised, when he assumed the agency, not to take on any new lines additional to Jack's, and if they find that he made this promise, and violated it, they should be instructed to find a verdict for the defendant.

In addition the jury should determine whether Brooks faithfully and efficiently carried out his part of the business. In this connection the jury should be instructed to consider the evidence tending to show the character of the salesmen selected by him, the frequent changes of personnel, his failure to render them the necessary services and to instruct them that they were his employees and not the employees of Jack's; and also the failure of Brooks to set up a headquarters' office for his agency. If the jury should find from a consideration of this evidence relating to these matters that Jack's had reasonable ground to terminate the agency, the verdict of the jury should be in its favor.[1]

It is not our intention to express any opinion on these controverted questions or to limit the jury to the consideration of the circumstances referred to above, but rather to outline the course to be followed upon the remand of the case, leaving to the District Judge to determine the bearing of the evidence, as it will be developed at the new trial upon the crucial issues in the case.

Reversed and remanded for new trial in accordance with the views expressed in this opinion.

Questions and Comments

1. Two distinct issues can be presented in a traditional common law case involving restrictions upon termination of franchise agreements.

---

1. There is no legal basis for the separate claim of the appellee for unjust enrichment.

A). Did the parties intend to be committed to each other for some time and that termination would be permitted only for good cause?

B). Was there consideration for this specific express or implied promise?

These questions can be interrelated. If there is some "special consideration" that was given by the franchisee beyond what was logically required to undertake the franchise duties, then this "additional" or "special" consideration could be the basis for finding an implied promise that the franchise would be non-terminable for some reasonable time. And that "special consideration" could also provide the bargained exchange that made enforceable the express or implied promise not to terminate.

2.   Du Pont made an express promise relating to termination only for cause and this promise was not enforced. Jack's may have made such promise but in any event one was implied and then enforced due to the "additional" or "special consideration" that was furnished by Mr. Brooks. Can you distinguish factually between what Brooks did and what Reno did in the Du Pont case? Is this simply a matter of different jurisdictions applying fundamentally different rules of law?

HUNT FOODS, INC. v. PHILLIPS AND H.W. LIHOLM

United States Court of Appeals, Ninth Circuit (1957)

248 F.2d 23

Partnership's action against food processor for breach of contract whereby partnership became exclusive distributor of processor's food to certain military establishments. Processor counterclaimed to recover unpaid balance on partnership's trade acceptances. The United States District Court for the Northern District of California, Southern Division, Louis E. Goodman, J., entered judgment for processor on counterclaim and for partnership on breach of contract claim and processor appealed. The Court of Appeals, Stephens, Chief Judge, held that processor was entitled to interest on trade acceptances from date of maturity, oral contract was not terminable at will because of lack of mutuality.

Affirmed in favor of appellees and remanded as to judgment in favor of appellant on cross-complaint.

STEPHENS, CHIEF JUDGE.

In this diversity case, appellees Wellington Phillips and H.W. Liholm, partners doing business under the name of Wellington Phillips & Co., seek damages for breach of contract. In 1951 appellees were engaged in the business of bidding for sales of canned goods and other products to military purchasing offices in California. Appellee Phillips was the chief moving force behind the partnership, having had some twenty-five years experience in various aspects of the grocery and canned food business. The appellees' bidding business in 1951, although fairly new, was profitable, and the outlook for the future was bright. Phillips, in August and September, 1951, talked to Mr. Flynn, Hunt Foods' Sales Manager for the Northern California District, as to the possibility of exclusively handling Hunt's products in the military commissaries. Various discussions later took place between Phillips, Flynn, Mr. Miller, District Sales Manager for all districts of Hunt Foods, Mr. Reed, Export and Government Supply Manager, and Mr. Church, Credit Manager for Hunt Foods. It was disputed at the trial as to the gist of those conversations. Phillips had critical discussions with Mr. Flynn, who was deceased at the time of the trial. Phillips alleged that he told Flynn that his then bidding business in 1951 was very profitable and he would earn $15,000 profit that year; that he told Flynn that he would be willing to act as jobber in sales of Hunt Foods products to the military commissary stores in Northern California if such appointment were exclusive and that he would sell no other brand of canned food products to such commissary stores. Phillips said he told Flynn that because Hunt Foods salesmen were presently selling at wholesale prices to the commissary stores, that it would take him a period of time to obtain a profit for himself on the resale of such products to the stores until changing market conditions or general price changes made it feasible to add or create a mark-up or percentage of profit for himself. Hunt Foods products were then selling considerably below the price of other brands for the same quantity, and it was the intention of Phillips to eventually obtain a fair profit margin by increasing the resale price of Hunt products more than would be done by competitors when there was a price increase, and to decrease Hunt resale prices less than the decrease of competitors when there was a general price decline. In both situations Hunt products would still be selling below that of competitors.

Phillips said he told Flynn that it would take two or three years to make up for early losses while he was building up sales and gradually increasing the resale price of the goods. Phillips said that Flynn agreed that Hunt salesmen would no longer sell to the commissaries, but that they would receive sales credit for all sales made by Phillips. Phillips said Flynn told him such arrangement was acceptable to him as District Sales Manager and that Phillips should talk to Mr. Miller, District Sales Manager for all districts, at the company's principal office at Fullerton, California. Phillips contacted Miller, who stated that any arrangements made by Flynn were acceptable to him. Phillips also arranged with Mr. Church, Credit Manager of appellant, for a certain amount of credit.

In November, 1951, Mr. Flynn signed and distributed, to Hunt salesmen in his area and to military commissaries, a letter confirming the appointment of Phillips as exclusive military service jobber.

Phillips commenced promotion and sales of Hunt products in December, 1951, and continued the jobber arrangement until April, 1953, at which time Hunt informed Phillips that it was terminating the arrangement. It was not disputed that, during the period of the arrangement, the sales of Hunt products to the military commissaries was doubled. The arrangement Hunt had with Phillips was unique, and Hunt had no similar arrangement with anyone else. Hunt terminated the arrangement with Phillips and turned over its entire nationwide sales to military commissaries to a nationwide firm.

Phillips, during the existence of the arrangement, did not promptly pay to Hunt all sums owing, for goods sold by Phillips and charged to him. But Hunt apparently was satisfied with the increased sales, and therefore did not press Phillips too hard as to credit problems. When Hunt did terminate the Agreement, Phillips owed Hunt approximately $25,000. After the termination, Phillips made payments to Hunt so that by July, 1953, he owed Hunt $13,319.37. Phillips then signed three written promises to pay, called trade acceptances, each in the sum of $4,439.79, representing the balance due to Hunt. Phillips paid $1,824.21 on the first trade acceptance, but the balance of the trade acceptance was never paid, nor were payments ever made on the other two acceptances. Phillips admitted liability on the acceptances for the balance of $11,495.16.

In November, 1954, Phillips sued Hunt Foods for breach of the oral contract. Hunt Foods also filed a counterclaim and cross-complaint seeking $11,495.16, based on the balance owing on the three trade acceptances signed by Phillips.

A non-jury trial was had in the District Court. The trial judge found that an oral agreement was entered into between the parties for an unspecified period of time commencing on December 1, 1951. The Court further held that Hunt Foods, Inc. violated and breached the oral agreement and awarded damages of $21,500 to appellees. Judgment was rendered in favor of appellant on its cross-complaint for $11,495.16, being the admitted balance then due and owing on the three trade acceptances signed by Phillips. Hunt Foods, Inc. appeals from the judgment.

THE APPEAL

Termination and Mutuality

Appellant argues that the arrangement with appellees was terminable at will and that the parties merely hoped that the arrangement would be mutually successful and would continue. The trial court took the view, based on the evidence, that appellant appointed appellees as exclusive military service jobber for an unspecified period of time and that before a reasonable time had elapsed, appellant unfairly terminated the contract. The trial court stated that *J.C. Millett Co. v. Park & Tilford Distillers Corp.*, D.C. N.D. Cal., 123 F. Supp. 484, 492, was not substantially dissimilar to the instant case. The *Millett* case involved a determination of the relationship of the parties under an oral agreement whereby plaintiff bought defendant's products as a wholesaler and resold them to retail outlets. In a well-reasoned opinion the court made the following comment in regard to the nature of the distributorship contract which we hold is applicable to the instant case.

'The distributorship contract in the case at bar is more than a contract of employment or agency. It is also a contract of sale. On the other hand, it is more than a mere sales contract. It partakes of the substantial aspects of both.

'At least one California case has applied the California rule pertaining to sales contracts of indefinite duration, *i.e.*, that the party seeking to terminate must give the other party reasonable notice thereof and such termination cannot be effected until at least a reasonable time has expired, to a contract in which plaintiff agreed to buy and exploit in California the warehouse receipts of defendant's distillery. The distributorship contract viewed as a contract of sales would require this result here.

'What of the contract's agency aspects? The California Courts hold that where a contract of employment or agency for an indefinite period is based on some consideration other than the services to be rendered it will continue for a reasonable period of time. While there is some conflict regarding contracts for permanent employment based on such independent consideration it is clear that they likewise continue for at least a reasonable period of time. The other consideration need not be unrelated to the services to be performed. The requirement is that the consideration be other than the service to be rendered as an employee or agent.

'The agency aspects of the distributorship contract required Millett to use its corporate best efforts to promote the sale of Park & Tilford products and to sell such products to the retail market. But in addition Millett agreed to and did buy Park & Tilford products, took title to them and thus assumed the risk of their destruction, maintained warehouse facilities and tied up a substantial amount of its capital in inventory and accounts receivable. While these functions are related to the services to be rendered they are not the aspects of the distributorship contract which are properly called agency. Factually, the agreement was an integrated whole. But for purposes of determining the applicability of the *Speegle* case (*Speegle v. Board of Fire Underwriters*, 1946, 29 Cal. 2d 34, 172 P.2d 867) the agency character of the relationship must be separated from its sales character. In my opinion the non-agency undertakings are sufficient additional consideration.'

Appellant argues that in the instant case there is no independent consideration. However, the trial court held in Finding of Fact V that:

'During the period from December 1, 1951, to the month of May, 1953, plaintiffs did substantially abandon plaintiffs' activity in said former bidding business in order to fully promote the sales of defendant's products during said period and in order to perform said oral agreement and did sell large quantities of defendant's products to said military installations at about plaintiffs' costs and without substantial gross profit.'

We hold that there was consideration other than the service to be rendered as an employee or agent. For a concise summary of the law on this point, *see Jack's Cookie Company v. Brooks*, 4 Cir., 227 F.2d 935. Appellees curtailed substantially their then existing bidding business in order to devote time and effort to the exclusive jobber contract. Appellees (with the understanding and knowledge of Hunt) agreed to sell appellant's products for a year or two without substantial profit. Appellees likewise maintained a stock of goods in inventory and agreed to refrain from selling competing lines to the commissaries. *Thacker v. American Foundry*, 78 Cal. App. 2d 76, 177 P.2d 322, 327, cited by appellant, is inapposite to the instant case, since in that case, the evidence indicated that the employee's prior position as an expediter was terminating because of the completion of its plant and that he would have to look for a job. Also in the Thacker case, the plaintiff did not allege any consideration which would have enabled the court to find any contract other than one terminable at will. *Ruinello v. Murray*, 1951, 36 Cal. 2d 687, 227 P.2d 251, is also of no aid to appellant since in that case the plaintiff did not allege any consideration which would indicate that the employment he gave up was anything other than an employment terminable at will. *Ford Motor Co. v. Kirkmyer Motor Co.*, 1933, 4 Cir., 65 F.2d 1001, is clearly distinguishable when read in its entirety and not out of context as done by appellant in its brief. The oral contract therein involved was held to be lacking in mutuality and too indefinite to form the basis of a binding obligation. The alleged oral contract referred to and inferentially incorporated a written contract, but it was pointed out that the written contract was terminable at will and also did not obligate the defendant to deliver a single car or truck. *E.I. Du Pont De Nemours & Co. v. Claiborne-Reno Co.*, 8 Cir., 64 F.2d 224, 228, 89 A.L.R. 238, likewise is inapposite since it was therein held that under the contract the Reno Company was in a position at any time to terminate the contract without incurring any liability therefor, and therefore the contract lacked mutuality and was terminable at will.

We likewise hold that the contract is not terminable at will because of lack of mutuality. We have already somewhat discussed this issue, but we now answer specific points raised by appellant. First, appellant argues that there is lack of mutuality because appellees were free to somewhat continue their brokerage business. In support of this argument, appellant cites *Hoffmann v. Pfingsten*, 1951, 260 Wis. 160, 50 N.W.2d 369, 372, 26 A.L.R.2d 1131, wherein by dictum the court substantiated its holding of lack of mutuality (because under the modified contract Hoffmann made no promise to order the product) by pointing out that Hoffmann had no obligation to give all his time to Old Tanner nor to prosecute its development vigorously * * *.' (Emphasis supplied.) Under the contract in the instant case, appellees agreed to do more than refrain from handling competitive products. They agreed to service the various military establishments, to depart from their existing bidding business, and to sell the line without profit for a year or two. In *J. C. Millett Co. v. Park & Tilford Distillers Corp.*, D.C., 123 F. Supp. 484, 490, it is stated:

> It is clear that Millett promised to do more than buy whatever amount of liquor it desired. In promising to take on the distributorship, it promised to perform the essential economic function of that position, *i.e.*, to use its corporate best efforts to promote the sale of Park & Tilford products. * * *

> The fact that Millett was in contemplation of both parties to sell other distillers' products does not mitigate against its covenant to use its best efforts. * * *

It is clear that appellant's representatives knew and acquiesced in appellees continuing their prior brokerage business. In fact, it is obvious that the parties intended that the brokerage business was to continue on a somewhat reduced scale until such time as appellees' sales of Hunt products enabled them to discontinue the prior business entirely. Finding of Fact IV is in accord with this view and is not clearly erroneous.

We find without merit the second argument of appellant that the contract lacks mutuality because appellant could not force appellees to buy any goods. Appellees were the exclusive jobber of appellant's products to the military establishments in Northern

California, and appellees were obligated to use their best efforts to promote the sales of appellant's goods. If appellees failed to use their best efforts, appellants could maintain an action against appellees for breach of contract. *E.I. Du Pont De Nemours & Co. v. Claiborne, supra*, is inapposite as previously discussed. *Curtiss Candy Co. v. Silberman*, 6 Cir., 45 F.2d 451, 452, is distinguishable since the court construed the negotiations of the parties as resulting only in a series of separate and independent sales, each complete in itself, and each consisting of its individual order, accepted and the sale completed on the part of defendant by delivery of the merchandise. The court likewise found no consideration or hardship or unfairness calling for application of Restatement of the Law of Contracts § 90. Other cases cited by appellant are either not persuasive or inapposite.

Reason for Termination

The trial court held in Finding of Fact VII that appellees duly and fully performed each and all of the obligations' under the oral contract and the trial court did not agree with appellant's claim that the termination was because Phillips had not promptly paid for the goods delivered upon Phillips' account. We can not substitute our judgment for that of the trial court.

Statute of Frauds

Appellant argues that the California Statute of Frauds is a defense to this action because the alleged oral contract was to continue for more than one year. The trial court held that recovery is not prevented by the statute of frauds, basing its decision on appellant being estopped to assert the statute. The trial court construed the oral contract to be one that was to continue for a reasonable time and that long before a reasonable time had elapsed, Hunt unfairly terminated the contract. The court held that the contract commenced December 1, 1951, and was breached by appellant on April 25, 1953.

(The court found facts supporting estoppel.)

Damages

Appellant raises a host of objections on the subject of damages. Appellant argues in essence that the damages were so speculative that they could not be assessed; that is, they were prospective damages for a new enterprise involving contingent future bargains. Appellant also argues that gross profit figures were used in assessing damages, and that there was a failure of proof of the ability of appellees to perform the contract.

The California rule is that where it clearly appears that a party has suffered damage, a liberal rule should be applied in allowing a court or jury to determine the amount; and that, given proof of damage, uncertainty as to the exact amount is no reason for denying all recovery. The fact that the amount of damage may not be susceptible of exact proof or may be uncertain, contingent or difficult of ascertainment does not bar recovery. *California Lettuce Growers v. Union Sugar Company*, 45 Cal. 2d 474, 289 P.2d 785, 49 A.L.R.2d 496; *James v. Herbert*, Cal. App., 1957, 309 P.2d 91; *Mann v. Jackson*, 141 Cal. App. 2d 6, 296 P.2d 120. It is also clear that in arriving at the amount of such damages in a situation involving loss of profits, net profits are to be considered and not gross anticipated profits. *West Coast Winery, Inc. v. Golden West Wineries, Inc.*, 69 Cal. App. 2d 166, 169, 158 P.2d 623, 625; *Olcese v. Davis*, 124 Cal. App. 2d 58, 268 P.2d 175, 177.

In the instant case appellees had acted as the exclusive jobber of appellant to retail distributors on military bases for some sixteen months before appellant terminated the arrangement, and during such time appellees had substantially increased the sales of Hunt products to the various military establishments in Northern California. It was the understanding of the parties that of necessity the profits of appellees at the outset of the arrangement would be meager. At the trial appellees presented evidence as to business experience as to three of the nineteen commissary stores in Northern California. Appellees presented this evidence in order to show what amounts were sold, the gross profit and the fact that the sales were increasing as time went along. The difference in gross profit at various times was also testified to by appellee Phillips. Appellee Phillips also testified that there was no relationship between the size of the orders he got from a particular military establishment and the cost of traveling expense to call on such establishment. Phillips also testified that his expenses were more or less static. We note particularly that appellees' partnership 1952 income tax return was admitted into evidence, which shows that during the year 1952 automobile and travel expenses' to be $6,576.82. Other expenses were listed in the tax return. It is also apparent from a reading of the transcript that appellees' sales of appellant's products were increasing rapidly at the time of the termination of the agreement and that gross profit was also rising. We hold that under the facts of the instant case, there was operating experience sufficient to permit a reasonable estimate of probable income and expense, and the trial court was justified in awarding damages for loss of prospective profits. *Jegen v. Berger*, 77 Cal. App. 2d 1, 174 P.2d 489; *Natural Soda Products Co. v. City of Los Angeles*, 23 Cal. 2d 193, 143 P.2d 12. *Schmitt v. Continental-Diamond Fibre Co.*, 7 Cir., 116 F.2d 779, which appellant cites out of context, is clearly distinguishable. There plaintiff based its damages for breach of a sales agency contract on the mere showing of the amount of defendant's sales and an assumption that a certain percentage of such sales would have originated in plaintiff's district for the years in question. Other cases cited by appellant are distinguishable and bear no relation to the facts of the instant case. It is clear from a reading of the record that the trial judge was aware of the proper standards for assessment of damages and that there is no evidence that gross profit was the sole basis for determining the award. We likewise find against appellant's claim that appellees did not show that they were able to perform the agreement; rather, the evidence showed just the opposite.

Other points raised by appellant we have examined and find without merit.

Judgment affirmed in favor of appellees on their complaint, and remanded as to the judgment in favor of appellant on its cross-complaint for a determination by the trial court as to the proper amount of interest allowable on such judgment.

VARNI BROS. CORPORATION ET AL., PLAINTIFFS AND APPELLANTS v. WINE WORLD, INC., DEFENDANT AND RESPONDENT

Court of Appeal, Fifth District, California (1955)
35 Cal. App. 4th 880, 41 Cal. Rptr. 2d 740, 26 UCC Rep. Serv. 2d 1054

HARRIS, J.

STATEMENT OF THE CASE AND FACTS

Wine World, Inc. (Wine World) is a producer and supplier of wines, including Beringer, Napa Ridge, Chateau Souverain and Meridian. Wine World distributes its wines through a network of independent distributors located throughout the United States. Brand Wines & Spirits, Inc. (Brand) and Varni Bros. Corporation (Varni) are former distributors for Wine World in the Fresno and Modesto areas, respectively. Varni began distributing for Wine World in 1975 and Brand began in 1985. The distributing arrangements were never formalized in written contracts.

Although Brand did not begin distributing for Wine World until 1985, Brand's founder, Harvey Braziel, had distributed for Wine World in the Fresno area while with a company called M & T Distributing Company. After consulting with Wine World in 1985, Brand and Wine World agreed that M & T would assign its distribution rights to Brand.

As wine distributors, Brand and Varni purchased wine from suppliers for resale to retailers in their assigned territories. The development of a market for the vintner's products was a joint effort between the vintner and the distributor. Distributors provided a wide variety of services to suppliers, including promotional sales calls on retailers, placement of advertising, and periodic removal of dated wine from retailers' shelves. Varni and Brand maintained warehouses and fleets of trucks and trained sales people to promote the portfolios of their suppliers, including Wine World. Wine World and other suppliers gave Varni and Brand written sales quotas or objectives to meet, and met periodically with them to evaluate their performances. In some instances, the duties of distributors were spelled out in written contracts. However, up until 1985 at the earliest, written distribution contracts were a rare exception in the wine industry. Rather, suppliers dealt with wholesale distributors on the basis of a handshake; everyone understood what a distributorship involved.

In 1989, Wine World decided to consolidate its distribution network in Northern California to a single distributor. Wine World terminated its distributing arrangements with both Varni and Brand on August 28, 1989, by 60 days' written notice.

It is undisputed that at the time Varni and Brand agreed to distribute for Wine World there were no substantive discussions regarding any terms of the distributorship arrangement. According to Wine World, it had no internal policy limiting the termination of its distributors and was not aware of any industry custom regarding termination. On the other hand, according to Braziel, he had been told it was Wine World's policy to build a record over the course of six months to a year to justify a termination.

While there was a dispute as to whether it was the prevailing custom at the time of the agreements that a supplier could not unilaterally terminate a distribution agreement except for poor performance or failure to pay invoices, there was no evidence proffered that any such custom continued to exist after 1985 or 1986. However, appellants proffered some evidence in an attempt to show that thereafter a custom and usage existed nonetheless requiring the supplier to pay some sort of severance compensation to the terminated distributor based on rendered services in establishing markets and sales volume for the supplier. In 1975 and 1985, respectively, when Varni and Brand agreed to distribute for Wine World, they expected they would not be terminated except for reasons established by the then prevailing industry custom.

A complaint was filed by Varni and Brand on July 25, 1991, alleging two causes of action, one for each plaintiff, for breach of implied contracts. The complaint alleged the contracts were only terminable for poor performance based on industry custom or trade usage, Wine World practices, and longevity of business relationships. Wine World answered by general denial and asserted several affirmative defenses.

Wine World filed separate summary judgment motions against Varni and Brand. Both motions were granted. Brand's motion for reconsideration was denied. Varni and Brand (collectively appellants) filed a timely notice of appeal.

DISCUSSION

I.

Termination

Appellants contend the trial court erred in granting Wine World's motions for summary judgment. The motions were granted on three alternative grounds: (1) parol evidence that there was an implied understanding between the parties that good cause would be required for termination under the agreements was not admissible; (2) appellants could not prevail on the merits because industry custom requiring termination for good cause applied only until 1985, and not up to 1989 when the relationship was terminated; and (3) because there was no agreement that the distributing arrangements would last for a fixed term of years, the contracts were of indefinite duration making them terminable at will under California Uniform Commercial Code section 2309.

Standard of Review

Summary judgment is proper if the supporting papers are sufficient to sustain a judgment in favor of the moving party as a matter of law and the opposing party presents no evidence giving rise to a triable issue as to any material fact. (Code Civ. Proc., § 437c, subd. (c).) . . .

Implied-in-fact Contract

The underlying basis for the breach of contract actions was the alleged existence of implied-in-fact contracts. Appellants rely on the case of *Bert G. Gianelli Distributing Co. v. Beck & Co.* (1985) 172 Cal. App. 3d 1020 [219 Cal. Rptr. 203] for the proposition that where a usage of trade exists, it may constitute a term of a contract. . . .

. . .

Here appellants had been distributing wine for Wine World for many years. Their course of conduct implies they had distribution agreements.[2] (Accord, *J. C. Millett Co. v. Park & Tilford Distillers*

---

2. A trier of fact might determine no contracts existed, but the evidence certainly raises a triable issue of fact on this point.

Corp. (N.D. Cal. 1954) 123 F. Supp. 484, 489–490 [rejected supplier's contention that distributing contract was not a contract at all but merely an arrangement under which the plaintiff was given the privilege of distributing defendant's products].) However, because no terms were ever expressed or discussed, they were not express written or oral contracts, but rather implied contracts, the terms of which must necessarily be determined by the parties' course of conduct. ... Thus, contrary to Wine World's contention, appellants are not seeking to create contracts by usage of trade. The implied distribution contracts exist, if at all, by the parties' course of conduct. Appellants only seek to establish a term of the alleged distribution agreements by usage of trade.

Custom and Usage

In addition, usage or custom may be looked to, both to explain the meaning of language and to imply terms, where no contrary intent appears from the terms of the contract. (1 Witkin, Summary of Cal. Law, *supra*, Contracts, § 696, p. 629; Civ. Code, § 1655.) . . .

. . .

It is undisputed in this case that there was no discussion regarding termination of the implied distributing contracts. Therefore, contrary to the trial court's ruling, custom and usage is admissible to prove that termination only for good cause was a term of the implied distributing agreements.

. . .

Duration of Contract

The trial court was correct in concluding that because there was no agreement that the distributing arrangements would last for a fixed term of years, the contracts were of indefinite duration, making them terminable at will under California Uniform Commercial Code section 2309 (hereafter section 2309).

Section 2309 provides in pertinent part: (2) Where the contract provides for successive performances but is indefinite in duration it is valid for a reasonable time but unless otherwise agreed may be terminated at any time by either party.

In addition to the above provision, it is well established by case law that where the nature of the contract and the totality of the circumstances give no suggestion as to any ascertainable term, the term of duration shall be at least a reasonable time and the contract shall be terminable at will upon reasonable notice. (*Consolidated Theatres, Inc. v. Theatrical Stage Employees Union* (1968)

69 Cal. 2d 713, 727 [73 Cal. Rptr. 213, 447 P.2d 325].) This rule applies, in particular, to distributorship agreements. (*Consolidated Theatres, Inc. v. Theatrical Stage Employees Union, supra*, 69 Cal. 2d at 728; *Reely v. Chapman, supra*, 177 Cal. App. 2d at 262.) Since the contracts in this case, as a matter of law, were at-will contracts, their duration was no longer or shorter than a reasonable time. They were thus in the nature of contracts renewable year to year or month to month, depending on what period may be determined to be a reasonable time.

Contrary to the trial court's conclusion, however, this does not end the inquiry. As explained in *Gianelli*, duration of a contract and the permissible reasons for termination are different concepts. (*Bert G. Gianelli Distributing Co. v. Beck & Co., supra*, 172 Cal. App. 3d at 1040.) While a contract may be indefinite in duration, thereby making it a contract at will as a matter of law, under *Gianelli* termination may nonetheless require good cause. Under *Gianelli*, a contract may continue to be indefinite in duration and at will until, for good cause or upon mutual consent, it is terminated.

As noted earlier, custom and usage is admissible to prove that termination only for good cause was a term implied in the implied distributing agreements. Appellants contend good cause is required by trade usage, and that by the application of trade usage the "unless otherwise agreed" language of section 2309 is satisfied. We will examine appellants' contentions in the following section of our discussion. We again note, however, and contrary to appellants' contention, the requirement of good cause for termination does not change the duration of the contracts. Rather, as explained above, the concepts of duration of a contract and the permissible reasons for termination are different. An at-will contract remains at will and indefinite in duration. Under section 2309, it is valid for a reasonable time.... Nonetheless, its termination may require good cause.

Sufficiency of Evidence of Custom or Usage

A more difficult question is whether the evidence proffered by appellants is sufficient to raise a triable issue of fact on the question of whether trade usage supports an implied term that termination must be for good cause. The trial court held it was not (and thus inadmissible) because the evidence established any trade usage to that effect had been abandoned years prior to the time of termination of the contracts. Thus the question is whether the trade usage that existed at the time of inception of the contracts governs when at the time of the termination, that trade usage no longer exists.

. . .

(The court stated that in a fixed term contract such as one for ten years, the trade usages that existed when the contract was formed continued in force for the life of the contract even if the industry modified its trade usages. However, in a contract terminable at will or is one that is valid only for a reasonable period of time, the contract is periodically renewed. Trade usages that are discontinued in the industry do not carry over to renewed versions of the contract. Therefore, since the facts show that in this case the trade usage requiring good cause for termination had been discontinued in the industry at least two years before this contract was terminated, that usage was no longer an implied term of the contract.)

The evidence presented in support of and in opposition to the motions for summary judgment establishes that the custom and usage existing at the time of the formation of the implied distributing contracts had changed or was in the process of changing three to four years before Wine World terminated the contracts in question. Good cause was no longer the standard for termination at that time. Rather, distributors were being terminated simply for purposes of consolidation. Thus, whatever may have been the custom and usage prior to 1989, it was irrelevant at the time these appellants' contracts were terminated. Applicable industry custom and usage thus does not support a conclusion that appellants' contracts were only terminable for good cause.

. . .

(The court concluded that there was insufficient evidence that Wine World's policies and practices were to not terminate a distributorship and in any case this policy had not been communicated to the plaintiffs, stating: "Thus a theory of detrimental reliance is not supported.")

II.

Nonbreach Severance Compensation

. . .

DISPOSITION

The judgments are affirmed. The parties shall bear their own costs on appeal.

Ardaiz, P. J., and Martin, J., concurred.

A petition for a rehearing was denied July 7, 1995, and the opinion was modified to read as printed above.

II. STATUTES PROTECTING THE RIGHTS OF AGENTS OR FRANCHISEES

In the absence of statutory protections, a franchisee often has many road blocks in the way of sustaining a cause of action for wrongful termination.

First, many franchise agreements are oral. When the issue is claimed long-term duration, the statute of frauds may preclude finding an enforceable contract or a remedy.

Second, written franchise agreements are generally drafted by the franchisor and often provide expressly that they are terminable at will and not subject to modification except by a signed writing. The contract may even require that the signature be that of someone with a specific title such as the CEO or president.

Third, the parol evidence rule may exclude collateral assurances given at the time of contracting and the "no oral modification" clause may well exclude proof of subsequent assurances. And even if the franchisee proves that an express or implied promise was given concerning duration, its enforcement may be denied on the grounds of lack of mutuality.

Finally, even when a franchisee is successful in establishing that the right to terminate was subject to limitation, there can still be difficulties establishing the duration and proving specific damages. Some cases find an implied term that the agreement would last for a reasonable time but this is a difficult term to define and can lead to an illogical result. The longer a franchise relationship has been in existence, the greater the likely investment that the franchisee has put into it. Yet if the franchise is implied to last only for a reasonable time, the longer it has been in existence, the less time there is for it to run. Compare this result to the European statutes which typically compensate the terminated franchisee using net income multiplied by a factor based upon how long the agreement has been in effect.

There are federal statutes and various state statutes that provide protection for commercial agents or franchisees. Many of these apply to only a specific industry such as the rather ineffective Automobile Dealers' Day in Court Act (15 U.S.C. §§ 1221–1225). Some only protect against bringing additional franchisees into the sales area. A franchise contract usually does not itself involve the sale of goods, however, an apparent majority of cases have found that UCC Article 2 does apply to franchises. Agents and franchisees might benefit from Code provisions such as the good faith requirements in Articles 1 and 2 and provisions of § 2–309(2) and (3) and perhaps § 2–306(2)). Some state enactments go much further substituting statutory terms for those provided for by the parties in their contracts and providing for administrative procedures to control franchise termination or the introduction of additional franchisees into sales territories.

The California Vehicle Code provides:

§ 3060. Termination of franchise

(a) Notwithstanding Section 20999.1 of the Business and Professions Code or the terms of any franchise, no franchisor shall terminate or refuse to continue any existing franchise unless all of the following conditions are met:

(1) The franchisee and the board have received written notice from the franchisor as follows:

(A) Sixty days before the effective date thereof setting forth the specific grounds for termination or refusal to continue.

(B) Fifteen days before the effective date thereof setting forth the specific grounds with respect to any of the following:

(i) Transfer of any ownership or interest in the franchise without the consent of the franchisor, which consent shall not be unreasonably withheld.

(ii) Misrepresentation by the franchisee in applying for the franchise.

(iii) Insolvency of the franchisee, or filing of any petition by or against the franchisee under any bankruptcy or receivership law.

(iv) Any unfair business practice after written warning thereof.

(v) Failure of the motor vehicle dealer to conduct its customary sales and service operations during its customary hours of business for seven consecutive business days, giving rise to a good faith belief on the part of the franchisor that the motor vehicle dealer is in fact going out of business, except for circumstances beyond the direct control of the motor vehicle dealer or by order of the department.

(C) The written notice shall contain, on the first page thereof in at least 12-point bold type and circumscribed by a line to segregate it from the rest of the text, one of the following statements, whichever is applicable:

[To be inserted when a 60-day notice of termination is given.]

"NOTICE TO DEALER: You have the right to file a protest with the NEW MOTOR VEHICLE BOARD in Sacramento and have a hearing in which you may protest the termination of your franchise under provisions of the California Vehicle Code.

You must file your protest with the board within 30 calendar days after receiving this notice or within 30 days after the end of any appeal procedure provided by the franchisor or your protest right will be waived."

[To be inserted when a 15-day notice of termination is given.]

"NOTICE TO DEALER: You have the right to file a protest with the NEW MOTOR VEHICLE BOARD in Sacramento and have a hearing in which you may protest the termination of your franchise under provisions of the California Vehicle Code. You must file your protest with the board within 10 calendar days after receiving this notice or within 10 days after the end of any appeal procedure provided by the franchisor or your protest right will be waived."

(2) Except as provided in Section 3050.7, the board finds that there is good cause for termination or refusal to continue, following a hearing called pursuant to Section 3066. The franchisee may file a protest with the board within 30 days after receiving a 60-day notice, satisfying the requirements of this section, or within 30 days after the end of any appeal procedure provided by the franchisor, or within 10 days after receiving a 15-day notice, satisfying the requirements of this section, or within 10 days after the end of any appeal procedure provided by the franchisor. When a protest is filed, the board shall advise the franchisor that a timely protest has been filed, that a hearing is required pursuant to Section 3066, and that the franchisor may not terminate or refuse to continue until the board makes its findings.

(3) The franchisor has received the written consent of the franchisee, or the appropriate period for filing a protest has elapsed.

(b)(1) Notwithstanding Section 20999.1 of the Business and Professions Code or the terms of any franchise, no franchisor shall modify or replace a franchise with a succeeding franchise if the modification or replacement would substantially affect the franchisee's sales or service obligations or investment, unless the franchisor has first given the board and each affected franchisee written notice thereof at least 60 days in advance of the modification or replacement. Within 30 days of receipt of the notice, satisfying the requirement of this section, or within 30 days after the end of any appeal procedure provided by the franchisor, a franchisee may file a protest with the board and the modification or replacement does not become effective until there is a finding by the board that there is good cause for the modification or replacement. If, however, a replacement franchise is the successor franchise to an expiring or expired term franchise, the prior franchise shall continue in effect until resolution of the protest by the board. In the event of multiple protests, hearings shall be consolidated to expedite the disposition of the issue.

(2) The written notice shall contain, on the first page thereof in at least 12-point bold type and circumscribed by a line to segregate it from the rest of the text, the following statement:

"NOTICE TO DEALER: Your franchise agreement is being modified or replaced. If the modification or replacement will substantially affect your sales or service obligations or investment, you have the right to file a protest with the NEW MOTOR VEHICLE BOARD in Sacramento and have a hearing in which you may protest the proposed modification or replacement of your franchise under provisions of the California Vehicle Code. You must file your protest with the board within 30 calendar days of your receipt of this notice or within 30 days after the end of any appeal procedure provided by the franchisor or your protest rights will be waived."

§ 3061. Good cause

In determining whether good cause has been established for modifying, replacing, terminating, or refusing to continue a franchise, the board shall take into consideration the existing circumstances, including, but not limited to, all of the following:

(a) Amount of business transacted by the franchisee, as compared to the business available to the franchisee.

(b) Investment necessarily made and obligations incurred by the franchisee to perform its part of the franchise.

(c) Permanency of the investment.

(d) Whether it is injurious or beneficial to the public welfare for the franchise to be modified or replaced or the business of the franchisee disrupted.

(e) Whether the franchisee has adequate motor vehicle sales and service facilities, equipment, vehicle parts, and qualified service personnel to reasonably provide for the needs of the consumers for the motor vehicles handled by the franchisee and has been and is rendering adequate services to the public.

(f) Whether the franchisee fails to fulfill the warranty obligations of the franchisor to be performed by the franchisee.

(g) Extent of franchisee's failure to comply with the terms of the franchise.

§ 3062. Establishing or relocating dealerships

(a)(1) Except as otherwise provided in subdivision (b), if a franchisor seeks to enter into a franchise establishing an additional motor vehicle dealership within a relevant market area where the same line-make is then represented, or seeks to relocate an existing motor vehicle dealership, the franchisor shall, in writing, first notify the board and each franchisee in that line-make in the relevant market area of the franchisor's intention to establish an additional dealership or to relocate an existing dealership within or into that market area. Within 20 days of receiving the notice, satisfying the requirements of this section, or within 20 days after the end of an appeal procedure provided by the franchisor, a franchisee required to be given the notice may file with the board a protest to the establishing or relocating of the dealership. If, within this time, a franchisee files with the board a request for additional time to file a protest, the board or its executive director, upon a showing of good cause, may grant an additional 10 days to file the protest. When a protest is filed, the board shall inform the franchisor that a timely protest has been filed, that a hearing is required pursuant to Section 3066, and that the franchisor may not establish or relocate the proposed dealership until the board has held a hearing as provided in Section 3066, nor thereafter, if the board has determined that there is good cause for not permitting the dealership. In the event of multiple protests, hearings may be consolidated to expedite the disposition of the issue.

(2) If a franchisor seeks to enter into a franchise that authorizes a satellite warranty facility to be established at, or relocated to, a proposed location that is within two miles of a dealership of the same line-make, the franchisor shall first give notice in writing of the franchisor's intention to establish or relocate a satellite warranty facility at the proposed location to the board and each franchisee operating a dealership of the same line-make within two miles of the proposed location. Within 20 days of receiving the notice satisfying the requirements of this section, or within 20 days after the end of an appeal procedure provided by the franchisor, a franchisee required to be given the notice may file with the board a protest to the establishing or relocating of the satellite warranty facility. If, within this time, a franchisee files with the board a request for additional time to file a protest, the board or its executive director, upon a showing of good cause, may grant an additional 10 days to file the protest. When a protest is filed, the board shall inform the franchisor that a timely protest has been filed, that a hearing is required pursuant to Section 3066,

and that the franchisor may not establish or relocate the proposed satellite warranty facility until the board has held a hearing as provided in Section 3066, nor thereafter, if the board has determined that there is good cause for not permitting the satellite warranty facility. In the event of multiple protests, hearings may be consolidated to expedite the disposition of the issue.

(3) The written notice shall contain, on the first page thereof in at least 12-point bold type and circumscribed by a line to segregate it from the rest of the text, the following statement:

"NOTICE TO DEALER: You have the right to file a protest with the NEW MOTOR VEHICLE BOARD in Sacramento and have a hearing on your protest under the terms of the California Vehicle Code if you oppose this action. You must file your protest with the board within 20 days of your receipt of this notice, or within 20 days after the end of any appeal procedure that is provided by us to you. If within this time you file with the board a request for additional time to file a protest, the board or its executive director, upon a showing of good cause, may grant you an additional 10 days to file the protest."

(b) Subdivision (a) does not apply to either of the following:

(1) The relocation of an existing dealership to a location that is both within the same city as, and within one mile from, the existing dealership location.

(2) The establishment at a location that is both within the same city as, and within one-quarter mile from, the location of a dealership of the same line-make that has been out of operation for less than 90 days.

(c) Subdivision (a) does not apply to a display of vehicles at a fair, exposition, or similar exhibit if actual sales are not made at the event and the display does not exceed 30 days. This subdivision may not be construed to prohibit a new vehicle dealer from establishing a branch office for the purpose of selling vehicles at the fair, exposition, or similar exhibit, even though the event is sponsored by a financial institution, as defined in Section 31041 of the Financial Code or by a financial institution and a licensed dealer. The establishment of these branch offices, however, shall be in accordance with subdivision (a) where applicable.

(d) For the purposes of this section, the reopening of a dealership that has not been in operation for one year or more shall be deemed the establishment of an additional motor vehicle dealership.

(e) As used in this section, the following definitions apply:

(1) "Motor vehicle dealership" or "dealership" means an authorized facility at which a franchisee offers for sale or lease, displays for sale or lease, or sells or leases new motor vehicles.

(2) "Satellite warranty facility" means a facility operated by a franchisee where authorized warranty repairs and service are performed and the offer for sale or lease, the display for sale or lease, or the sale or lease of new motor vehicles is not authorized to take place.

§ 507. Relevant market area

The "relevant market area" is any area within a radius of 10 miles from the site of a potential new dealership.

§ 3063. Good cause

In determining whether good cause has been established for not entering into or relocating an additional franchise for the same line-make, the board shall take into consideration the existing circumstances, including, but not limited to, all of the following:

(a) Permanency of the investment.

(b) Effect on the retail motor vehicle business and the consuming public in the relevant market area.

(c) Whether it is injurious to the public welfare for an additional franchise to be established.

(d) Whether the franchisees of the same line-make in that relevant market area are providing adequate competition and convenient consumer care for the motor vehicles of the line-make in the market area which shall include the adequacy of motor vehicle sales and service facilities, equipment, supply of vehicle parts, and qualified service personnel.

(e) Whether the establishment of an additional franchise would increase competition and therefore be in the public interest.

Vehicle Code section 3066(b) places the burden of proof regarding grounds to cancel upon the franchisor and the burden of proof regarding a challenge to a relocation or new franchise upon the franchisee. The effect of these laws is to allow existing car dealers to file a paper that says "I protest" and thereby delay the entry of a new franchise into its market area. A constitutional challenge (14th amendment due process) to this process was rejected in the case of *New Motor Vehicle Bd. v. Orrin W. Fox Co.*, 439 U.S. 96 (1978). One of the effects of the 2009 bankruptcies of General Motors and Chrysler was to permit the avoidance of contracts with selected franchisees which the companies wanted to terminate.

III. EUROPEAN UNION LEGISLATION

Before the enactment in 1986 of Council Directive 86/653/EEC, most countries in the EU had national statutes on the subject of the protection of a commercial agent's interests and these rules varied from country to country. The very definitions of what constituted a commercial agent's relationship to his principal differed, to say nothing of the protection given to such an agent. The United Kingdom treated a commercial agent as an independent sales agent who seeks orders for, or concludes sales on behalf of, his principal (Lidgard, Rohwer & Campbell, *A Survey of Commercial Agency*, Kluwer (1984) at 105; hereinafter *Survey*.) In Italy, however, an agent was merely a person who undertakes to promote the conclusion of contracts for his principal, but who has no authority to bind that principal. *(Survey* at 156.) The national approaches to duration and remedies for termination varied widely.

These differences created serious problems when an agent's territory crossed international borders, and they were not conducive to the smooth functioning of a common European market. They were viewed as "detrimental both to the protection available to commercial agents vis-à-vis their principals and to the security of commercial transactions" (Preamble, Council Directive 86/653/ EEC). In order to create a more uniform set of rights, obligations, and protections for commercial agents, Council Directive 86/653/ EEC was promulgated in 1986. Under this directive, the two disparate definitions of agents are brought under the same regime. To that end, the Directive defines a commercial agent as "a self-employed intermediary who has continuing authority to negotiate the sale or the purchase of goods on behalf of [the principal], *or* to negotiate and conclude such transactions on behalf and in the name of that principal" *(Art. 1(2)).* Distributorships are therefore specifically excluded from this Directive, and in general the protections given to commercial agents in Europe are much more substantial. Jacques Sales, *Termination of Sales Agents and Distributors in France*, 31 International Lawyer (Fall, 1997) 823, 824 (hereinafter 31 Int'l Law 823)

In general, the Directive attempts to protect the sales agent, as the weaker party, from any prejudice vis-à-vis the principal both during the course of his agency and upon termination. During the course of his agency, the agent is specifically entitled not only to a commission for transactions in which he is involved, but also to "goodwill remuneration." *(Survey* at 324). This is a concept found in Dutch law, but one that runs throughout the Directive. This form of remuneration compensates the agent "where the transaction is concluded with a third party whom (the agent) has previously acquired as a customer for transactions of the same kind." Council Directive 86/653/EEC, Art. 7(1)(b). The Directive specifically mandates the preservation of the agent's territory (Art. 7(2)), and the agent is entitled to his commission for bringing his principal a contract even if the principal ends up repudiating or breaching. (Arts. 10(1)(b) and (11)(1)).

Most significantly, the Directive provides for extensive protection upon termination of the agency relationship. The Directive allows either the agent or the principal to terminate the relationship at any time with varying consequences. (Art. 15(1)). First, there is again a notion of "goodwill remuneration," whereby, in addition to those transactions which the agent has partially performed, the principal must pay a commission to the agent on transactions with customers the agent was responsible for bringing to the principal for a reasonable time after termination. (Art. 8). Second, the party seeking to terminate the relationship must give the other party notice of their intent to terminate. This notice can be anywhere from one to three months depending on the length of the relationship and may be extended to as long as six months by national legislation. (Art. 15(2)and (3)). This sliding scale, where one year of service requires one month of notice, two years two months notice, etc., is reminiscent of the Italian sliding scale enacted before the Directive's mandate. (*Survey* at 174). This minimum notice period cannot be contracted around. The parties may contract for longer periods of notice, but in no case can the notice period be shorter for the principal's decision to terminate than for that of the agent. (Art. 15(4)).

Upon termination, even when given the required period of notice, the principal must indemnify his former agent (Art. 17). This indemnity is based on the amount of goodwill the agent has generated for his principal, as well as that which "is equitable having regard to all the circumstances" (Art. 17(2)(a)). In no case should this indemnity exceed one year's commission that the agent has previously received, but in addition he may receive "damages" for his termination. These damages include additional indemnity when the principal has not given the mandated period of notice. The agent is also entitled to have any uncompensated benefits disgorged from the principal, and to be reimbursed for any investments he has made "on the principal's advice" (Art. 17(3)). This form of compensation for investments made in the agent's reliance on the principal's representations is similar to the compensation given under Italian law before the Directive (*Survey* at 175).

While the compensation due to the agent is denominated "indemnity" and "damages," Articles 17(4) and 18 provide that the indemnity and damages are payable in the event of termination by the agent's death or termination by the agent due to age, infirmity or illness. This goes beyond the traditional concept of compensation for breach by the principal.

The Directive was implemented into French law in 1991. (Jacquez Sales, *Termination of Sales Agents and Distributors in France,* 31 Int'l Law, 823, 825–826). The indemnity mandated by the Directive is calculated by the French courts "on the arbitrary basis of twice the agent's annual commission, determined by averaging the preceding two or three years' commissions." *Id.* at 826–827. This is despite the Directive's provision in Article 17 fixing indemnity equal to one year's commission. This indemnity could be more or less depending on the circumstances of the case, but "courts are also likely to consider other additional factors ... such ... as the extent to which the agent increased the principal's business; the amount of the agent's investment; the extent of the agent's specialized qualifications; the portion of the agent's time devoted to the principal's business; and the cost to the agent of the termination of employment and other contracts resulting from the termination of the sales agency relationship" in determining the principal's liability. *Id.*

In addition to such indemnity, French courts are likely to award "supplementary compensation if the termination is regarded as 'abusive'." While what is "abusive" is a matter of judicial discretion, "when the agent [can] show an element of wantonness or unfairness in the termination" he will likely recover these supplementary damages as well. *Id.* What is more, even when there has been no termination by words or act of the principal and the contract has simply ended, this "mere expiration of [the] fixed-term contract would entitle the agent to indemnity." *Id.* at 830.

Nothing in the Directive is meant to change the national laws providing for termination of the agent for cause. However, while cause for the termination would result in the agent forfeiting his right to indemnity or damages (Art. 18), in practice finding cause for termination is difficult. Specifically, "the fault that would deprive the sales agent of a termination indemnity [is] unlikely to exist unless the sales agent engaged in some intentional wrongdoing or gross negligence." *Id.* at 828. Therefore, while the Directive leaves this area of national European law untouched, an agent who does not meet his sales quotas is unlikely to suffer forfeiture of his right to indemnity or damages.

THE EUROPEAN UNION DIRECTIVE

COUNCIL DIRECTIVE of 18 December 1986 on the coordination of the laws of the Member State relating to self-employed commercial agents (86/653/EEC)

CHAPTER I

Scope

Article 1

1. The harmonization measures prescribed by this Directive shall apply to the laws, regulations and administrative provisions of the Member States governing the relations between commercial agents and their principals.

2. For the purposes of this Directive, 'commercial agent' shall mean a self-employed intermediary who has continuing authority to negotiate the sale or the purchase of goods on behalf of another person, hereinafter called the 'principal', or to negotiate and conclude such transactions on behalf of and in the name of that principal.

3. A commercial agent shall be understood within the meaning of this Directive as not including in particular:

- a person who, in his capacity as an officer, is empowered to enter into commitments binding on a company or association,

- a partner who is lawfully authorized to enter into commitments binding on his partners,

- a receiver, a receiver and manager, a liquidator or a trustee in bankruptcy.

Article 2

1. This Directive shall not apply to:

- commercial agents whose activities are unpaid,

- commercial agents when they operate on commodity exchanges or in the commodity market, or

- the body known as the Crown Agents for Overseas Governments and Administrations, as set up under the Crown Agents Act 1979 in the United Kingdom, or its subsidiaries.

2. Each of the Member States shall have the right to provide that the Directive shall not apply to those persons whose activities as commercial agents are considered secondary by the law of that Member State.

CHAPTER II

Rights and obligations

Article 3

1. In performing his activities a commercial agent must look after his principal's interests and act dutifully and in good faith.

2.　In particular, a commercial agent must:

(a) make proper efforts to negotiate and, where appropriate, conclude the transactions he is instructed to take care of;

(b) communicate to his principal all the necessary information available to him;

(c) comply with reasonable instructions given by his principal.

Article 4

1.　In his relations with his commercial agent a principal must act dutifully and in good faith.

2.　A principal must in particular:

(a) provide his commercial agent with the necessary documentation relating to the goods concerned;

(b) obtain for his commercial agent the information necessary for the performance of the agency contract, and in particular notify the commercial agent within a reasonable period once he anticipates that the volume of commercial transactions will be significantly lower than that which the commercial agent could normally have expected.

3.　A principal must, in addition, inform the commercial agent within a reasonable period of his acceptance, refusal, and of any non-execution of a commercial transaction which the commercial agent has procured for the principal.

Article 5

The parties may not derogate from the provisions of Articles 3 and 4.

CHAPTER III

Remuneration

Article 6

1.　In the absence of any agreement on this matter between the parties, and without prejudice to the application of the compulsory provisions of the Member States concerning the level of remuneration, a commercial agent shall be entitled to the remuneration that commercial agents appointed for the goods forming the subject of his agency contract are customarily allowed in the place where he carries on his activities. If there is no such customary practice a commercial agent shall be entitled to reasonable remuneration taking into account all the aspects of the transaction.

2. Any part of the remuneration which varies with the number or value of business transactions shall be deemed to be commission within the meaning of this Directive.

3. Articles 7 to 12 shall not apply if the commercial agent is not remunerated wholly or in part by commission.

(Ed: While the goal is to provide for uniform rules to be applicable throughout the EU, the provisions in Article 6.1 permitting member states to continue legal rules that provide for greater protection are not uncommon.)

Article 7

1. A commercial agent shall be entitled to commission on commercial transactions concluded during the period covered by the agency contract:

(a) where the transaction has been concluded as a result of his action; or

(b) where the transaction is concluded with a third party whom he has previously acquired as a customer for transactions of the same kind.

2. A commercial agent shall also be entitled to commission on transactions concluded during the period covered by the agency contract:

- either where he is entrusted with a specific geographical area or group of customers,

- or where he has an exclusive right to a specific geographical area or group of customers, and where the transaction has been entered into with a customer belonging to that area or group.

Member States shall include in their legislation one of the possibilities referred to in the above two indents.

Article 8

A commercial agent shall be entitled to commission on commercial transactions concluded after the agency contract has terminated:

(a) if the transaction is mainly attributable to the commercial agent's efforts during the period covered by the agency contract and if the transaction was entered into within a reasonable period after that contract terminated; or

(b) if, in accordance with the conditions mentioned in Article 7, the order of the third party reached the principal or the commercial agent before the agency contract terminated.

Article 9

A commercial agent shall not be entitled to the commission referred to in Article 7, if that commission is payable, pursuant to Article 8, to the previous commercial agent, unless it is equitable because of the circumstances for the commission to be shared between the commercial agents.

Article 10

1. The commission shall become due as soon as and to the extent that one of the following circumstances obtains:

(a) the principal has executed the transaction; or

(b) the principal should, according to his agreement with the third party, have executed the transaction; or

(c) the third party has executed the transaction.

2. The commission shall become due at the latest when the third party has executed his part of the transaction or should have done so if the principal had executed his part of the transaction, as he should have.

3. The commission shall be paid not later than on the last day of the month following the quarter in which it became due.

4. Agreements to derogate from paragraphs 2 and 3 to the detriment of the commercial agent shall not be permitted.

Article 11

1. The right to commission can be extinguished only if and to the extent that:

- it is established that the contract between the third party and the principal will not be executed, and

- that fact is due to a reason for which the principal is not to blame.

2. Any commission which the commercial agent has already received shall be refunded if the right to it is extinguished.

3. Agreements to derogate from paragraph 1 to the detriment of the commercial agent shall not be permitted.

Article 12

1. The principal shall supply his commercial agent with a statement of the commission due, not later than the last day of the month following the quarter in which the commission has become due. This statement shall set out the main components used in calculating the amount of commission.

2.   A commercial agent shall be entitled to demand that he be provided with all the information, and in particular an extract from the books, which is available to his principal and which he needs in order to check the amount of the commission due to him.

3.   Agreements to derogate from paragraphs 1 and 2 to the detriment of the commercial agent shall not be permitted.

4.   This Directive shall not conflict with the internal provisions of Member States which recognize the right of a commercial agent to inspect a principal's books.

CHAPTER IV

Conclusion and termination of the agency contract

Article 13

1.   Each party shall be entitled to receive from the other on request a signed written document setting out the terms of the agency contract including any terms subsequently agreed. Waiver of this right shall not be permitted.

2.   Notwithstanding paragraph 1 a Member State may provide that an agency contract shall not be valid unless evidenced in writing.

Article 14

An agency contract for a fixed period which continues to be performed by both parties after that period has expired shall be deemed to be converted into an agency contract for an indefinite period.

Article 15

1.   Where an agency contract is concluded for an indefinite period either party may terminate it by notice.

2.   The period of notice shall be one month for the first year of the contract, two months for the second year commenced, and three months for the third year commenced and subsequent years. The parties may not agree on shorter periods of notice.

3.   Member States may fix the period of notice at four months for the fourth year of the contract, five months for the fifth year and six months for the sixth and subsequent years. They may decide that the parties may not agree to shorter periods.

4.   If the parties agree on longer periods than those laid down in paragraphs 2 and 3, the period of notice to be observed by the principal must not be shorter than that to be observed by the commercial agent.

5. Unless otherwise agreed by the parties, the end of the period of notice must coincide with the end of a calendar month.

6. The provision of this Article shall apply to an agency contract for a fixed period where it is converted under Article 14 into an agency contract for an indefinite period, subject to the proviso that the earlier fixed period must be taken into account in the calculation of the period of notice.

(Ed: Note the basic thrust of the formula providing for more compensation for termination following a longer relationship. Compare the typical US common law approach that provides for duration of a "reasonable time" with the result that the longer the relationship has existed, the less compensation is due on termination. The European approach is designed to compensate for what? The American approach is designed to compensate for what?)

Article 16

Nothing in this Directive shall affect the application of the law of the Member States where the latter provides for the immediate termination of the agency contract:

(a) because of the failure of one party to carry out all or part of his obligations;

(b) where exceptional circumstances arise.

Article 17

1. Member States shall take the measures necessary to ensure that the commercial agent is, after termination of the agency contract, indemnified in accordance with paragraph 2 or compensated for damage in accordance with paragraph 3.

2(a) The commercial agent shall be entitled to an indemnity if and to the extent that:

- he has brought the principal new customers or has significantly increased the volume of business with existing customers and the principal continues to derive substantial benefits from the business with such customers, and

- the payment of this indemnity is equitable having regard to all the circumstances and, in particular, the commission lost by the commercial agent on the business transacted with such customers. Member States may provide for such circumstances also to include the application or otherwise of a restraint of trade clause, within the meaning of Article 20;

(b) The amount of the indemnity may not exceed a figure equivalent to an indemnity for one year calculated from the commercial agent's average annual remuneration over the preceding five years and if the contract goes back less than five years the indemnity shall be calculated on the average for the period in question;

(c) The grant of such an indemnity shall not prevent the commercial agent from seeking damages.

3. The commercial agent shall be entitled to compensation for the damage he suffers as a result of the termination of his relations with the principal.

Such damage shall be deemed to occur particularly when the termination takes place in circumstances:

- depriving the commercial agent of the commission which proper performance of the agency contract would have procured him whilst providing the principal with substantial benefits linked to the commercial agent's activities,

- and/or which have not enabled the commercial agent to amortize the costs and expenses that he had incurred for the performance of the agency contract on the principal's advice.

4. Entitlement to the indemnity as provided for in paragraph 2 or to compensation for damage as provided for under paragraph 3, shall also arise where the agency contract is terminated as a result of the commercial agent's death.

5. The commercial agent shall lose his entitlement to the indemnity in the instances provided for in paragraph 2 or to compensation for damage in the instances provided for in paragraph 3, if within one year following termination of the contract he has not notified the principal that he intends pursuing his entitlement.

6. The Commission shall submit to the Council, within eight years following the date of notification of this Directive, a report on the implementation of this Article, and shall if necessary submit to it proposals for amendments.

Article 18

The indemnity or compensation referred to in Article 17 shall not be payable:

(a) where the principal has terminated the agency contract because of default attributable to the commercial agent which would justify immediate termination of the agency contract under national law;

(b) where the commercial agent has terminated the agency contract, unless such termination is justified by circumstances attributable to the principal or on grounds of age, infirmity or illness of the commercial agent in consequence of which he cannot reasonably be required to continue his activities;

(c) where, with the agreement of the principal, the commercial agent assigns his rights and duties under the agency contract to another person.

Article 19

The parties may not derogate from Articles 17 and 18 to the detriment of the commercial agent before the agency contract expires.

Article 20

1. For the purposes of this Directive an agreement restricting the business activities of a commercial agent following termination of the agency contract is hereinafter referred to as a restraint of trade clause.

2. A restraint of trade clause shall be valid only if and to the extent that:

(a) it is concluded in writing; and

(b) it relates to the geographical area or the group of customers and the geographical area entrusted to the commercial agent and to the kind of goods covered by his agency under the contract.

3. A restraint of trade clause shall be valid for not more than two years after termination of the agency contract.

4. This Article shall not affect provisions of national law which impose other restrictions on the validity or enforceability of restraint of trade clauses or which enable the courts to reduce the obligations on the parties resulting from such an agreement.

CHAPTER V

General and final provisions

Article 21

Nothing in this Directive shall require a Member State to provide for the disclosure of information where such disclosure would be contrary to public policy.

Article 22

1. Member States shall bring into force the provisions necessary to comply with this Directive before 1 January 1990. They shall forthwith inform the Commission thereof. Such provisions shall apply at least to contracts concluded after their entry into

force. They shall apply to contracts in operation by 1 January 1994 at the latest.

2.   As from the notification of this Directive, Member States shall communicate to the Commission the main laws, regulations and administrative provisions which they adopt in the field governed by this Directive.

3.   However, with regard to Ireland and the United Kingdom, 1 January 1990 referred to in paragraph 1 shall be replaced by 1 January 1994.

With regard to Italy, 1 January 1990 shall be replaced by 1 January 1993 in the case of the obligations deriving from Article 17.

(Ed: Note the introductory comment immediately preceding Article 1 concerning transitional periods.)

Article 23

This Directive is addressed to the Member States.

Done et Brussels, 18 December 1986.
For the Council
The President

PROBLEM

Analyze the fundamental difference in approaches that have been taken by the US and the EU. Assume that you were to engage in a discussion with a lawyer familiar with the EU approach. Explain how the US approaches differ. If a debate ensues, you might consider advancing ideas relating to the economic advantages of an open labor market where it is easy to hire and fire and easy to terminate a distributor and turn to a different system—or replacement distributor. Is this philosophically consistent with those state laws that deny enforcement to covenants not to compete except in cases involving sales of businesses? (*E.g.*, Cal. Bus. and Prof. Code sections 16000 et seq.) This raises assorted issues relating to protection against economic bruises at the expense of free markets.

Council Directive 86/653/EEC covers agents and does not cover distributorships or franchisees. As one might imagine, defining who is and is not an agent is a common threshold issue in litigation in the EU (*Termination of Sales Agents and Distributors in France*, Jacquez Sales, 31 Int'l Law, 823, 824). What policy considerations might explain the decision to draw this distinction?

Assume that your client ("Client" herein) has invented a "better mousetrap" and is planning to sell this new device all over the world. You are retained to participate in the planning of a distribution scheme in the United States and in foreign countries. There are numerous possibilities, for example:

1. Client could hire salaried employees to handle sales and distribution transactions in Client's name and on Client's behalf.

2. Client could hire employees who work on salary or commission or some combination of the two to solicit orders which Client might then accept or reject.

3. Client could hire employees or independent contractors who work on salary or commission and who have authority to conclude transactions on behalf of Client.

4. Client could contract with independent contractors who would act as franchisees buying mousetraps from Client and reselling those goods for their own account to willing buyers.

What advice would you give to your client as to how to proceed hiring distributors or sales agents in the US? What different advice might you give in Europe? Using contract labels that describe parties as "independent contractors" is not going to be effective if they are in fact employees. The controls that Client might want to assert over these people may be the very factors that would cause a court to classify them as employees and agents. (*See N.L.R.B. v. Hearst Publications*, 322 U.S. 111, 64 S. Ct. 851 (1944).) Classification as agents is obviously a fundamental difference under EU law, but it also produces very substantial differences in the US. Employee status affects assorted matters ranging from the right to form unions and bargain collectively (*N.L.R.B. v. Hearst*) to the right to participate in company employee plans relating to such matters as retirement benefits and health care.

Chapter 6

EXTRATERRITORIALITY; ENFORCEMENT AND CLAW BACK LAWS

Territory and nationality provide the traditional basis for the sovereign jurisdiction of a nation. However, one effect of having a global economy is that conduct in one jurisdiction often has an impact in others. This inevitably leads to governments wanting not to be limited to territorial sovereignty but seeking to take action to punish or prevent conduct occurring outside its borders which produce unwanted effects at home. Extraterritorial jurisdiction can thus be proper, but there is not common agreement as to its limits.

Assume that two executives from different automobile companies meet on a golf course outside of Tokyo and agree upon a method by which their companies can fix a higher price for auto parts and thereafter their respective companies followed through with this scheme. Assume that if these actions had occurred in the United States they would be in violation of US antitrust laws potentially subjecting the individuals and corporations involved to criminal and civil sanctions. The car parts involved will be exported all over the world including the US and the actions described will cause American businesses and individuals to pay higher prices. Have the Japanese individuals and corporations involved broken US law? Are they subject to prosecution in the United States?

The Restatement (Third) of the Law: Foreign Relations Law of the United States (1987) indicates that US law can be applied extraterritorially where the conduct in question produces the requisite "effect" upon the legislating state and where enforcement would meet a test of "reasonableness." This approach was first recognized in the *Alcoa* case (*United States v. Aluminum Co. of America*, 148 F.2d 416 (2d Cir. 1945)), and in subsequent decisions,

163

American courts have developed the concept that US law could extend where Congress intended to reach if the conduct in question produces the necessary effect upon the US economy or to US interests and application of US law to this extraterritorial activity would be reasonable. The courts have developed a test involving the "balancing of interests," but of course this balancing is being done by the American judges who are being asked to determine whether subjecting this wrongdoer to justice in this judge's court is "reasonable" after balancing the foreign government's abstract interest in sovereignty with US interests in protecting our citizenry. The answer to that question is predictable.

The United States stands apart from almost all of its principal trading partners on the question of how far its laws and courts can reach. The problem is compounded in the area of enforcement of competition laws (antitrust laws) for three reasons.

US antitrust laws are very broad and are interpreted liberally.

US antitrust laws provide for multiplying actual damages by three which produces a punitive damage effect.

US antitrust law permits and encourages private enforcement actions. Thus, bilateral or multilateral agreements that other countries enter with the US are effective only with respect to actions brought by the government but over ninety percent of the antitrust actions in the US are brought by private plaintiffs.

In the early 1970's, the world demand for uranium declined and prices fell precipitously. In response, the governments of countries that were major producers encouraged and assisted in the formation of a cartel involving over twenty producers in countries such as Canada, South Africa, France, Great Britain and Australia. The purpose was to limit production and allocate markets and this action was successful in producing a very substantial increase in world prices. Westinghouse, a major US corporation, had entered long-term fixed price contracts for uranium with American utilities that were operating nuclear energy plants. The price increase placed Westinghouse in a very difficult position as absorbing the price increase threatened it with insolvency and refusal to perform subjected it to liability that could reach $2 billion. Westinghouse sued the members of the cartel for antitrust violations and using the statutory treble damage provision, the total claim was in the range of $6–7 billion. (There is more than one reported opinion, but the most relevant relating to cross-border discovery issues is: *In re Uranium Antitrust Litigation, Westinghouse Electric Corporation v. Rio Algom Limited, et al*, 480 F. Supp. 1138.)

Foreign governments that had participated in or encouraged the creation of the cartel were outraged at what they considered to be an assault on their sovereignty. Sovereign nations have engaged in economic cartel activity from time to time such as OPEC and the oil production cartel that it administers. Several nations including the United Kingdom, Canada, Australia and later the European Union struck back at the assertion of jurisdiction by US courts adopting laws with three main purposes:

First, to prevent US courts or plaintiffs from gaining access to documents located in the enacting country and to prevent the compulsion of testimony from citizens of that country.

Second, to prevent enforcement of US judgments, or in some circumstances the punitive portions of US judgments in the enacting country. (This is referred to as "blockage.")

Third, to give to all of its businesses and citizens against whom US judgments had been enforced the right to an automatic judgment for the full amount of the judgment (or in some cases only the extra multiplier portion) plus all costs incurred in defending the action. (This is referred to as "claw back.")

The Canadian law is a fair example and it is set forth below. Note the efforts made to prevent individuals from being directly or indirectly forced to testify or produce "records" requested by the foreign (US) courts.

Canada Federal Statutes

Foreign Extraterritorial Measures Act

An Act to authorize the making of orders relating to the production of records and the giving of information for the purposes of proceedings in foreign tribunals, relating to measures of foreign states or foreign tribunals affecting international trade or commerce and in respect of the recognition and enforcement in Canada of certain foreign judgments

S.C. 1995, c. 5, s. 25; 1996, c. 28, ss. 1–8; 1997, c. 18, s. 127 (Fr.); 2001, c. 4, ss. 86 (Fr.), 87.

1. Short title

This Act may be cited as the *Foreign Extraterritorial Measures Act.*

2. Definitions

In this Act,

"antitrust law" means a law of a foreign jurisdiction of a kind commonly known as an antitrust law, and includes a law having directly or indirectly as a purpose the preservation or enhancement of competition between business enterprises or the prevention or repression of monopolies or restrictive practices in trade or commerce; *("loi antitrust")*

"foreign state" means a country other than Canada, and includes

(a) any political subdivision of the foreign state,

(b) the government, and any department, of the foreign state or of a political subdivision thereof, and

(c) any agency of the foreign state or of a political subdivision thereof;

("État étranger")

"foreign trade law" means a law of a foreign jurisdiction that directly or indirectly affects or is likely to affect trade or commerce between

(a) Canada, a province, a Canadian citizen or a resident of Canada, a corporation incorporated by or under a law of Canada or a province or a person carrying on business in Canada,

and

(b) any person or foreign state;

("loi commerciale étrangère")

"foreign tribunal" means a tribunal of a foreign state or of an organization of states; *("tribunal étranger")*

"judgment" includes a decree or order; *("jugement")*

"record" includes any correspondence, memorandum, book, plan, map, drawing, diagram, pictorial or graphic work, photograph, film, microform, sound recording, videotape, machine readable record, and any other documentary material, regardless of physical form or characteristics, and any copy or portion thereof; *("document")*

"tribunal" includes any court, body, authority or person having authority to take or receive information, whether on its or his behalf or on behalf of any other court, body, authority or person. *("tribunal")*

2.1   Power of Attorney General

The Attorney General of Canada may, with the concurrence of the Minister of Foreign Affairs, by order, amend the schedule

(a) by adding the name of a foreign trade law or a reference to any provision of a foreign trade law if the Attorney General of Canada is of the opinion that that law or provision is contrary to international law or international comity; or

(b) by removing a name or reference to any provision set out in the schedule if the Attorney General of Canada is of the opinion that it is appropriate to do so.

3.

3(1) Orders of Attorney General relating to production of records and giving of information

Where, in the opinion of the Attorney General of Canada, a foreign tribunal has exercised, is exercising or is proposing or likely to exercise jurisdiction or powers of a kind or in a manner that has adversely affected or is likely to adversely affect significant Canadian interests in relation to international trade or commerce involving a business carried on in whole or in part in Canada or that otherwise has infringed or is likely to infringe Canadian sovereignty, or jurisdiction or powers that is or are related to the enforcement of a foreign trade law or a provision of a foreign trade law set out in the schedule, the Attorney General of Canada may, by order, prohibit or restrict

(a) the production before or the disclosure or identification to, or for the purposes of, a foreign tribunal of records that, at any time while the order is in force, are in Canada or are in the possession or under the control of a Canadian citizen or a person resident in Canada;

(b) the doing of any act in Canada, in relation to records that, at any time while the order is in force, are in Canada or are in the possession or under the control of a Canadian citizen or a person resident in Canada, that will, or is likely to, result in the records, or information as to the contents of the records or from which the records might be identified, being produced before or disclosed or identified to, or for the purposes of, a foreign tribunal; and

(c) the giving by a person, at a time when that person is a Canadian citizen or a resident of Canada, of information before, or for the purposes of, a foreign tribunal in relation to, or in relation to the contents or identification of, records that, at any time while the order is in force, are or were in Canada or under the control of a Canadian citizen or a person resident in Canada.

3(2) Restriction in relation to tribunals in Canada

Where production before or disclosure or identification to, or for the purposes of, a foreign tribunal of a record and the giving by a person of information before, or for the purposes of, a foreign tribunal in relation to, or in relation to the contents or identification of, a record is prohibited or restricted by an order made under subsection (1), a tribunal in Canada shall not, for the purposes of proceedings before the foreign tribunal,

(a) where the order is in the nature of a prohibition, receive the record or information; or

(b) where the order is in the nature of a restriction, receive the record or information if, as a result of so doing, the order may be contravened.

3(3) Form of orders

An order made under this section may

(a) be directed to a particular person or to a class of persons;

(b) relate to a particular foreign tribunal or to a class of foreign tribunals; and

(c) relate to a particular record or to a class of records.

4. Seizure of records for safe-keeping

Where, on an application by or on behalf of the Attorney General of Canada, a superior court is satisfied that an order made under section 3 may not be complied with in relation to some or all of the records in Canada to which it relates, the court may issue a warrant authorizing a person named therein or a peace officer to seize those records and to deliver them to the court or a person designated by the court for safe-keeping while the order remains in force, on such terms as to access to the records or return of all or any of the records as are fixed by the court having regard to the object to which the order is directed.

5.

5(1) Orders of Attorney General relating to measures of a foreign state or foreign tribunal

Where, in the opinion of the Attorney General of Canada, a foreign state or foreign tribunal has taken or is proposing or is likely to take measures affecting international trade or commerce of a kind or in a manner that has adversely affected or is likely to adversely affect significant Canadian interests in relation to international trade or commerce involving business carried on in whole or in part in Canada or that otherwise has infringed or is likely to infringe Canadian sovereignty, the Attorney General of Canada may, with the concurrence of the Minister of Foreign Affairs, by order,

(a) require any person in Canada to give notice to him of such measures, or of any directives, instructions, intimations of policy or other communications relating to such measures from a person who is in a position to direct or influence the policies of the person in Canada; or

(b) prohibit any person in Canada from complying with such measures, or with any directives, instructions, intimations of policy or other communications relating to such measures from a person who is in a position to direct or influence the policies of the person in Canada.

5(2) Measures

For the purposes of subsection (1), measures taken or to be taken by a foreign state or foreign tribunal include laws, judgments and rulings made or to be made by the foreign state or foreign tribunal and directives, instructions, intimations of policy and other communications issued by or to be issued by the foreign state or foreign tribunal.

5(3) Form of orders

An order made under this section may be directed to a particular person or to a class of persons.

6.

6(1) Service

An order made under section 3 or 5

(a) may be served on a person, other than a corporation, to whom it is directed by delivering it personally to him or, if that person cannot conveniently be found, by leaving it for him at his latest known address with any person found therein who appears to be at least sixteen years of age; or

(b) may be served on a corporation to which it is directed by delivering it personally to the manager, secretary or other executive officer of the corporation or of a branch thereof.

6(2) Idem

Where, on an application by or on behalf of the Attorney General of Canada, a superior court is satisfied that an order made under section 3 or 5 that is directed to a class of persons cannot reasonably be served in the manner described in paragraph (1)(a) or (b) on all or any of the persons included in the class, the court may, by order, authorize service of the order on those persons in such other manner as it considers appropriate.

6(3) Idem

An order varying or revoking an order made under section 3 or 5 may be served on the person to whom it is directed in any manner in which the order could have been served on that person.

7.

7(1) Offence and punishment

Every person who contravenes an order made under section 3 or 5 that is directed to the person and that has been served on the person in accordance with section 6 is guilty of an offence and liable

(a) on conviction on indictment,

(i) in the case of a corporation, to a fine not exceeding $1,500,000, and

(ii) in the case of an individual, to a fine not exceeding $150,000 or to imprisonment for a term not exceeding five years, or to both; or

(b) on summary conviction,

(i) in the case of a corporation, to a fine not exceeding $150,000, and

(ii) in the case of an individual, to a fine not exceeding $15,000 or to imprisonment for a term not exceeding two years, or to both.

7(2) Offence outside Canada

A contravention of an order made under paragraph 3(1)(a) or (c) or 5(1)(a) or (b) that would be punishable as an offence under subsection (1) if committed in Canada is, if committed outside Canada, an offence under this Act that may be tried and punished in Canada as if it were committed in Canada, and proceedings in respect of such an offence may be instituted, tried and determined at any place in Canada.

7(3) Consent to prosecution required

No proceedings with respect to an offence under this Act may be instituted without the consent of the Attorney General of Canada.

7(4) Factors to take into account

In taking into account the circumstances of the offence when determining the sentence for an offence referred to in subsection (1), the court shall have regard, among other things, to the degree of premeditation in its commission, the size, scale and nature of the offender's operations and whether any economic benefits have, directly or indirectly, accrued to the offender as a result of having committed the offence.

7.1　Cuban Liberty and Democratic Solidarity (LIBERTAD) Act of 1996

Any judgment given under the law of the United States entitled *Cuban Liberty and Democratic Solidarity (LIBERTAD) Act of 1996* shall not be recognized or enforceable in any manner in Canada.

8.

8(1) Attorney General may declare antitrust judgments not to be recognized or enforceable

Where a foreign tribunal has given a judgment in proceedings instituted under an antitrust law and, in the opinion of the Attorney General of Canada, the recognition or enforcement of the judgment in Canada has adversely affected or is likely to adversely affect significant Canadian interests in relation to international trade or commerce involving a business carried on in whole or in part in Canada or otherwise has infringed or is likely to infringe Canadian sovereignty, the Attorney General of Canada may

(a) in the case of any judgment, by order, declare that the judgment shall not be recognized or enforceable in any manner in Canada; or

(b) in the case of a judgment for a specified amount of money, by order, declare that, for the purposes of the recognition and enforcement of the judgment in Canada, the amount of the judgment shall be deemed to be reduced to such amount as is specified in the order.

8(1.1) Attorney General may declare certain foreign judgments not to be recognized or enforceable

Where a foreign tribunal has given a judgment in proceedings instituted under a foreign trade law or a provision of a foreign trade law set out in the schedule and, in the opinion of the Attorney General of Canada, the recognition or enforcement of the judgment in Canada has adversely affected or is likely to adversely affect significant interests in Canada, the Attorney General of Canada may

(a) in the case of any judgment, by order, declare that the judgment shall not be recognized or enforceable in any manner in Canada; or

(b) in the case of a judgment for a specified amount of money, by order, declare that, for the purposes of the recognition and enforcement of the judgment in Canada, the amount of the judgment shall be deemed to be reduced to such amount as is specified in the order.

8(2) Publication and coming into force

Every order made under subsection (1) or (1.1) shall be published in the *Canada Gazette* and each order comes into force on the later of the day it is published and a day specified in the order as the day on which it is to come into force.

8(3) Effect of order

While an order made under subsection (1) or (1.1) is in force,

(a) in the case of an order made under paragraph (1)(a) or (1.1)(a), the judgment to which it relates shall not be recognized and is not enforceable in Canada; and

(b) in the case of an order made under paragraph (1)(b) or (1.1)(b), the judgment to which it relates may, if enforceable apart from this Act, be recognized and enforced in Canada as if the amount specified in the order were substituted for the amount of the judgment, and not otherwise.

8(4) No inference where order not made

In any proceedings in Canada to recognize or enforce a judgment given by a foreign tribunal in proceedings instituted under an antitrust law, or a foreign trade law or a provision of a foreign trade law set out in the schedule, or to enforce a concurrent or subsequent judgment for contribution or indemnity related to that judgment, no inference shall be drawn from the fact that the Attorney General of Canada has not made an order under subsection (1) or (1.1) in respect of the judgment.

8.1 Judgments satisfied outside Canada

Where an order may not be made under section 8 in respect of a judgment because the judgment has been satisfied outside Canada, or where a judgment has been given under the law of the United States entitled *Cuban Liberty and Democratic Solidarity (LIBERTAD) Act of 1996*, the Attorney General of Canada may, on application by a party against whom the judgment was given who is a Canadian citizen, a resident of Canada, a corporation incorporated by or under a law of Canada or a province or a person carrying on business in Canada, by order, declare that that party may recover, under the provisions of section 9 that the Attorney General identifies, any or all amounts obtained from that party under the judgment, expenses incurred by that party, or loss or damage suffered by that party.

9.

9(1) Recovery of damages and expenses

Where a judgment in respect of which an order has been made under section 8 has been given against a party who is a Canadian citizen, a resident of Canada, a corporation incorporated by or under a law of Canada or a province or a person carrying on business in Canada, or an order has been made under section 8.1 in favour of such a party in respect of a judgment, that party may, in Canada, sue for and recover from a person in whose favour the judgment is given

(a) in the case of an order made under paragraph 8(1)(a) or (1.1)(a),

(i) any amount obtained from that party by that person under the judgment,

(ii) all expenses incurred by that party in the course of defending the proceedings in which the judgment was awarded and in instituting proceedings under this Act, including all solicitor-client costs or judicial and extrajudicial costs, and

(iii) any loss or damage suffered by that party by reason of the enforcement of the judgment; and

(b) in the case of an order made under paragraph 8(1)(b) or (1.1)(b),

(i) any amount obtained from that party by that person under the judgment that is in excess of the amount to which the judgment is deemed to be reduced,

(ii) the amount that the Attorney General of Canada may specify in respect of the expenses incurred by that party in the course of defending the proceedings in which the judgment was awarded,

(iii) the expenses incurred by that party in instituting proceedings under this Act, including all solicitor-client costs or judicial and extrajudicial costs, and

(iv) such proportion of any loss or damage suffered by that party by reason of the enforcement of the judgment as the Attorney General may specify.

9(1.1) Recovery of expenses before final judgment

Where proceedings are instituted under an antitrust law, or a foreign trade law or a provision of a foreign trade law set out in the schedule, and no final judgment has been given under those proceedings against a party who is a Canadian citizen, a resident of Canada, a corporation incorporated by or under a law of Canada or a province or a person carrying on business in

Canada, that party may, in Canada, with the consent of the Attorney General of Canada, at any time during the proceedings sue the person who instituted the action and recover from that person all expenses incurred by the party in defending those proceedings and in instituting proceedings under this Act, including all solicitor-client costs or judicial and extrajudicial costs.

9(2) Seizure and sale of property and shares

A court that renders judgment in favour of a party pursuant to subsection (1) or (1.1) may, in addition to any other means of enforcing judgment available to the court, order the seizure and sale of any property in which the person against whom the judgment is rendered, or any person who controls or is a member of a group of persons that controls, in law or in fact, that person, has a direct or indirect beneficial interest. The property that may be seized and sold includes shares of any corporation incorporated by or under a law of Canada or a province, regardless of whether the share certificates are located inside or outside Canada.

10. Tabling

An order made under section 2.1, 3, 5, 8 or 8.1 shall be laid before each House of Parliament within fifteen sitting days after it is made.

11. Coming into force

This Act shall come into force on February 14, 1985.

Schedule

[1]

The number in square brackets has been editorially added by Carswell.

	Column I	Column II	Column III
	Foreign Trade Law	Enacting Jurisdiction	Provisions
Item			
1.	*Cuban Liberty* and Democratic Solidarity *(LIBERTAD) Act of 1996*	United States	All

Notes

Canada's law is typical in that it vests the Attorney General with apparently very broad authority to decide what foreign legal actions justify retaliation. Note, however, that Canada also requires "concurrence" of the Minister of Foreign Affairs which is evident recognition of the political nature of these issues. There is an "Antitrust Cooperation Agreement" in force between Australia and the United States which requires notification and consultation if Australia or the US Department of Justice or Federal Trade Commission undertake an antitrust investigation. However, such requirements are not applicable to the majority of litigation in the United States which is initiated by private parties.

Other laws involving evidence, blockage and claw back can be found at:

Protection of Trading Interests Act, 1980 (Eng.)

Foreign Proceedings (Excess of Jurisdiction) Act, 1984, Act No.3 of 1984 as amended (Austl.)

Council Regulation (EC) 2271/96, Protecting Against the Effects of the Extra–Territorial Application of Legislation Adopted by a Third Country and Actions Based Thereon or Resulting Therefrom, 1996 O.J. (L309), Art 5 (European Union).

Helms-Burton Act and D'Amato Act

A second area of discord between the US and its principal trading partners has arisen as a result of US efforts to prevent certain aspects of commercial activity involving properties seized in or about 1960 by the Cuban Government (the Helms-Burton Act, Cuban Liberty and Democratic Solidarity (LIBERTAD) Act of 1996, 22 U.S.C.§§ 6021–6091) and oil development contracts with Libya and Iran (the D'Amato Act, Iran and Libya Sanctions Act of 1996, Pub. L. No. 104–72, 110 Stat. 1541 (1996)). These acts involve foreign policy matters rather than trade issues, however the issues regarding national sovereignty are similar, and the treble damage provisions and the private action provisions are again present.

Helms-Burton is designed to recover back the value of private properties nationalized when the Castro Government came to power. It gives US citizens the right to sue anyone who has "trafficked" in confiscated property and provides for recovery of costs and treble damages in some cases. It also requires the Secretary of State to deny entry to the US of any non-US national who has trafficked in confiscated property including officers or controlling shareholders of corporations that have so trafficked. ("Trafficking" is defined in § 6023(13).) Helms-Burton comes in for special mention in the Canadian laws. Note articles 7.1 and 8.1 in the Foreign Extraterritorial Measures Act quoted above.

The D'Amato Act imposes penalties upon those who invest in the Libyan or Iranian petroleum industry or sell certain listed goods to those countries.

Chapter 7

MICROFINANCE

I. INTRODUCTION: THE ORIGINS AND MANY FORMS OF MICROFINANCE

Anthropologist Marguerite S. Robinson defines microfinance as follows:

Microfinance refers to small-scale financial services— primarily credit and savings—provided to people who farm or fish or herd; who operate small enterprises or microenterprises where goods are produced, recycled, repaired, or sold; who provide services; who work for wages or commissions; who gain income from renting out small amounts of land, vehicles, draft animals, or machinery and tools; and to other individuals and groups at the local levels of developing countries, both rural and urban.[1]

"Microenterprise" is the name that is commonly given to a business venture that is funded by microcredit. Philanthropists Phil Smith and Eric Thurman define microenterprises as follows:

Microenterprises are small-scale versions of the same types of businesses found in developed countries. Twenty hens and a coop constructed from scrap material become a poultry enterprise. A produce store may be a rickety wooden cart piled with mangos picked that morning by the driver or purchased from a local farmer. Hives, bees, and a collection of mismatched used jars are a honey factory. A 40-year-old truck is used to transport both goods for sale and paying passengers. A pedal-powered sewing machine is the local equivalent of a clothing factory. An outdoor clay oven is the local bakery. With a microloan providing working capital, these businesses can sup-

---

1. MARGUERITE S. ROBINSON, THE MICROFINANCE REVOLUTION: SUSTAINABLE FINANCE FOR THE POOR 9 (2001).

176

port families and boost the grassroots economy for the whole community.[2]

Modern microfinance had its origins in the early 1970s. Among the very first microfinance institutions [MFIs] were the Self Employed Women's Association in India, ACCIÓN International in Latin America, Opportunity International in Latin America and Indonesia, and Grameen Bank in Bangladesh.[3] Since that time, the field has expanded enormously. Because an MFI can be "a village credit co-operative with 75 customers," "a regulated bank serving more than 6 million microborrowers," or anything in between, there seems to be no way to know exactly how many MFIs are currently in existence.[4] Even so, the industry has clearly reached a significant size: Microfinance Information Exchange, Inc.[5] (MIX) had collected data on more than 2,200 MFIs by the end of its fiscal year 2008.[6]

As Phil Smith and Eric Thurman have noted, "microcredit has an impressive record of changing lives."[7] Consider the following excerpt from testimony by New Jersey Representative Christopher Smith before Congress in 2005:

2. PHIL SMITH & ERIC THURMAN, A BILLION BOOTSTRAPS: MICROCREDIT, BAREFOOT BANKING, AND THE BUSINESS SOLUTION FOR ENDING POVERTY 41 (2007).

3. For a self-titled "Very Brief History of Microcredit," see id. at 179–182. See also Rebecca Farrar, Exploring the Human Rights Implications of Microfinance Initiatives, 36 INT'L J. LEGAL INF. 447, 454 (2009) ("While Muhammad Yunus is often credited as having created microfinance, . . . the Self Employed Women's Association (SEWA) predated Yunus' first loan and Grameen Bank.").

4. MICROFINANCE INFORMATION EXCHANGE, INC., ANNUAL REPORT FY 2008 12 (2008).

5. MIX is a private, not-for-profit company that was founded by the Consultative Group to Assist the Poor (CGAP), in partnership with a number of entities, including the Citigroup Foundation, the Deutsche Bank Americas Foundation, and others. MICROFINANCE INFORMATION EXCHANGE, INC., supra note 4, at 4. Its major funders include, among several others, the Bill and Melinda Gates Foundation. Id. at 5. MIX collects data from MFIs, who participate on a voluntary basis, and uses that information to produce industry benchmarks. Id. at 12. MIX sources indicate that "[a]cademic researchers, investment banks, private sector investors and

funders, multi-lateral and bi-lateral development organizations, . . . governments[, and mainstream media sources]" regularly rely on MIX data. Id. at 2. Although MIX does not capture data from every MFI in the world, it employs what it describes as a "top down strategy," which is intended to ensure that MIX data includes the leading and most influential MFIs. Id. at 12, 15. MIX's global online platform is called MIX Market. In addition to MIX Market, MIX maintains a second database called The MicroBanking Bulletin (MBB), in which data is reported in a way that is not individually identifiable to any MFI, to maintain confidentiality. RICHARD ROSENBERG, ET AL., THE NEW MONEYLENDERS: ARE THE POOR BEING EXPLOITED BY HIGH MICROCREDIT INTEREST RATES? 3 (2009). Most MFIs are represented in both databases. Id.

6. MICROFINANCE INFORMATION EXCHANGE, INC., supra note 4, at 19. Another source suggests the numbers may be considerably higher: according to Nimal Fernando, a Principal Finance Specialist for Asian Development Bank, there were more than 3,100 MFIs by the end of 2005. NIMAL A. FERNANDO, MICROFINANCE INDUSTRY: SOME CHANGES AND CONTINUITIES 1 (May 2007).

7. SMITH & THURMAN, supra note 2, at 49.

Success stories from the beneficiaries of microenterprise are quite numerous. Take, for example, Dorothy Eyiah from Ghana. Dorothy was resourceful, but she had no idea how she was going to support her AIDS-stricken sister and family when she brought them into her home in Ghana. She used to support herself selling ice, but that wasn't going to pay for the food and medicines she now needed. She started praying. All doors seemed shut until Dorothy met some women within her village who are part of an Opportunity International Trust Bank.[8] The Trust Bank could help her grow a small business, providing her with financing, training, and support. Five loans later, Dorothy is the secretary of her Trust Bank and runs three businesses, employing nine people from her village. She is content, her sister is comfortable, all the children are in school, and their needs are being met. "God has been so good to me," she says. Success stories such as this are what microfinance and the Microenterprise Results and Accountability Act of 2004 are all about.[9]

The Act to which Representative Smith refers, and which he sponsored, became law in December of 2004.[10] Among other things, the Act "[a]uthorizes microenterprise development grant assistance in developing countries for: (1) expanding credit, savings, and other financial services; (2) training, technical assistance, and business development services; (3) capacity-building; and (4) policy and regulatory programs at the country level that improve the environment for microenterprise institutions serving the poor and very poor."[11]

A second example of microfinance's potential comes from Darfur, a region of Sudan where 40 to 80 ethnic groups share a body of land about the size of Texas. The conflict that has raged in Darfur since 2003 has affected at least three quarters of the region's population, and hundreds of thousands have died.

In rural Darfur, many women have lost family members, their homes, all their personal possessions, and their livelihoods as the result of militia attacks on their villages. Some have

8. For more information on Opportunity International, which currently provides microloans to clients in over 25 countries through over 40 different programs, visit its web site, http://www.opportunity.org.

9. Testimony of Representative Christopher Smith, Implementing the Microenterprise Results and Accountability Act of 2004, Hearing Before the Subcommittee on Africa, Global Human Rights and International Operations of the Committee on International Relations House of Representatives, 109 Congress, First Session. September 20, 2005. Serial No. 109–84 Transcript available at http://www.house.gov/international-relations.

10. Microenterprise Results and Accountability Act of 2004, Pub. L. No. 108–484, 118 Stat. 3922.

11. From the Library of Congress bill summary available at http://thomas.loc.gov/cgi-bin/bdquery/z?d108:HR03818:@@@D&summ2=m&.

endured four to five years in "temporary" shelters in under-supplied camps for displaced people. They've become the heads of their remaining households. And many have suffered multiple rapes. Darfuri women and girls are at the center of one of the most serious human rights and women's health crises in the world today.[12]

In response, a nonprofit, nonsectarian organization called Darfur Peace and Development has created a women's center as "a secure place for women to gather for supportive services and programs."[13] The organization describes its mission as follows:

> The guiding principle of the Center is equipping Darfuri women with the resources to recover personal strength and develop resources to rebuild productive lives. The Center integrates social, educational, and income-generation services by providing:
>
> • A safe environment that encourages peer support in group activities;
>
> • Facilitation of micro-enterprises to ensure continuing income for women supporting households;
>
> • Training in first aid, literacy, vocational skills—as requested by the women.[14]

The pilot Women's Center opened in Kassab IDP camp in April 2008, and a second site opened in Abu–Shouk in September 2009. In addition, a basket-weaving cooperative, which generates income for its members, has been in existence since September 2007, and the organization's solar cooker program, which was begun in 2006, provides a safer and more environmentally friendly means of cooking. Fatiah F., a twenty-eight-year-old woman with six siblings whose mother is ill and father is deceased, describes her experience with the Center as follows:

> The part of our women community that is at the center benefited a lot from it. Most of these women no longer go to collect fire wood which could lead to them being attacked because they now have solar cookers to cook with. The women

12. From the Darfur Peace & Development web site. http://www.darfurpeace.org/programs/womens-center. The organization describes itself as follows:

Darfur Peace & Development is a nonprofit, non-sectarian organization with headquarters in Washington, DC and offices in Khartoum and El Fasher, Sudan. DPDO provides humanitarian and development assistance to the victims of conflict in Darfur, Sudan without regard to ethnicity, gender, age or religious beliefs. DPDO works to foster reconciliation, to facilitate just governance and to enable Darfurians to rebuild their homeland in effective, sustainable ways. DPDO also promotes awareness of the crisis in the United States and advocates for a peaceful resolution of the conflict.

http://www.darfurpeace.org/.

13. *Id.*

14. *Id.*

at the center make traditional baskets and when they sell these baskets, it helps them to finance their lives. Every time they sell a basket or receive a solar cooker they don't have to leave the camp for fire wood. This center has changed my role in the community. It gave me the chance to speak out and report on everything that is going on in the center. Also now the women come to me for help, I have become from a normal woman in the camp to one which makes decisions regarding the welfare of women in the camp.[15]

Dorothy and Fatiah's stories display some themes that characterize microfinance at its best: a disadvantaged woman transcends poverty and abuse and improves her children's life prospects as well as her own.[16]

Microfinance takes place within many different contexts: formal MFIs, NGOs,[17] co-operatives, conventional banks, nonfinancial companies, and "facilitators" like Kiva, to name a few.[18] Especially given the fact that so many different kinds of organizations are involved in microfinance, it has been unclear whether microfinance should be viewed as its own financial sector, or whether it should be seen instead as the lower end of the conventional banking sector. On the one hand are arguments that microfinance is its own industry, especially given the "double bottom line" that MFIs traditionally face, "aim[ing] for both social and financial returns."[19] In addition, MFIs are traditionally characterized by "excellent asset quality, high net interest margins (NIMs), high operating costs,[20] and longer term funding available from developmental investors,"[21] as compared with conventional financial institutions. On the other

---

15. *Id.*

16. *Id.* at 187.

17. "Typically, NGO MFIs are 'credit only' institutions by law, in that they are prohibited from offering financial services beyond their microlending and, in particular, are forbidden to raise capital in the form of deposits. NGO MFIs have no owners and are typically governed by a board elected by a general assembly of members or a self-perpetuating board. Often, NGO MFIs rely almost exclusively on donated capital, although many are legally permitted to borrow funds if they can find a willing lender." Timothy R. Lyman, *Supporting Microfinance Abroad: Introductory Legal Issues for U.S. Grantmakers*, 2 INT'L J. NOT-FOR-PROFIT L. (June 2000), *available at* http://www.icnl.org/knowledge/ijnl/vol2iss4/ig_2.htm.

18. FERNANDO, *supra* note 6, at 2–3. Kiva was founded in October 2005 and

has grown to be one of the largest "microcredit facilitators" in the world. Additional information about Kiva is available on its website, http://www.kiva.org. For an alternative listing of various forms an MFI can take, including NGO MFIs, finance companies, savings-and-credit associations, microfinance banks, and conventional financial institutions, *see* Lyman, *supra* note 17.

19. O'DONOHOE, *infra* note 68, at 1. *See also* Hall, *infra* note 23, at 39 ("The law has an important role to play in creating an architecture for microfinance that considers not just the bottom line, but also the bottom person.").

20. ROSENBERG, ET AL., *supra* note 5, at 13 (reporting that "[t]he worldwide median operating expense was 11.4 percent of GLP," or gross loan portfolio).

21. O'DONOHOE, *infra* note 68, at 1.

hand are arguments that microfinance is just like any other growing industry, and indeed just like any other sector of banking.
Arguably, "the tools used to build strong [MFI] institutions are the
same as those in other industries—data collection, analysis, bench-
marking, trend setting, and . . . financial transparency."[22]

With this basic background information in mind, consider the
following perspective from commentator Margaux Hall, who has
called for greater regulation of microfinance:

> To date, the microfinance industry has been able to operate
> largely independent of government regulations. Indeed, micro-
> finance has been viewed as an important tool for financial
> development in countries suffering from weak or corrupt gov-
> ernments. Microfinancial institutions can still operate in these
> environments and, if they are responsible in their operations,
> can provide valuable services. Yet, the absence of governance in
> this arena stands to not only hinder microfinance institutions'
> sustainable growth; it also has the potential to severely harm
> the persons microfinance was intended to empower. The Unit-
> ed Nations commented that "[a]ccess to microfinance is stifled
> by a lack of fiscal, regulatory and supervisory policies to
> promote rather than stunt deep, broad and inclusive financial
> sectors." A report to the United Nations Secretary General
> noted that legal and regulatory structures are necessary in
> order to allow small and medium businesses to be successful.
> These include commercial laws to create and protect contracts
> and enforce property rights.[23]

The following excerpt from a 2007 Business Week article helps
to explain why Hall and others are concerned about MFI regulation:

> [Eva Yanet] Hernandez [Caballero], 29, the daughter of a small
> farmer, says her mother purchased several knitting machines
> in 1992, but lacked cash for yarn. The equipment remained idle
> for years. A loan, Hernandez thought, would enable her to buy
> nylon and more machines. She aimed to lure home her brother
> and two sisters, who she says are undocumented workers with
> restaurant and hotel jobs in the US. Over four years, beginning
> in 2001, she, her mother, and a sister took out a series of loans

22. MICROFINANCE INFORMATION EX-
CHANGE, INC., *supra* note 4, at 10.

23. Margaux Janine Hall, *Banking
for the Poor: Building a New International Legal Architecture for Microfinance*, 2 J. GLOBAL CHANGE & GOVER-
NANCE 29–30 (2009), *available at* http://
www.jgcg.org/. Hall compares the mi-

crofinance and subprime markets and
concludes that "the rapid and largely
unregulated growth taking place in microfinance must be checked in order to
ensure that microfinance operates in a
responsible and viable manner. *Id.* at
38.

[from an MFI called Compartamos][24] ranging from $200 to $1,800, at an APR[25] of 105%. They rolled one into the next and used the money to increase their weekly output from 800 dozen pairs of socks to 1,500 dozen. At their peak, they say they brought in $800 a week, more than enough to sustain an extended family of six.

Then things unraveled. Wholesale customers fell behind on payments. Compartamos' steep interest rates took an unremitting toll, as Hernandez and her relatives each missed several $130 payments to the lender. That was a lot for the rest of the 23-member borrowing circle[26] to make up. Resentment surfaced. Soon after Compartamos trumpeted her story in 2005, Hernandez and her family were banished from the group.

Lacking capital, she has seen her production and earnings plunge to 500 dozen pairs of socks and $270 a week. Her siblings remain north of the border. Stoic about her tarnished accomplishments, she is uncertain about the future. "It's been a huge effort," she says, "and we're barely afloat now." [27]

PROBLEM 1

Assume that you work for a United States Senator who chairs the Senate Subcommittee on International Trade, Customs and Global Competitiveness, and he or she has asked you to prepare a memorandum addressing whether American MFIs should be regulated in the same manner as conventional banks. What is your initial instinct as to what the correct answer to the Senator's question should be, and why?

II. MICROFINANCE AND SOCIAL CHANGE

Reading the following excerpt from the Nobel Peace Prize acceptance speech of Grameen Bank founder Muhammad Yunus is a good way to get both an introduction to microfinance and a sense

24. Compartamos commenced operations in 1990 as an NGO and was transformed into a commercial bank in 2006. To learn more about the company, visit http://www.compartamos.com and view the various documents under "About Compartamos Banco" on the home page.

25. According to the Federal Reserve Bank of New York, "APR," which stands for "Annual Percentage Rate," "includes, as a percent of the principal, not only the interest that has to be paid on a loan, but also some other costs, particularly 'points' on a mortgage

loan." Federal Reserve Bank of New York, Interest Rates: An Introduction, *available at* http://www.ny.frb.org/education/define.html#aps.

26. Peer lending groups, of which this "borrowing circle" is an example, are discussed in Part IV of this chapter.

27. Keith Epstein & Geri Smith, *Compartamos: From Nonprofit to Profit: Behind its Gentle Image is a Tough, Highly Lucrative Bank*, 4064 Bus. Wk. 45, 45 (2007), *quoted in* Hall, *supra* note 23, at 3.

of Yunus' own vision and passion for microcredit. By way of background, Yunus was a professor of economics in his native Bangladesh before he founded what became the world's largest and best-known MFI. In his Nobel remarks, he speaks not only of his background as a professor, but also the way in which Grameen Bank began with forty-two loans totaling only twenty-seven dollars. Today, the typical loan size for an MFI may be as small as fifty dollars or less, if the MFI targets very-low-income borrowers, or as high as several thousand dollars for an MFI that targets established small businesses.[28]

Poverty is a Threat to Peace

December 10, 2006

Oslo City Hall, Norway

Ladies and Gentlemen:

By giving us this prize, the Norwegian Nobel Committee has given important support to the proposition that peace is inextricably linked to poverty. Poverty is a threat to peace.

[The w]orld's income distribution gives a very telling story. Ninety-four percent of the world income goes to forty percent of the population while sixty percent of people live on only six percent of world income. Half of the world population lives on two dollars a day. Over one billion people live on less than a dollar a day. This is no formula for peace.

* * *

Poverty is Denial of All Human Rights

Peace should be understood in a human way—in a broad social, political and economic way. Peace is threatened by unjust economic, social and political order, absence of democracy, environmental degradation and absence of human rights.

Poverty is the absence of all human rights. The frustrations, hostility and anger generated by abject poverty cannot sustain peace in any society. For building stable peace we must find ways to provide opportunities for people to live decent lives.

The creation of opportunities for the majority of people—the poor—is at the heart of the work that we have dedicated ourselves to during the past 30 years.

Grameen Bank

I became involved in the poverty issue not as a policymaker or a researcher. I became involved because poverty was all around

---

28. Hardy et al., *infra* note 84, at 6–
7.

me, and I could not turn away from it. In 1974, I found it difficult to teach elegant theories of economics in the university classroom, in the backdrop of a terrible famine in Bangladesh. Suddenly, I felt the emptiness of those theories in the face of crushing hunger and poverty. I wanted to do something immediate to help people around me, even if it was just one human being, to get through another day with a little more ease. That brought me face to face with poor people's struggle to find the tiniest amounts of money to support their efforts to eke out a living. I was shocked to discover a woman in the village, borrowing less than a dollar from the money-lender, on the condition that he would have the exclusive right to buy all she produces at the price he decides. This, to me, was a way of recruiting slave labor.

I decided to make a list of the victims of this money-lending "business" in the village next door to our campus.

When my list was done, it had the names of forty-two victims who borrowed a total amount of twenty-seven US dollars. I offered twenty-seven US dollars from my own pocket to get these victims out of the clutches of those money-lenders. The excitement that was created among the people by this small action got me further involved in it. If I could make so many people so happy with such a tiny amount of money, why not do more of it?

That is what I have been trying to do ever since. The first thing I did was to try to persuade the bank located in the campus to lend money to the poor. But that did not work. The bank said that the poor were not creditworthy. After all my efforts, over several months, failed I offered to become a guarantor for the loans to the poor. I was stunned by the result. The poor paid back their loans, on time, every time! But still I kept confronting difficulties in expanding the program through the existing banks. That was when I decided to create a separate bank for the poor, and in 1983, I finally succeeded in doing that. I named it Grameen Bank or Village Bank.

Today, Grameen Bank gives loans to nearly seven million poor people, ninety-seven percent of whom are women, in 73,000 villages in Bangladesh. Grameen Bank gives collateral-free income generating, housing, student and micro-enterprise loans to the poor families and offers a host of attractive savings, pension funds and insurance products for its members. Since it introduced them in 1984, housing loans have been used to construct 640,000 houses. The legal ownership of these houses belongs to the women themselves. We focused on women because we found giving loans to women always brought more benefits to the family.

In a cumulative way the bank has given out loans totaling about six billion US dollars. The repayment rate is ninety-nine percent. Grameen Bank routinely makes profit. Financially, it is self-reliant and has not taken donor money since 1995. [The d]eposits and own resources of Grameen Bank today amount to 143% of all outstanding loans. According to Grameen Bank's internal survey, fifty-eight percent of our borrowers have crossed the poverty line.

* * *

Second Generation

It is thirty years now since we began. We keep looking at the children of our borrowers to see what has been the impact of our work on their lives. The women who are our borrowers always gave topmost priority to the children. One of the Sixteen Decisions developed and followed by them was to send children to school. Grameen Bank encouraged them, and before long all the children were going to school. Many of these children made it to the top of their class. We wanted to celebrate that, so we introduced scholarships for talented students. Grameen Bank now gives 30,000 scholarships every year.

Many of the children went on to higher education to become doctors, engineers, college teachers and other professionals. We introduced student loans to make it easy for Grameen students to complete higher education. Now some of them have Ph.D's. There are 13,000 students on student loans. Over 7,000 students are now added to this number annually.

We are creating a completely new generation that will be well equipped to take their families way out of the reach of poverty. We want to make a break in the historical continuation of poverty.

Beggars Can Turn to Business

In Bangladesh eighty percent of the poor families have already been reached with microcredit. We are hoping that by 2010, one hundred percent of the poor families will be reached.

Three years ago we started an exclusive programme focusing on the beggars. None of Grameen Bank's rules apply to them. Loans are interest-free; they can pay whatever amount they wish, whenever they wish. We gave them the idea to carry small merchandise such as snacks, toys or household items, when they went from house to house for begging. The idea worked. There are now 85,000 beggars in the program. About

5,000 of them have already stopped begging completely. Typical loan to a beggar is twelve dollars.

We encourage and support every conceivable intervention to help the poor fight out of poverty. We always advocate microcredit in addition to all other interventions, arguing that microcredit makes those interventions work better.[29]

Questions

1. In an excerpted portion of his speech that appears below, Dr. Yunus claims that global initiatives to end poverty were put on hold following September 11, 2001, and the start of the Iraq war:

> The new millennium began with a great global dream. World leaders gathered at the United Nations in 2000 and adopted, among others, a historic goal to reduce poverty by half by 2015. Never in human history had such a bold goal been adopted by the entire world in one voice, one that specified time and size. But then came September 11 and the Iraq war, and suddenly the world became derailed from the pursuit of this dream, with the attention of world leaders shifting from the war on poverty to the war on terrorism. Until now over $530 billion has been spent on the war in Iraq by the USA alone.
>
> I believe terrorism cannot be won over by military action. Terrorism must be condemned in the strongest language. We must stand solidly against it, and find all the means to end it. We must address the root causes of terrorism to end it for all time to come. I believe that putting resources into improving the lives of the poor people is a better strategy than spending it on guns.[30]

    After reading this excerpt and the other portions of Dr. Yunus' speech that appear on the preceding pages, why, in your own words, does he contend that "poverty is a threat to peace?"

2. In the preceding excerpt, Dr. Yunus has described poverty as "the absence of all human rights."[31] Irene Khan, Secretary General of Amnesty International, has expressed a similar view, and has "identified several dimensions to the experience of living in poverty, including insecurity, being shut out by official institutions, and being denied a voice and ignored"[32] as particular examples. With which of these can microcredit most clearly make a difference, and how?

29. Muhammad Yunus, Nobel Peace Prize Acceptance Speech: Poverty is a Threat to Peace (Dec. 10, 2006), *available at* http://nobelprize.org/nobel_dprizes/peace/laureates/2006/yunus-lecture-en.html.

30. *Id.*

31. *See supra* page 183.

32. IRENE KHAN, THE UNHEARD TRUTH: POVERTY AND HUMAN RIGHTS 13 (2009).

3. Eric Thurman and Phil Smith, whose work in microfinance and philanthropy was mentioned earlier in the chapter, have identified each of the following as proven best practices in the field of microfinance:

    a. Small loans, normally between $50 and $500.

    b. Small groups of entrepreneurs who cross-guarantee the loans of other group members.

    c. Short terms of four to six months.

    d. Frequent payments. Weekly payments are the norm, although some programs require daily payments.

    e. The potential for larger loans if the small initial loans are repaid in a timely fashion.[33]

    How, in your opinion, could each of these practices tend to support a successful microcredit model? Are there some with which you tend to disagree?

4. Dr. Yunus has his own theory as to why loans to low-income persons generally have very high repayment rates. He recounts a conversation in which he explained to a bank employee, "The poorest of the poor work twelve hours a day. They need to sell and earn income to eat. They have every reason to pay you back, just to take another loan and live another day! That is the best security you can have—their life."[34] Do you agree? Are there other possible explanations?

PROBLEM 2

Imagine that you have been retained by a client who is seeking to start an MFI and, quite by coincidence, shortly thereafter find yourself sitting next to Dr. Yunus on a plane. If you had an opportunity to conduct an informal impromptu interview with him during the flight, what would you want to ask him? How would your questions help your client?

PROBLEM 3

Imagine that you are designing an MFI, which you plan to name Opportunity, Inc., around a "facilitated" model like Kiva's. How would the "double bottom line"[35] you face affect such considerations as whom you would hire and where Opportunity, Inc.'s headquarters would be? To the extent that it would be useful to do

---

33. SMITH & THURMAN, *supra* note 2, at 52–53.

34. MUHAMMAD YUNUS, BANKER TO THE POOR: MICRO-LENDING AND THE BATTLE AGAINST WORLD POVERTY 54 (1999).

35. *See supra* text accompanying note 19.

so in crafting your answer, research Kiva by checking out its website (http://www.kiva.org) and other resources.

For Further Exploration

1. To learn more about the Sixteen Decisions to which Dr. Yunus' speech makes reference, visit Grameen Bank's website, http://www.grameen-info.org, and select "Sixteen Decisions" under the "Methodology" tab on the front page.

2. In his Nobel speech, Dr. Yunus mentions a program targeted to beggars, whom Grameen Bank calls "struggling members" of the bank. To learn more about this program, visit http://www.grameen-info.org, and select "Know More" under the "Founder" tab on the front page.

III. MEETING THE DEMAND FOR MICROFINANCE AND CREATING SUSTAINABLE INSTITUTIONS

The following excerpt from Marguerite Robinson's book *The Microfinance Revolution* discusses some of the major challenges and opportunities currently facing MFIs and their borrowers:

There are differences among countries and regions in the availability of microfinance services and in the level of unmet demand for these services. There are also differences in demand among small businesses, microenterprises, farmers, laborers, low-income salaried employees, and others. Common to nearly all parts of the developing world, however, is a lack of commercial microfinance institutions—a shortcoming that unnecessarily limits the options and lowers the financial security of poor people throughout the world.

But this pattern is changing. The *microfinance revolution* is emerging in many countries around the world. As it is used here, this term refers to the large-scale, profitable provision of microfinance services—small savings and loans—to economically active poor people by sustainable financial institutions. These services are provided by competing institutions at the local level—near the homes and workplaces of the clients—in both rural and urban areas. Financial services delivered at the local level refer to those provided to people living in villages and other types of rural settlements and to people living in low-income neighborhoods in semiurban or urban areas. *Large scale* as used here means coverage by multiple institutions of millions of clients; or, for small countries or middle-and high-income countries with low demand, outreach to a significant portion of the microfinance market. *Profitability* means covering all costs and risks without subsidy and returning a profit to the institution.

In aggregate, commercial microfinance institutions can provide outreach to a significant segment of their country's poor households. In a few countries this has already occurred; in others it is at various stages of progress. . . .

Estimating the Demand for Microfinance

The microfinance revolution is best understood in the context of the population and income levels of developing countries, and of estimates of unmet global demand for formal sector commercial financial services.

According to the World Bank's *World Development Report 1999/2000: Entering the 21st Century,* in 1998 about 1.2 billion people—24 percent of the population in developing and transition economies—lived on less than $1 a day. In 1999, 4.5 billion people, or 75 percent of the world's population, lived in low-and lower-middle-income economies. Of these, 2.4 billion were from low-income economies with an average annual GNP[36] per capita of $410, while 2.1 billion lived in lower-middle-income economies with an average annual GNP per capita of $1,200.

The following are crude but conservative assumptions:

· Some 80 percent of the world's 4.5 billion people living in low-and lower-middle-income economies do not have access to formal sector financial services. (It is probably more accurate to say 90 percent, but these are conservative estimates.)

· Among these 3.6 billion people, the average household size is five people (720 million households).

· Half of these households (360 million) account for the unmet demand for commercial savings or credit services from financial institutions.[37]

In the following section, which continues the preceding excerpt, Robinson explains how she believes access to financial services can greatly improve the lives of millions of people. In doing so, she emphasizes some of the unique characteristics of the informal businesses that are typically associated with microfinance.

---

36. "GNP," or "gross national product," is "the total value of the goods and services produced in a nation during a specific period (as a year) and also comprising the total of expenditures by consumers and government plus gross private investment." WEBSTER'S THIRD NEW INTERNATIONAL DICTIONARY UNABRIDGED 1002 (2002).

37. ROBINSON, *supra* note 1, at 10–11.

The average productivity of these households could be increased substantially with access to appropriate institutional savings and credit services delivered locally. Because the benefits of financial services would also extend to the dependents of microfinance, clients, the economic activities and the quality of life of more than 1.8 billion people could be improved by providing them with local access to formal commercial microfinance.

This is not a scale that can be reached by government-or donor-funded institutions. Microfinance demand can be met on a global scale only through the provision of financial services by self-sufficient institutions.

Most of the demand for microfinance comes from households and enterprises operating in the unregulated, informal sector of the economy. Yet there is "no clear-cut division between a 'formal' and an 'informal' sector. The complex reality could be better described as a continuum with sliding transitions."[38] Thus, in the labor markets of developing countries, some microenterprises combine informal and formal characteristics, and some move back and forth between the two sectors.

Still, a number of features generally associated in aggregate with informal enterprises tend to be absent from formal enterprises. These include scarcity of capital, family ownership, small-scale operations, nonlegal status, lack of security of business location, operation in unregulated markets, relatively easy entry into markets, labor-intensive production modes, nonformal education and low skill levels, irregular work hours, small inventories, use of indigenous resources, and domestic sales of products, often to end users. But the informal sector is far from homogeneous. It includes people who collect and recycle cigarette butts and people who subcontract for large industrial concerns—and many others in between (such as petty traders, carpenters, brickmakers, recyclers of paper and metal, shoemakers, and tailors).

The formal financial sector has generally been self-deterred from financing informal enterprises by characteristics typically associated with such businesses, including the nonlegal status of enterprises, the frequent lack of an authorized business location, the unavailability of standard forms of collateral, the small size of transactions (and associated high cost per transaction), and the perceived riskiness of such businesses.

* * *

38. Here, Robinson is quoting Dieter Weiss. DIETER WEISS, THE INFORMAL SECTOR IN METROPOLITAN AREAS OF DEVELOPING COUNTRIES 61 (1998).

Yet microenterprises provide an income stream for poor entrepreneurs. They create employment. They recycle and repair goods that would otherwise become waste, And they provide cheap food, clothing, and transportation to poor people—including those at the lower levels of the formal sector—who would not otherwise be able to live on their salaries. Microentrepreneurs accomplish all of this despite severe obstacles, since they typically lack capital, skills, legal status, and business security. But they generally have strong survival skills: shrewd business sense, long experience of hard work, knowledge of their markets, extensive informal support and communication networks, and a fundamental understanding of flexibility as the key to microenterprise survival.

* * *

The growing interest in commercial microfinance is related to the recent recognition on the part of some policymakers that the informal sector is very large, it is here for the foreseeable future, it provides employment and contributes to the economy, and its performance can be improved with the removal of legal and financial obstacles. Thus, increasing microenterprise access to financial services—both credit and savings—has become a priority for many governments and donors. With this has come awareness that the demand for commercial microfinance is far larger than was previously understood.[39]

In the next excerpt, Robinson discusses the means of financing that have historically been available to low-income persons through informal commercial moneylenders. She notes that the moneylenders provide an essential service, but also suggests ways in which microfinance may provide a better alternative.

Informal Commercial Moneylenders and Their Interest Rates

Financial institutions that provide commercial microfinance help poor people manage enterprise growth and diversification and raise their household incomes. Yet informal commercial lenders—local traders, employers, and landlords, commodity wholesalers, pawnbrokers, and moneylenders of various types—provide loans to the poor in many developing countries. Why, then, are formal commercial loans so crucial for social and economic development? Why fix a system that seems to work?

* * *

While it is true that informal commercial moneylenders provide important financial services to the poor, they typically

<hr/>

39. ROBINSON, *supra* note 1, at 11–13.

charge very high interest rates to low-income borrowers in developing countries. The reasons for the high interest rates have been hotly debated, but the evidence for the high rates is unmistakable. While the transaction costs of obtaining a loan are normally higher for a borrower who obtains credit from a commercial microfinance institution than from an informal moneylender, the difference in interest rates is often so large that the total cost to the borrower is much lower at the [MFI]. . . .

* * *

Each moneylender tends to have a range of interest rates that he or she charges to different customers. Poor borrowers are usually charged the higher rates for two main reasons: because poor borrowers have few other options and low bargaining power, and because for lenders the transaction costs for making small loans are essentially the same as for large loans. If the interest rates were the same, small loans would be less profitable. In some cases there is also a third reason: moneylenders may consider poor borrowers risky and so add a premium to cover the extra risk. In my experience, however, this factor is generally considered less important than the other two. Outside of risks that borrowers may face because of collective shock in the region—drought, hyperinflation, war—moneylenders normally do not lend to poor borrowers who pose high risks.

Informal credit from moneylenders is often provided in the context of interlinked transactions; the borrower is also the lender's commodity supplier, employee, tenant, or sharecropper, for example. In such situations the lenders have good information about the borrowers and a variety of methods for ensuring loan repayment.

Moneylenders typically calculate interest rates on a flat rate basis—that is, on the original loan balance. This is in contrast to most standard banks, where the effective interest rate is used, calculated on the (declining) outstanding loan balance. Converting moneylenders' stated rates to effective monthly interest rates enables comparison with the rates of commercial microfinance institutions. In general, moneylenders' rates tend to be much higher than those of commercial microfinance institutions. In many parts of the developing world informal commercial lenders typically charge nominal effective interest rates of 10 percent to more than 100 percent a month, while sustainable microfinance institutions usually charge nominal effective rates between 2 and 5 percent a month. Moreover, some moneylenders charge even higher rates, especially to poor borrowers.

Nominal interest rates for small one-day loans can range from 5 percent to more than 20 percent, and many such borrowers continue to borrow on the same terms, day after day.... In parts of Latin America and Asia *five-six* terms[40] are especially common. A borrower receives, for example, a loan of $10 in the morning and repays $12 at the end of the day—a 20 percent interest rate for a one-day loan. This can represent a monthly effective interest rate of more than 20,000 percent....[41]

* * *

The following portion of Professor Robinson's book calls to mind Dr. Yunus' Nobel acceptance speech excerpted earlier in this chapter, in which he describes some of the societal harms associated with poverty. Robinson does the same, and then also goes on to explain that poverty is not monolithic, and not all poor persons are equally well situated to benefit from microfinance.

The Economically Active Poor and the Extremely Poor

Poverty comes in many forms and causes multiple harms. The poor may suffer from lack of food and water, unemployment or underemployment, disease, abuse, homelessness, degradation, and disenfranchisement. The results among those affected often include physical, mental, and emotional disability, limited skills and education, low self-esteem and lack of self-confidence, and fear, resentment, aggression, and truncated vision. Some individuals break out of poverty.

Some societies have social safety nets that prevent the poor from reaching destitution. Impoverished refugees face special problems. The effects of poverty combine in different ways and in varying degrees, affecting the poor differently depending on the society and the individual. While all such people are poor by the standards of the wider society, there are substantial differences among them. Those who are severely food-deficit, bonded laborers whose full-time work pays only the interest on their loans, and displaced refugees are different from poor people who have some land, employment, or a microbusiness— except that in many cases the latter were once the former. Sometimes it works the other way around. At any level of

---

40. "So-called because of the manner in which they lend, five-six (5–6) moneylenders charge a nominal interest rate of 20 percent over an agreed period of time. A person who borrows 5 pesos from a 5–6 moneylender over a period of one week pays 6 pesos, including 1 peso interest." Mari Kondi, *The "Bombay 5–* 6": *Last Resource Informal Financiers for Philippine Micro-Enterprises,* KYOTO REV. SOUTH EAST ASIA (Oct. 2003), *available at* http://kyotoreview.cseas.kyoto-u. ac.jp/issue/issue3/article_298.html.

41. ROBINSON, *supra* note 1, at 13–17.

poverty, however, women and some minorities tend to be the poorest, with girls typically the most deprived.

Overall, as Nobel Prize winner Amartya Sen[42] has observed, "poverty must be seen as the deprivation of basic capabilities rather than merely as low incomes."

Though there are multiple degrees and kinds of poverty, here we distinguish only between the extremely poor and the economically active poor. The World Bank defines extreme poverty as living on less than 75 cents a day; about two-thirds of the people defined as poor by the $1 a day standard are classified as extremely poor.

People living in extreme poverty exist below the minimum subsistence level; they include those who are unemployed or severely underemployed, as well as those whose work is so poorly remunerated that their purchasing power does not permit the minimum caloric intake required to overcome malnutrition. Also included are people who live in regions severely deprived of resources; those who are too young, too old, or too disabled to work: those who for reasons of environment, ethnic identity, politics, gender, and the like have little or no employment opportunities—and who have no earning assets or household members to support them; and those who are escaping from natural or human made catastrophes.

As Henry Mayhew[43] put it in 1861, people who "cannot work" include those who are incapacitated from want of power—the old, the young, the ill, the insane, and the untaught; those who are incapacitated from want of means (having no tools, clothes, "stock money," materials, or workplace); and those who are incapacitated from want of employment (because of a business glut or stagnation, a change in fashion, the introduction of machinery, or the seasonality of the work). These categories are still relevant for identifying the extremely poor in many developing countries.

The term *economically active poor,* in contrast, is used in a general sense to refer to those among the poor who have some form of employment and who are not severely food-deficit or destitute. . . .

* * *

42. Dr. Sen won the 1998 Nobel Prize in Economics "for his contributions to welfare economics." For information on Dr. Sen, including links to his Nobel speech and autobiography, visit http://nobelprize.org/nobel_prizes/economics/laureates/1998/index.html.

43. For more information on Mayhew, an "adventurous English journalist," and others with similar views on poverty and its effects, *see* Leon Radzinowicz, *Ideology and Crime: The Deterministic Position*, 65 Colum. L. Rev. 1047, 1051 (1965).

Poverty contains many anomalies. Imprecise as they are, however, the two general categories of the economically active poor and the extremely poor can be usefully distinguished in the planning and implementation of effective strategies for overcoming poverty. The delineation of an official poverty line, defined by consumption or by a basket of goods, can be a useful tool for governments and donors in making policy decisions and in planning long-term development strategies. But the poverty line concept is not directly relevant for microfinance. Savers are commonly found on both sides of the official line, and many borrowers below the line are creditworthy, while many above the line are not.

In commercial microfinance the critical distinctions among the poor are those that differentiate the economically active poor from the extremely poor, and the poor who participate in a cash economy from those who do not (some pastoralists, subsistence agriculturalists, and hunters and gatherers). There is also a crucial distinction between creditworthy and noncreditworthy borrowers.

On the savings side, people with incomes that provide for their most minimal needs often save in small amounts in whatever forms are appropriate for their purposes and conveniently available. The demand among even the lowest levels of the economically active poor for secure, convenient, and appropriately designed financial savings services is well documented from many parts of the world. Such facilities are often more in demand among the poor than are credit services.

While the extremely poor may not be directly affected by commercial microfinance, they can benefit indirectly from its development. Thus microfinance helps to create employment; some of the extremely poor may find jobs if kin and neighbors among the economically active poor have access to commercial financial services. And if commercial microfinance is made locally available, the very poor who become employed will eventually be able to make use of its services.

A Poverty Alleviation Toolbox

Alleviating poverty requires many tools, including food, shelter, employment, health and family planning services, financial services, education, infrastructure, markets, and communication. The key to reducing poverty is knowing how to use these tools.

Credit is a powerful tool that is used effectively when it is made available to the creditworthy among the economically active poor participating in at least a partial cash economy—people with the ability to use loans and the willingness to repay them.

But other tools are required for the very poor who have prior needs, such as food, shelter, medicine, skills training, and employment. It is sometimes forgotten—although generally not by borrowers—that another word for credit is debt. When loans are provided to the very poor, the borrowers may not be able to use the loans effectively because they lack opportunities for profitable self-employment, and because the risks involved in using the credit may be unacceptably high. For example, extremely poor households living in small, isolated communities in areas that lack basic infrastructure and markets may be unable to use credit in any way that would enable them to repay loan principal and interest.

Placing in debt those who are too poor to use credit effectively helps neither borrowers nor lenders. Food-deficit borrowers without opportunities to use credit or to market their output may have no choice but to eat their loans. This can, in turn, lead to humiliation and the diminishing of an already low level of self-confidence. Lenders to the extremely poor also face difficulties because low repayment rates caused by borrowers who cannot repay prevent the development of sustainable financial institutions.

The poorest of the poor should not be the responsibility of the financial sector. The food, employment, and other basic requirements needed to overcome desperate poverty are appropriately financed by government and donor subsidies and grants. These tools are properly the responsibility of ministries of health, labor, social welfare, and others, as well as of donor agencies and private charities.

But credit subsidies to the economically active poor—who could make good use of commercial credit—prevent them from having widespread access to available loans because subsidized loans are usually rationed. In addition, this approach uses scarce donor and government funds that would be better spent on other forms of poverty alleviation, The use of tools in these ways—providing credit to the extremely poor and credit subsidies to the economically active poor—is like trying to build a house by using a saw to hammer the nails and a screwdriver to cut the boards.[44]

In this final excerpt, Professor Robinson describes two very different approaches to microlending—the "poverty lending" model and the "financial systems" approach—and explains why she contends the "financial systems" model is superior.

44. ROBINSON, *supra* note 1, at 17–20.

The Financial Systems Approach and the Poverty Lending Approach: A Fork in the Road

Microfinance in the 1990s was marked by a major debate between two leading views: the financial systems approach and the poverty lending approach. The financial systems approach ... emphasizes large-scale outreach to the economically active poor—both to borrowers who can repay microloans from household and enterprise income streams, and to savers. The financial systems approach focuses on institutional self-sufficiency because, given the scale of the demand for microfinance worldwide, this is the only possible means to meet widespread client demand for convenient, appropriate financial services.

The poverty lending approach concentrates on reducing poverty through credit, often provided together with complementary services such as skills training and the teaching of literacy and numeracy, health, nutrition, family planning, and the like. Under this approach donor-and government-funded credit is provided to poor borrowers, typically at below-market interest rates.

The goal is to reach the poor, especially the extremely poor—the poorest of the poor—with credit to help overcome poverty and gain empowerment. Except for mandatory savings required as a condition of receiving a loan, the mobilization of local savings is normally not a significant part of the poverty lending approach to microfinance.

Bangladesh's Grameen Bank and some of its replicators in other countries represent leading examples of the poverty lending approach. The microbanking division of Bank Rakyat Indonesia (BRI),[45] BancoSol in Bolivia,[46] and the Association for Social Advancement (ASA) in Bangladesh[47] are at the forefront of the financial systems approach.

* * *

Substantial contributions to the development of institutional microfinance have been made through both approaches. Some institutions using the poverty lending approach to microcredit have successfully reached poor people with donor-and government-subsidized credit services. These institutions have helped their borrowers develop their enterprises and increase their incomes, and they have had high repayment rates. But the literature on both microfinance and rural finance is filled with

45. For more information about BRI, visit its website, http://www.bri.co.id, and select "English."

46. For more information on Banco Sol in Bolivia, visit its website, http:// www.bancosol.com.bo/, and select "English."

47. For more information on ASA, visit its website, http://www.asa.org.bd/.

examples showing that most institutions that provide subsidized credit fail. And even successful institutions following the
poverty lending approach, in aggregate, can meet only a small
portion of the demand for microfinance.

* * *

The poverty lending approach uses subsidies primarily to fund
loan portfolios. The financial systems approach uses subsidies
primarily to disseminate lessons from the best practices of fully
sustainable microfinance systems and to finance the development of financially self-sufficient microfinance institutions.
These institutions then finance their microloan portfolios com-
mercially, enabling them to multiply outreach by leveraging
additional capital. One road leads toward donor-dependent
microcredit institutions that cannot meet the demand for credit
and do not meet the demand for savings services. The other
leads to self-sufficient financial intermediaries and large-scale
microfinance outreach. . . . [48]

Questions

1. As Robinson states, "Informal credit from moneylenders is often
   provided in the context of interlinked transactions; the borrower is
   also the lender's commodity supplier, employee, tenant, or sharecropper, for example. In such situations the lenders have good
   information about the borrowers and a variety of methods for
   ensuring loan repayment."[49] What are some of the risks and
   benefits of an interlinked transaction, as compared with one in
   which the borrower and lender have no relationship with one
   another outside of the loan transaction?

2. Although not discussed in these materials, "predatory lending" is a
   common catch phrase in the popular media. Which aspects of
   traditional moneylenders' practices might fairly be called predatory? Which could fairly be termed savvy business practices?

3. In your own words, what is the distinction between the "poverty
   lending" and "financial systems" approaches to microfinance? Why
   does Robinson favor the latter? Based on what you have read, do
   you agree?

4. In what ways might "the benefits of financial services . . . extend
   to the dependents of microfinance clients"? How might an MFI
   seek to maximize the chances that this would happen?

5. How do Dr. Yunus and Professor Robinson deal differently with
   the poorest of the poor, including those who beg for subsistence?
   Which approach do you prefer, and why?

48. ROBINSON, *supra* note 1, at 22–27.   **49.** *Id.* at 16.

6. Why is it significant that microbusinesses tend to be informal enterprises?

7. How, according to Robinson, is it possible for someone to be below the poverty line and yet creditworthy? How would you determine whether a potential MFI borrower was creditworthy, assuming that no formal credit reporting is available?

8. Is making a profit immoral in the MFI context when an MFI serves persons who are below the poverty line? Why or why not?

9. Why, according to Robinson, can the world's unmet demand for microfinance not be met by government or donor-funded institutions?

10. From what you have read, would Dr. Yunus agree with Robinson's description of Grameen Bank as following a "poverty lending" model? Why or why not? If so, what would explain Grameen Bank's apparent success with what Professor Robinson has called an unsustainable model?

11. Irene Kahn, Secretary General of Amnesty International, has stated, "Muhammad Yunus once said to me that, had he been a delegate at the United Nations in 1948 when the universal declaration [of human rights] was being drafted, he surely would have insisted on a right to microcredit as an alternative form of social security."[50] Based on what you have read, do you think Robinson would concur? Why or why not? Would you?

PROBLEM 4

Assume you are designing an MFI, which you plan to call Beyond Banking, Inc., that will adopt a "conventional banking" model. How would your institution respond to each of the groups who, according to Henry Mayhew, "cannot work?" Which (if any) groups would you have to admit you cannot serve, and why?

PROBLEM 5

Building on the prior problem, would Beyond Banking, Inc. limit its lending to a particular demographic, industry, or geographic location? What would be some of the risks and benefits of specialization as compared with diversification?

For Further Exploration

1. How can Robinson's distinction between the "economically active poor" and the "extremely poor" be understood in the

50. KAHN, *supra* note 32, at 75.

context of Abraham Maslow's[51] famous study of the hierarchy of human needs? If it is useful to you in formulating your answer, you might skim his famous article, *A Theory of Human Motivation*, 50 Psychol. Rev. 370–396 (1943). The article is easily found on the internet.

2. Building on the prior question, industry analyst Nimal Fernando has argued that microcredit should be extended to a group he deems "the vulnerable nonpoor."[52] Who might fall within such a group, and what could be some of the advantages and disadvantages of extending microcredit to them, rather than focusing wholly on the "economically active poor," as Robinson suggested?

IV. PEER LENDING GROUPS, RELATIVELY HIGH INTEREST RATES, AND OTHER CHARACTERISTICS OF MICROFINANCE

According to the Microfinance Information Exchange, Inc., three of the five largest MFIs (as measured by the number of borrowers) are located in Bangladesh.[53] In fact, Asia dominates the global microfinance market at this time.[54] By one estimation, more than half of the microfinance institutions in existence at the end of 2005 were located in Asia and the Pacific area.[55] The Middle East and Northern Africa, by contrast, are a much less developed market for microfinance.[56] The largest number of microfinance borrowers

---

51. Abraham Maslow was a U.S. psychologist whose "hierarchy of human motives challenged psychologists' assumptions by placing physiological needs (such as hunger and thirst) at the bottom, with the need for safety, a sense of belonging and love, and esteem in the middle and self-actualization at the top. He argued that lower needs dominate behavior unless fulfilled, and that an individual must defy society's pressure to conform in order to achieve self-actualization." EDWARD VERNOFF & RIMA SHORE, THE PENGUIN INTERNATIONAL DICTIONARY OF CONTEMPORARY BIOGRAPHY 565 (2001).

52. FERNANDO, *supra* note 6, at 2.

53. These three, in descending order of size, are Grameen Bank, BRAC, and ASA. The other two rounding out the top five are VBSP, the Vietnam Bank for Social Policies, and BRI, Bank Rakyat Indonesia. When measured by gross loan portfolio, the three largest MFIs are BRI, VBSP, and Grameen Bank, in that order. *See also* Matthew Swibel, *The 50*

Top Microfinance Institutions, Dec. 20, 2007, *available at* http://www.forbes.com.

54. MICROFINANCE INFORMATION EXCHANGE, INC., *supra* note 4, at 24.

55. FERNANDO, *supra* note 6, at 1 (noting that 1,652 of 3,133 MFIs in existence at that time were in Asia and the Pacific area). *See also* HARDY ET AL., *infra* note 84, at 5 ("MFIs are not equally distributed worldwide. They appear to be especially well developed in certain Asian and Latin American countries, such as Bangladesh, Bolivia, and Indonesia.").

56. "[M]icrofinance hasn't worked nearly so well in Africa as it has in Asia. That may be because it is newer there and the models haven't been adjusted, or because populations are more rural and dispersed, or because the underlying economies are growing more slowly and so investment opportunities are fewer." NICHOLAS D. KRISTOF & SHERYL WUDUNN, HALF THE SKY: TURNING OPPRESSION INTO OPPORTUNITY FOR WOMEN WORLDWIDE 191 (2009).

comes from Indonesia, Vietnam, Mexico, and Bangladesh, in that order, while most lenders are found in Latin America and the Caribbean.[57]

Regardless of where an MFI is headquartered, most MFIs have three characteristics in common: high rates of repayment, a much higher incidence of lending to women than men, and relatively high interest rates.[58] In 2007, ASA reported a write-off rate of .30%, with Grameen Bank and BRAC[59] reporting rates of .56% and 1.35%, respectively. According to one source, an MFI with an annual loan loss rate of more than 5% would be considered unsustainable.[60]

Data from the world's five largest MFIs shows that women dominate the ranks of borrowers. According to MIX data, in 2007, 96.87% of Grameen Bank's borrowers, 80.16% of ASA's borrowers, and 47.82% of BRI's borrowers were women. In 2008, according to the same source, 95.40% of BRAC's borrowers and 64.79% of VBSP's borrowers were women.[61] Consider the following excerpt from Dr. Geeta Rao Gupta's testimony before the United States Senate Committee on Foreign Relations, in which she addresses the role of microfinance in preventing violence against women:

> Violence against women occurs in epidemic proportions in many countries around the world. It cuts across socioeconomic, religious, and ethnic groups, as well as geographic areas. The United Nations estimates that one in three women around the world will be beaten, raped, or otherwise abused during her lifetime. One in four women will be physically or sexually abused while she is pregnant.
>
> * * *
>
> Developing strategies that lead to a better economic standing for women can ultimately help thwart violence. The violence they face is rooted in inequitable power dynamics within a household—men own the land, the home, all of the productive assets, and control the income, even when women are the

---

57. Microfinance Information Exchange, Inc., *supra* note 4, at 27.

58. Data from the world's five largest MFIs bears this out, at least in significant measure. According to MIX data, in 2007, 96.87% of Grameen Bank's borrowers, 80.16% of ASA's borrowers, and 47.82% of BRI's borrowers were women. *Id.* In 2008, according to the same source, 95.40% of BRAC's borrowers and 64.79% of VBSP's borrowers were women. *Id. See also* Fernando, *supra* note 6, at 1 (noting that, insofar as

Asian and Pacific MFIs are concerned, approximately two-thirds of the clients served through December 2005 were women).

59. BRAC, which is now known by its acronym, was formerly called the Bangladesh Rural Advancement Committee and was established in 1972. For more information, visit its website, http://www.brac.net.

60. Rosenberg et al., *supra* note 5, at 12.

61. *See supra* note 58.

source of that income. Increasing a woman's economic independence can provide her the leverage to negotiate protection or leave a violent relationship. Additionally, women are more likely than men to spend their income on the well-being of their families, including more nutritious foods, school fees for children, and health care.

One successful mechanism that is proven to empower women and reduce violence is microfinance .... Statistics show that women who received loans pay them back at rates close to 99 percent.

The benefits of these economic activities extend beyond the participants to their families and communities. Families can afford three meals a day rather than one. They can pay school fees and buy uniforms to send their children to school. They can expand their businesses and hire other community members as employees.

When microfinance is distributed in combination with other community programs, it can actually prevent violence. This is most clearly demonstrated by the Intervention with MicroFinance for AIDS and Gender Equity Project (IMAGE Project) in South Africa.[62] Through the Small Enterprise Foundation, the program distributed small loans to women to start or expand small businesses and generate household income. The program also provided training and skills-building sessions on HIV prevention, gender norms, cultural beliefs, communication, and intimate partner violence. A random, controlled trial found that, two years after completing the program, participants reported a 55 percent reduction in incidence of violence by their intimate partners in the previous 12 months than did members of a control group. Women also reported higher confidence, autonomy in decision making, better relationships with their partners and other household members, and improved communication skills.[63]

---

62. For more information on the IMAGE Project, which is a research initiative of University of the Witwatersrand, Johannesburg, visit http://web.witz.ac.za/academic/health/publichealth/radar/socialinterventions/intervetionwithmicrofinanceforAIDSgenderequity.htm.

63. Geeta Rao Gupta, Ph.D, *The Economic Costs of Violence Against Women in the Developing World* (Oct. 1, 2009) (testimony submitted by Gupta, who is the president of the International Center for Research on Women, to the Committee on Foreign Relations, United States Senate). Dr. Gupta adds a cau-

tionary note later in her testimony, acknowledging "evidence from Bangladesh and other parts of the world that programs increasing a woman's access to economic resources can put her at risk of increased violence, ... particularly ... in settings where a woman's status is low, because increasing her income can lead to greater conflict within the family." *Id.* at 6. She notes, "One of the ways to mitigate the risk of this kind of backlash by men is to engage them in economic development programs from the start." *Id.* at 7.

Consistent with Dr. Gupta's testimony, one source has gone so far as to claim that "[m]icrofinance has done more to bolster the status of women, and to protect them from abuse, than any laws could accomplish.[64]

In addition to notably high rates of loan repayment and a particular emphasis on loaning to women, microlending is typically associated with relatively high interest rates. This aspect of microfinance has generated considerable concern and controversy. Interest is a very large component of MFI revenue; compared with conventional banks in emerging markets, which have an average net interest margin[65] of about 6%, MFIs have an average NMI of about 22%.[66] According to a white paper issued by J.P. Morgan and the Consultative Group to Assist the Poor (CGAP),[67] the average lending rate for MFIs worldwide in 2006 was 24.8%.[68]

It is important to understand the reasons behind these relatively high interest rates, which may sometimes be exaggerated by coverage in the popular media. The following quotation from MFI rating agency Planet Rating attempts to put these rates into context:

> The interest rates of microfinance institutions are high as MFIs grant many more small loans than traditional banks do, using a rigorous methodology that results in higher operating and processing costs.
>
> The interest rates cover: the cost of the money to be reimbursed, the costs associated with risk of non-reimbursement and expenses relating to the microcredit administrative and processing tasks (time spent selecting and accompanying clients, the processing of requests for financing, payment collection . . . .) It is estimated that operating costs represent 25% of the average amount of a MFI[69] portfolio, whereas in India, for example, commercial loans post operating costs of approximately 5 to 7% of their outstanding loans.[70]

64. Kristoff & WuDunn, *supra* note 56, at 187.

65. See *supra* note 20 and accompanying text.

66. O'Donohoe, *infra* note 68, at 7. Another source asserts that "the median interest income for sustainable MFIs in MIX . . . was 26.4 percent of loans outstanding." Consultative Group to Assist the Poor, Data Download: Interest Rates, Operating Costs, and Profits (Feb. 15, 2009), *available at* http://www.cgap.org/p/site/template.rc/1.26.5403/.

67. CGAP has been described as "a consortium of multilateral and bilateral development agencies and few private foundations working together to build financial systems for the poor in developing countries." Fernando, *supra* note 6, at 2. For more information on CGAP, visit its website, http://www.cgap.org.

68. Nicholas P. O'Donohoe et al., Shedding Light on Microfinance Equity Valuation: Past and Present 7 (Feb. 2009).

69. According to another source, "[o]perating expenses represent over three-quarters of all expenses of MFIs." Microfinance Information Exchange, Inc., *supra* note 4, at 19.

Lack of competition may also tend to drive up interest rates.[71] Thus, as the microfinance industry continues to develop, resulting in increased MFI competition and reduced operating costs,[72] it is probably reasonable to expect that interest rates will fall at least somewhat.[73] Furthermore and not surprisingly, the interest rates for self-sustaining MFIs are higher than for those supported by a donor pool or government.[74] In addition, as one source has pointed out, interest rates for microloans may be more affordable than they seem—"even a monthly interest rate of 6% [may] represent[ ] only 0.4 to 3.4% of a microentrepreneur's operating costs."[75] Microloans also sometimes have very high upside growth potential: for microloans based in India, Kenya, and the Philippines, "the average annual rate of the return on investment in microenterprises ranges from 117 to 847%."[76]

Some authors have spoken out strongly against reforms that would cap interest rates for microfinance. Nimal Fernando of the Asian Development Bank, for example, has expressed his concern that caps would cause MFIs to incur losses if rates were set lower than required to cover costs, thus "reducing an MFI's willingness and ability to expand operations, and discouraging potential inves-

70. PLANET FINANCE GROUP, HOW MICROFINANCE WORKS, *available at* http://www.planetfinancegroup.org/EN/micro finance.php. PlaNet Rating, an MFI rating agency, is part of the NGO PlaNet Finance and has been in existence since 1999, now having offices in Paris, Dakar, Nairobi, Beirut, Lima, and Madrid. PLANET RATING, ACTIVITY REPORT 2008 2, 8 (2008). *See also* O'DONOHOE, *supra* note 68, at 7 ("Microlending incurs relatively higher costs than traditional lending, with higher personal and administrative expenses because of the location of clients, small transaction size, and frequent interaction with MFI staff.").

71. O'DONOHOE, *supra* note 68, at 7 ("Despite the rapid growth of microfinance in most markets, there are still relatively few financial institutions that serve low-income people, and competition on lending rates is limited.").

72. FERNANDO, *supra* note 6, at 4, 5 (noting that "[m]ost leading MFIs have managed to reduce their operating expense ratios (OERs) significantly in recent years" and "[a] number of major MFIs in India have ... reduced their interest rates in part due to to competition"). *See also* O'DONOHOE, *supra* note 68, at 9 ("[T]he cost structure of MFIs tends to improve over time as a result of economies of scale, better loan technology, and an increase in the average loan size."); ROSENBERG ET AL., *supra* note 5, at 14 ("Worldwide, the ratio of operating expense to loan portfolio declined about 1 percentage point per year, from 15.6 percent in 2003 to 12.7 percent in 2006. This pattern held for all regions except South Asia, where operating costs were already quite low in 2003.").

73. ROSENBERG ET AL., *supra* note 5, at 9 (reporting data from two different studies showing average interest rates drops of 2.3 percentage points per year for the period from 2003 to 2006, and 3.4 percentage points per year from the period from 2000 to 2005, respectively).

74. *Id.* at 3 ("The average interest yield (weighted by loan portfolio) for MFIs reporting to MIX in 2006 was 28.1 percent for sustainable MFIs, compared with 20.5 percent for unsustainable MFIs.").

75. *See also* O'DONOHOE, *supra* note 68, at 7 ("Microenterprises have the potential to generate high returns, which enables clients to pay higher interest rates to MFIs.").

76. PLANET FINANCE GROUP, *supra* note 70.

tors from supporting the industry."[77] Fernando continues, "Rate ceilings will reduce the creditworthiness of MFIs, reducing their ability to borrow from the market to finance their operations, and prompting a decline in the supply of credit, contrary to expectations of policy makers who seek such a ceiling."[78] Even so, Fernando acknowledges that MFIs have not been able to reach "a majority of the poorest people and [microfinance] is not widely used for financing farming activities" because of its high cost, and thus lower interest rates are desirable.[79] To this end, Fernando has encouraged policymakers to focus on other means of reducing interest rates, such as "promoting an enabling environment for MFIs, encouraging the entry of different kinds of institutions into the industry, and laying the foundations for more competitive markets."[80]

Peer lending groups are another important and sometimes controversial aspect of many microlending models.[81] Of 890 MFIs reporting to MIX in 2007, 440 (or about half) use both "solidarity lending" (also known as peer lending) and individual lending, while 277 use only individual lending and 79 only peer lending.[82] 94 use a model called "village banking."[83] Some data suggests that peer lending is declining as the microcredit industry continues to develop.[84] According to MIX data from this same period, peer lending tends to promote higher repayment rates: MFIs employing only solidarity lending reported a write-off ratio of .3%, while those

---

77. NIMAL A. FERNANDO, UNDERSTANDING AND DEALING WITH HIGH INTEREST RATES ON MICROCREDIT: A NOTE TO POLICY MAKERS IN THE ASIA AND PACIFIC REGION 4 (May 2006). Fernando's work provides a perspective on a region where MFI interest rates are particularly high. As Fernando notes, "[t]he nominal interest rates charged by most MFIs in the region range from 30% to 70% per year," while "[t]he effective interest rates are even higher because of commissions and fees charged by MFIs." *Id.* at 1. Fernando adds that "[o]ther factors—such as the compulsory deposits for obtaining a loan, frequency of repayments, and the systems adopted to collect repayments—also raise the effective interest rates." *Id.*

78. *Id.* at 4–5.

79. *Id.* at 7.

80. *Id.* at 8–9.

81. Professor Daryl Levinson's article *Collective Sanctions* provides an interesting overview of some of the risks and benefits of joint and several liability in a variety of contexts, including microlending. Daryl J. Levinson, *Collec-*

tive Sanctions, 56 STAN. L. REV. 345, 396–398 (2003). *See also* Denitsa Vigenina & Alexander S. Kritikos, *The Individual Micro-Lending Contract: Is it a Better Design than Joint Liability?,* 28 ECON. SYSTEMS 155, 173 (2004).

82. MICROFINANCE INFORMATION EXCHANGE, INC., MICROBANKING BULLETIN 35 (Autumn 2008).

83. "Village banking" is a form of microlending first employed by the Foundation for International Community Assistance (FINCA), and characterized by support groups of ten to fifty persons, group loan guarantees, and democratic governance. For more information on FINCA and village banking, visit http://villagebanking.org and select "Frequently Asked Questions" under the "About FINCA International" tab.

84. DANIEL C. HARDY ET AL., MICROFINANCE INSTITUTIONS AND PUBLIC POLICY 5 (2002) ("Group guarantees were an especially common feature in the early days of microcredit, but they seem to have been partially supplanted by more advanced techniques of loan evaluation and enforcement.").

employing only individual lending reported a rate of 1.4%. MFIs using a hybrid of both reported a write-off ratio of 1.1%.[85] At the same time, there are concerns with peer-group lending. As Rebecca Farrar has noted, because "[i]t is up to members to select their own group members, ... often the poorest members of the community are excluded."[86] Farrar goes on to describe how women living with either HIV or AIDS were "systematically excluded" according to one field study because the other women "believed [the women with HIV or AIDS] could die and jeopardize their existing loan and access to future loans."[87]

With these statistics and concerns in mind, consider the following excerpt in which Professor Daryl Levinson describes some attractive features of peer-group lending:

> Microcredit institutions, like the highly publicized Grameen Bank in Bangladesh, have been an intriguing, and in some cases stunningly successful, innovation in international development. These institutions have succeeded in extending credit to desperately poor populations in developing countries in Africa, Asia, and Latin America that historically have had no access to productive capital. Rural credit markets in developing countries have been undermined not only by the poverty of the borrowers but also by the lack of institutional infrastructure. Property rights are poorly defined and enforced, credit histories are undocumented, legal systems are costly and unreliable, and complementary insurance markets are, for similar reasons, nonexistent. As a result, banks cannot assess credit risks, hold collateral, or legally enforce repayment. Village moneylenders, who loan only to a handful of individuals and cannot diversify their portfolios or capture economies of scale, charge usurious interest rates. For many of the world's poorest people, therefore, formal sector credit is unavailable and informal sector credit is unaffordable.

> Microcredit institutions overcome these barriers by using a strategy of collective sanctions borrowed from nineteenth-century European credit cooperatives. Their key innovation is group lending. In the case of the Grameen Bank, loans are granted not to individuals but to self-selected groups of five borrowers who are held collectively accountable for repayment and whose eligibility for future loans depends on successful repayment by all group members. Group lending has a number of advantages.

---

85. MICROFINANCE INFORMATION EX-
CHANGE, INC., *supra* note 82, at 41.

86. Farrar, *supra* note 3, at 459.

87. *Id.*

At the stage of group formation, peer selection by borrowers mitigates the huge information asymmetries inherent in under-developed credit markets. While assessing the credit risks of Bangladeshi villagers would be prohibitively costly for a bank, the villagers themselves are intimately acquainted with each other's honesty, financial status, and work ethic. They are also well-situated to assess the local economy and the prospects of fellow borrowers' business plans. Borrowers who risk losing their own capital if someone in their group fails to make payments will carefully screen potential group members and select for good credit risks. Specifically, group lending affects group composition through assortative matching. Because low-risk borrowers will refuse to cross-subsidize high-risk borrow-ers, borrowers of the same risk level will sort themselves into homogeneous groups. And because the cost of credit for any individual will depend on the risk of default presented by the other members of her group, the effective interest rate will be calibrated to her risk of repayment. At an appropriately fixed nominal interest rate, therefore, low-risk borrowers will select into the group-lending scheme and high-risk borrowers will select out. More simply, any group that does apply for credit will quickly be cut off, at minimal cost to the bank, as soon as the first individual loan is not repaid.

The benefits of group lending extend through the course of the loan and beyond. Microcredit loans are usually made for invest-ment in productive capital put to use in small-scale enterprises (looms, livestock, and the like). Collective responsibility gives group members an incentive to help out with each other's businesses, for example, by contributing labor, money, or ad-vice in times of need. It also gives them an incentive to mobilize group-level sanctions against members who fail to repay loans. In contrast to the financial sanctions available to traditional banks when borrowers default, which are useless as applied to a borrowing population without wages or collateral, peer pressure brought by fellow villagers, especially when aug-mented by cultural and religious norms of communal responsi-bility, may create powerful incentives to repay loans. By lever-aging group solidarity in selection, assistance, and sanctioning, the Grameen Bank has maintained repayment rates of well over ninety percent.[88]

88. Levinson, *supra* note 81, at 395–396.

Questions

1. Grameen Bank, like most MFIs, focuses on lending to women. Dr. Yunus explains this phenomenon by stating, "We focused on women because we found giving loans to women always brought more benefits to the family."[89] Why might this statement be true? Could focusing on lending to men be an equally valid—or perhaps even more successful—strategy, or do you tend to agree with Dr. Yunus' assertion? Is it a form of discrimination to favor women over men?

2. What factors should an MFI consider in deciding whether to subsidize its' clients' interest rates?

3. Nimal Fernando has suggested that farming is generally a less attractive match for microfinance than other business ventures are. What characteristics of farming would support such an assertion? What others might tend to disprove it?

4. The Levinson excerpt presents a favorable perspective on peer group lending. What counter-arguments would you anticipate? What kinds of borrowers would be most (and least) drawn to such a model?

PROBLEM 6

Imagine you are crafting a press release for an MFI client that charges an interest rate of 30% per annum and has decided to employ peer-group lending. What would you hope to be able to say about your client with respect to each of these decisions? What questions would you need to ask first to make sure your perceptions are accurate?

For Further Exploration

1. For a "real world" example of how peer-group lending can help to "mitigate [ ] the huge information asymmetries inherent in underdeveloped credit markets," as Professor Levinson has stated, you may wish to view the Public Broadcasting Service's Frontline episode entitled, "Uganda: A Little Goes a Long Way," paying particular attention to the discussion of a prospective borrower named Molly and her son. The episode can be viewed at http://www.pbs.org/frontlineworld/stories/uganda601/video_index.html.

V. MICROFINANCE IN THE UNITED STATES

Up to this point, this chapter's discussion of microfinance has focused on the experience of other countries. As the following

---

89. See *supra* pages 184–185.

excerpt from Federal Reserve Chairman Ben Bernanke's 2007 speech at a microfinance summit indicates, microfinance is a relatively recent development in the United States and faces some special challenges. Chairman Bernanke emphasizes the fact that microentrepreneurs in other countries tend to operate in the informal sector—a factor that the Robinson excerpt also emphasized—while those in the United States are less likely to do so.

Chairman Ben S. Bernanke

At the ACCIÓN Texas Summit on Microfinance in the United States,

San Antonio, Texas

November 6, 2007

Microfinance in the United States

* * *

The microfinance, or microcredit, movement has spread throughout the world—to other parts of Asia, Africa, Latin America, and, more recently, to the United States. Although the social and economic contexts differ widely across countries, the fundamental purpose of microfinance programs remains the same: to offer small loans and other financial services to low-income people to help them increase their incomes through entrepreneurship and self-employment.

* * *

The Development of the U.S. Microfinance Movement

Although the United States came relatively late to the microfinance movement, experimentation in the 1980s and 1990s laid the groundwork for the lively network of programs we see today....

Of course, the operational details of US microfinance programs differ significantly from those in overseas programs, but as I mentioned, they share similar goals and core values. As it does in developing countries, the microfinance movement in the United States seeks to expand economic opportunities for individuals and to foster community economic development by providing small loans and other business services to people who have been traditionally underserved by mainstream financial institutions. Loan features—including size, collateral requirements, and repayment terms—are typically more flexible than those of standard bank loans and are tailored to the needs of low- and moderate-income entrepreneurs.

In the United States, however, credit is only one part of the microfinance package. To a greater extent than overseas, microfinance programs here have expanded their offerings to deliver education, training, and various other services to nascent entrepreneurs. The goals of these supplemental activities are twofold: to improve the survival rate of the borrowers' start-up businesses and to mitigate credit risks for the lender. Several factors have driven the US microfinance industry to diversify beyond simply lending. The complexity of the US market for financial services requires greater financial management skills than are typically needed in developing countries. Here, even very small businesses are likely to have to deal with factors—such as taxes, licenses, and zoning laws—that can prove daunting hurdles to the inexperienced, aspiring business owner. By contrast, entrepreneurs in developing countries tend to operate in the informal sector, often out of the sight of regulators and tax authorities. Yet another difference between the US context and that of the developing world is that, in the United States, aspiring entrepreneurs may have access to alternative sources of credit. Although they may not be able to obtain traditional small business loans, some can qualify for credit cards, home equity credit lines, or other alternatives to microcredit, whereas many of Grameen Bank's clients in Bangladesh, for example, have no such alternatives. Thus, while lending remains a very important part of US microfinance programs, it is not as central to the broader mission as is typically the case in the developing world.

In helping local enterprises get under way, microfinance organizations help deliver the social benefits often associated with such businesses. For example, microentrepreneurs often involve their family members in their businesses, providing them valuable work experience; and extra income can confer important advantages on future generations, such as a chance for a better education. In addition, entrepreneurs may benefit communities and local economies in multiple ways, as this story of a woman who resides in one of Houston's poorest neighborhoods illustrates. Observing the lack of grocery stores in her community, she approached Acción Texas [MFI] for funds to open a small organic food store and restaurant. With the help of the microloan, she created a viable business while also improving the options for food shopping in her community. She also provides various services, including neighborhood cooking classes that promote healthy eating habits.

The Place of Microfinance in the Landscape of Small Business Finance

* * *

Small businesses, generally defined as firms having fewer than 500 employees, have always played a vital role in the US economy. Together, they employ more than half of private-sector workers and produce more than half of private-sector output. The enterprises that micro lenders finance are, of course, the very smallest of small businesses, but such firms make up a substantial share of the US small business sector: 20 percent of small businesses in the United States have only one individual working in the firm, and 40 percent have two to four people working. Among these smaller firms, nearly 25 percent were founded or acquired by a new owner within the past four years.

Thus microenterprises not only provide a path to economic self-reliance for owner-entrepreneurs and benefit their local communities, but they are also important for the economy as a whole. There is some truth to the popular image of the successful firm which had its beginnings in someone's garage. Microenterprises can grow into small businesses, and small businesses can grow into large firms. Thus, microfinance plays the role of business incubator by compensating for the difficulties faced by very small firms and startups in obtaining credit from established financial intermediaries. These difficulties arise because lending to small businesses is typically considered riskier and more costly than lending to larger firms. Small businesses are often more susceptible to changes in the broader economy and generally have a much higher rate of failure than larger operations, although the survival rate of small firms increases with age. Collateral may be used to help mitigate the risk to lenders, but the smallest and youngest firms often have few assets available to pledge. Besides being riskier, lending to small firms can be more expensive. It costs more per dollar loaned both to evaluate their credit applications and to monitor their ongoing performance. Many small businesses lack detailed balance sheets and other financial information used by underwriters in making lending decisions. And the small firm does not issue publicly traded debt or other securities whose values in the marketplace serve as a signal of its profit expectations.

Of course, despite these challenges, many smaller businesses do manage to obtain the credit and capital they need. Community banks, which rely on personal relationships and knowledge of the local market to assess credit risks, have long been a source of funding for small business. The development of more sophisticated techniques in small business loan underwriting, including the use of credit scoring, has helped make small business lending more attractive to larger institutions as well. And research demonstrates that internal finance—that is, financing from the personal resources of owners, family, friends, and business associates—can help offset a lack of access to capital and is crucial to both new and established small enterprises. For some potential low-income entrepreneurs, however, none of these options is feasible. Microfinance was designed to bridge this gap.

The Future of Microfinance in the United States

As I have emphasized, microenterprise development programs in the United States are about much more than the extension of credit, though access to credit remains a central concern. Many programs take a holistic approach, offering interconnected services that complement lending activities and are targeted at entrepreneurs at each stage of business development. Services being offered include up-front business training; specialized technical assistance; mentoring programs; sector-specific advice and support; networking opportunities; coordinated sales and marketing programs; and the development of formal links with banks, local community colleges, and other institutions. Of course, many start-up businesses don't make it; that's an inescapable aspect of the risks that small business entrepreneurs face. But the services provided by microenterprise programs offer borrowers a strong foundation in the fundamentals of running a business and give their businesses a better chance to grow and flourish in a competitive marketplace.

These services benefit the lender by making the borrowers more creditworthy, but providing these services to budding entrepreneurs is labor intensive and requires considerable expertise. Because microfinance clients are rarely able to pay for these services, the costs have generally been underwritten by philanthropic efforts and public-private partnerships. Whether US microfinance programs can become financially self-sustaining is a key question for the future.

Currently, microenterprise organizations are experimenting with business models in the effort to promote self-sustainability. Some are trying to enhance their profitability by offering a wider array of fee-based services, such as check cashing and the facilitation of remittances.[90] Others have turned to technology to reduce their costs. Acción USA, for instance, has reduced transaction, underwriting, and servicing costs through an Internet lending initiative. It has also reduced its training costs through online and distance-learning courses. Another web-

---

90. As the term "remittance" is used in this context, it means "[t]he action or process of sending money to another person or place." BLACK'S LAW DICTIONARY 1321 (8th ed. 2004).

based effort, MicroMentor, matches inexperienced entrepreneurs with more experienced businesspeople, thereby providing important assistance to new business owners at a relatively low cost (http://www.micromentor.org). The Association for Enterprise Opportunity, the principal trade association for microenterprise programs, serves as a forum for learning about innovations, developments, and best practices in this field (http://www.microenterpriseworks.org).

Another promising avenue for the future of microfinance is the development of more partnerships with mainstream banking institutions. Mainstream banks typically don't offer the array of supportive services found at microlenders. But by partnering with a microlender that incubates very small businesses, mainstream institutions can gain new customers when the borrowers "graduate" from the microfinance program and seek larger loans. And these new customers will be more creditworthy borrowers because of the early support they received from the microfinance organization. Acción Texas and other microfinance organizations have established several mutually beneficial partnerships with large banking institutions. Such partnerships serve as two-way referral systems between the microlenders and large banks and help break down the barriers between mainstream institutions and underserved entrepreneurs.

Conclusion

To sum up, I want to affirm the important role that microfinance plays in bringing the opportunity for entrepreneurship to people who otherwise might not have it. Although some businesses will inevitably fall by the wayside, those that flourish and grow are likely to have better management and better long-term prospects than they would have without the support of microenterprise programs. Successful microbusinesses provide jobs as well as valuable products and services to their communities. Not least important, they can provide economic independence and self-reliance for the owner-entrepreneurs. The full benefits of this movement are difficult to calculate. Indeed, one important challenge for the future is to find ways to better measure the impact and cost effectiveness of microfinance programs. What is clear is that the microfinance movement has grown and adapted considerably during its short history in the United States. I hope that microfinance organizations will sustain their energetic spirit of innovation and experimentation as they strive to become more self-sufficient and adapt to our ever-changing economy.[91]

91. Ben S. Bernanke, Acción Texas Summit on Microfinance in the United States: Microfinance in the United States (Nov. 6, 2007), *available at* http://

In addition to the challenges Chairman Bernanke mentioned, small start-up businesses in the US have also historically faced high interest rates. With the debate regarding MFI interest rates described in the prior section in mind, consider the following excerpt from an article written by historians Mark Haller and John Alviti, which builds upon some of the concepts introduced in the Bernanke speech by describing some of the historical challenges in the early 1900s associated with affordable, sustainable small-business lending in the United States.

> Campaigns against loan sharks had three goals: to assist those persons already in debt, to drive out the salary lenders,[92] and finally to provide legal sources of small loans so that borrowers would no longer be dependent upon loan sharks. In important respects, the campaign against loan sharks involved a questioning of previous attitudes toward indebtedness. Opponents of loan sharks argued that borrowing by persons of modest means was often necessary to tide a family over temporary crises and that indebtedness was not evidence of moral failure. The reason for usurious salary lending, they maintained, was the existence of a market for small loans; the solution to the problem was to provide legal, adequately regulated sources of small loans at rates that were reasonable for the borrower yet profitable for the lender. Because loan shark opponents stressed the legitimacy of borrowing, their campaigns contributed to the process by which America changed from a society of frugal producers to a society of borrowers and consumers.
>
> Campaigns against loan sharks were fought on several fronts. In many cities businessmen attempted to persuade their fellow employers not to fire employees found to be in debt, for such a policy did not prevent employees from borrowing but, ironically, made the employers unintended collectors for loan shark debts. In a number of cities, local district attorneys undertook campaigns to prosecute salary lenders on criminal charges for violation of usury laws. The attempts at prosecution often disclosed the weaknesses of usury laws and thus triggered efforts to strengthen them. Many wrestled with the problem that wage assignments were often used to circumvent usury laws.[93] A few states passed laws to forbid wage assignments.

www.federalreserve.gov/newsevents/ speech/bernanke20071106a.htm.

92. Haller and Alviti differentiate between "salary lenders," who operated "with the appearance of legality" and whose lending, "so far as can be determined, had no connection with gambling syndicates or other 'organized crime' ac-

tivities," and "loansharks," who "made little or no pretense of legality" and whose transactions included the understanding that violent sanctions for nonpayment were possible. Haller & Alviti, *infra* note 95, at 125.

93. As Haller and Alviti note, one way that the salary lender created the

Others tried some form of regulation: for instance, a requirement that a wage assignment not be legal unless approved by the borrower's spouse or employer. In a number of cities, charitable organizations or legal aid societies provided legal representation for borrowers entangled in debts or faced with suits.

Campaigns to combat salary lending were the most exciting and publicized strategy in the short run. In the long run, however, significant change resulted chiefly from laws designed to create alternative lending institutions. In this the Russell Sage Foundation provided crucial national leadership. The Foundation sponsored several careful and scholarly studies of the loan shark problem. Under its auspices, experts drafted a model small-loan act that would permit licensed institutions to offer small loans at rates high enough to earn a profit. The model act provided for a state body to license small lenders, forbade small loans by unlicensed institutions, required that the borrower receive a copy of all documents in the transaction, prohibited all charges other than the stated interest, and set a maximum interest rate. Studies soon suggested that a rate of 3/½ percent monthly was necessary for a profitable small loan business. Despite opposition from salary lenders, by 1933 twenty-seven states, mostly outside the South, had passed satisfactory small loan acts.

In the 1910's and 1920's, then, a variety of small loan systems emerged in American cities. Corporations and labor unions established credit unions for their employees or members. Ethnic benevolent societies, especially among Jewish and Catholic immigrants, set up loan funds, on a profit-making or self-sustaining basis, to tide persons over temporary financial difficulties. Under the new small loan laws, a variety of licensed small loan companies developed. Chattel loan companies, for instance, often supported passage of model small loan acts and then became licensed lenders. In the same period, Morris Plan Banks[94]—and analogous institutions—appeared in a number of cities. Finally, by the 1920's and 1930's commercial bankers, recognizing both the profitability and respectability of the small loan market, opened small loan departments. Gradually sources of credit became available for middle income groups,

appearance of legality was by treating the loan as a " 'purchase' of the borrower's future salary." *Id* at 125.

94. According to a 1933 article from Time Magazine, "Morris Plan Banks . . . make loans of $50 to $5,000 largely on character, earning power, and two endorsements—a type of business which many commercial banks find unprofitable." *Business: New Morris Plan*, TIME (Nov. 13, 1933), *available at* http://time.com/time/magazine/article/0,9171, 746327,00.html.

especially those with the highest incomes and most stable employment records.

* * *

As a result of the small loan acts in New York, Illinois, and other states, salary lenders could no longer threaten court action to collect loans and were easily subject to prosecution as unlicensed lenders. By the late 1930's and 1940's, they remained active chiefly in the southern states, extending from Florida and the Carolinas to Texas, where small loan acts had not yet been passed. Here the relationships of salary lenders and lower courts remained strong, while the movement to pass the model small loan act generally faltered. The interstate chains of salary lenders now located their headquarters in cities like Atlanta, Miami, Memphis, and Dallas. In the South, campaigns against salary lending, completed in other states ten or twenty years earlier, still remained to be fought out.

Although model small loan laws gradually drove out illegal salary lenders, the new legal lending institutions did not, as had been expected, meet the needs of persons desiring small, short-term loans—the group serviced earlier by illegal salary lenders. Despite the fact that in many states lenders were permitted to charge a "profitable" interest rate of $3\frac{1}{2}$ percent monthly, lenders faced declining profits, brought on by the inflationary pressures of the 1920's and by the risks of making loans for personal needs. Licensed small lenders, however, were specifically forbidden to adopt profit-maximizing strategies of earlier salary lenders, such as penalty and service fees, chain debt tactics, or higher interest rates. Instead, an increase in the average size of loans became the chief method by which lending companies could protect profits. As a result, the average size of a legal small loan in Massachusetts rose from $26 in 1915 to $150 in 1931; average loans in New Jersey grew from $55 to $240 in the same period; and in Illinois average size increased from $89 in 1918 to $149 in 1931. The upward shift was made possible, in part, by servicing a newly-created, somewhat more affluent class of borrowers who desired larger loans and had the financial stability to make repayments. Emergence of the new class of borrowers reflected, in turn, a continued breakdown during the 1920's of traditional moral obstacles against borrowing money for consumer purposes. Because the needs of small borrowers were often unmet by legal lenders, the small loan market remained in major cities; and this market came gradually to be serviced by a new type of illegal lender: the racketeer loan shark.[95]

95. Mark H. Haller & John V. Alviti, *Loansharking in American Cities: Historical* Analysis of a Marginal Enter-   prise, 21 Am. J. Legal Hist. 125, 136–141 (1977).

Questions

1. Based on the Bernanke excerpt, how is microlending in the United States different from the model that has commonly been effective in other countries, and why?

2. What does Chairman Bernanke suggest about the special role, and special risks, of small businesses in the United States? Are there reasons to believe that this picture is in some way unique to the United States?

3. Chairman Bernanke suggests several ways in which some small businesses gain credit and capital without microfinance. Are these resources equally available to women and men?

4. Toward the end of his speech, Chairman Bernanke describes several "promising avenue[s] for the future of microfinance." Which sound most (and least) promising to you, and why?

5. After having read the Haller & Alviti excerpt, how have American attitudes toward borrowing changed since the early 1900s?

6. What kinds of regulations might a modern, international version of the Russell Sage Foundation propose for MFIs? Who would need to be included in the process to ensure that the recommendations would meet with success?

7. What, if any, analogue to the ethnic benevolent societies that Haller and Alviti describe exists in the MFI context?

8. Which reform attempts failed—and which succeeded—in the age of the salary lenders Haller and Alviti describe? What, if any, lessons might be drawn for modern MFIs?

PROBLEM 7

Assume you have been given the task of opening Beyond Banking, Inc's first branch in the United States. How, if at all, would you change your model for this new context, and what challenges would you expect to encounter?

VI. THE ROAD AHEAD: WEATHERING FINANCIAL AND POLITICAL CHALLENGES

It will be interesting to see how the field of microfinance weathers a recession.[96] MFIs may be more resilient than conventional banks in a time of economic downturn, particularly if, as

---

96. MICROFINANCE INFORMATION EX-
CHANGE, INC., *supra* note 4, at 3 ("Liquidi-
ty shortages, currency dislocations and global recession are likely to affect mi-

some suggest, MFIs are normally less highly leveraged than conventional banks.[97] According to a white paper issued by JP Morgan and CGAP,

> [m]icrolending has proven to be resilient to economic shocks in the past, such as during financial crises in East Asia and Latin America. This is because microfinance customers tend to operate in the informal sector and to be less integrated into the global economy. They also often provide essential products, such as food or basic services, that remain in high demand even in times of crisis.[98]

In addition, MFIs may compare favorably with conventional banks with respect to returns on assets (ROAs) and returns on equity (ROEs).[99] Likewise, the JP Morgan/CGAP report claims that "[p]ublicly listed low-income financial institutions (LIFIs) have outperformed traditional banks," at least for the past five years.[100] Even so, and especially given the current trends toward increased leveraging[101] and the fact that it is difficult to get a clear sense of how leveraged MFIs currently are,[102] it is not clear how the industry will fare.

MFIs face a number of business risks, some of which are shared with conventional banks and others of which are not. These include "rising competition, over-indebtedness, foreign currency funding, transformation, regulation or mission drift."[103] Seeing how the investment market views MFIs is one potential way of analyzing the industry's fiscal health. MFI ratings firm PlaNet Finance reported that, in 2008, approximately 33% of the MFIs it rated were considered "investment grade," while about 50% were considered "speculative" investments.[104]

In addition to financial challenges, the field of microfinance faces political challenges as well. MFIs have received considerable attention due to concerns about financial assistance to foreign terrorist organizations. Professor Nina Crimm describes some of the relevant legal issues as follows:

> Although Congress enacted 18 U.S.C. § 2339A in 1994 to criminalize the direct or indirect provision of financial or other material support or resources by any person "knowing or

crofinance institutions and their clients. The global crisis will test the assumption that microfinance is resilient to economic shocks and can continue to access funding and maintain high quality loan portfolios in time of turmoil.").

97. O'DONOHOE, *supra* note 68, at 10. *See also* ROSENBERG ET AL., *supra* note 5, at 10, 12.

98. O'DONOHOE, *supra* note 68, at 8.

99. FERNANDO, *supra* note 6, at 7.

100. O'DONOHOE, *supra* note 68, at 1.

101. *Id.* at 10.

102. MICROFINANCE INFORMATION EXCHANGE, INC., *supra* note 4, at 33.

103. PLANET RATING, *supra* note 70, at 3.

104. *Id.* at 14.

intending" their use for terrorist activities, the USA Patriot Act[105] enhanced this provision. It expanded the breadth of the "material support or resources" definition, which appears now to contemplate grants, microfinance assistance, and many types of technical assistance. The USA Patriot Act also extended the maximum prison sentence imposed on any person who commits an offense under § 2339A.

The USA Patriot Act also strengthened 18 U.S.C. § 2339B, which is applicable to anyone who financially supports or provides other assistance to a "foreign terrorist organization" (FTO).[106] The statute imposes harsh criminal sanctions on anyone, including a financial contributor who "knowingly" provides, or attempts or conspires to provide, "material support or resources," including grants, microfinance assistance, and many types of technical assistance, to a designated FTO.

The constitutionality of the scienter requirement of 18 U.S.C. § 2339B has been challenged multiple times, resulting in differing judicial positions. The Ninth Circuit and Fourth Circuit Courts of Appeals held that the *mens rea* required for a conviction under the statute is defendant's knowledge of either (1) the organization's underlying designation as a FTO, or (2) the FTO's unlawful activities that caused its designation (even if unaware of the FTO's designation). By contrast, a federal district court in Florida interpreted the necessary *mens rea* for conviction to additionally require defendant's specific intent to provide material support to further the FTO's illegal activities. Congress proposed, as part of the Tools to Fight Terrorism Act of 2004 (TFTA), to adopt the approach of the Fourth and Ninth Circuits, thus clearly giving the anti-terrorism statute a broad reach.

Section 2339B further specifically targets any "financial institution" that becomes aware that it possesses or controls funds in which a FTO or its agent has an interest. It requires such a financial institution to retain possession or control over such funds and to report the holdings to the Secretary of the Treasury. To date, although the definition of "financial institution" has been interpreted to include primarily traditional entities, such as banks, it is possible to stretch the interpretation to include § 501(c)(3) organizations in their capacities as

105. *USA Patriot Act,* Pub. L. No. 107–56, 115 Stat. 272 (2001).

106. "The term foreign terrorist organization means an organization designated or redesignated as a foreign terrorist organization, or with respect to which the Secretary of State has notified

Congress of the intention to designate as a foreign terrorist organization, under U.S.C. § 1189(a)." 31 C.F.R. § 597.309. For a list of entities that had been designated as FTOs as of April 30, 2008, visit http://www.state.gov/s/ct/rls/crt/2007/ 103714.htm.

collectors and disseminators of cash donations. Pursuant to the statute, noncompliance by a financial institution triggers a civil penalty of the greater of either $50,000 per violation or twice the amount of funds at issue.[107]

The statutes Professor Crimm cites in this excerpt provide in relevant part as follows:

18 U.S.C. § 2339A.

Providing material support to terrorists

(a) Offense.—Whoever provides material support or resources or conceals or disguises the nature, location, source, or ownership of material support or resources, knowing or intending that they are to be used in preparation for, or in carrying out, a violation of section 32, 37, 81, 175, 229, 351, 831, 842(m) or (n), 844(f) or (i), 930(c), 956, 1114, 1116, 1203, 1361, 1362, 1363, 1366, 1751, 1992, 2155, 2156, 2280, 2281, 2332, 2332a, 2332b, 2332f, or 2340A of this title, section 236 of the Atomic Energy Act of 1954 (42 U.S.C. 2284), section 46502 or 60123(b) of title 49, or any offense listed in section 2332b(g)(5)(B) (except for sections 2339A and 2339B) or in preparation for, or in carrying out, the concealment of an escape from the commission of any such violation, or attempts or conspires to do such an act, shall be fined under this title, imprisoned not more than 15 years, or both, and, if the death of any person results, shall be imprisoned for any term of years or for life. A violation of this section may be prosecuted in any Federal judicial district in which the underlying offense was committed, or in any other Federal judicial district as provided by law.

(b) Definitions.—As used in this section—

(1) the term "material support or resources" means any property, tangible or intangible, or service, including currency or monetary instruments or financial securities, financial services, lodging, training, expert advice or assistance, safehouses, false documentation or identification, communications equipment, facilities, weapons, lethal substances, explosives, personnel (1 or more individuals who may be or include oneself), and transportation, except medicine or religious materials;

(2) the term "training" means instruction or teaching designed to impart a specific skill, as opposed to general knowledge; and

---

107. Nina J. Crimm, *Post-September 11 Fortified Anti-Terrorism Measures* *Compel Heightened Due Diligence*, 25 PACE L. REV. 203, 208–210 (2005).

(3) the term "expert advice or assistance" means advice or assistance derived from scientific, technical or other specialized knowledge.[108]

18 U.S.C. § 2339B.

Providing material support or resources to designated foreign terrorist organizations

(a) Prohibited activities.—

(1) Unlawful conduct.—Whoever knowingly provides material support or resources to a foreign terrorist organization, or attempts or conspires to do so, shall be fined under this title or imprisoned not more than 15 years, or both, and, if the death of any person results, shall be imprisoned for any term of years or for life. To violate this paragraph, a person must have knowledge that the organization is a designated terrorist organization (as defined in subsection (g)(6)), that the organization has engaged or engages in terrorist activity (as defined in section 212(a)(3)(B) of the Immigration and Nationality Act), or that the organization has engaged or engages in terrorism (as defined in section 140(d)(2) of the Foreign Relations Authorization Act, Fiscal Years 1988 and 1989).

(2) Financial institutions.—Except as authorized by the Secretary, any financial institution that becomes aware that it has possession of, or control over, any funds in which a foreign terrorist organization, or its agent, has an interest, shall—

(A) retain possession of, or maintain control over, such funds; and

(B) report to the Secretary the existence of such funds in accordance with regulations issued by the Secretary.

(b) Civil penalty.—Any financial institution that knowingly fails to comply with subsection (a)(2) shall be subject to a civil penalty in an amount that is the greater of—

(A) $50,000 per violation; or

(B) twice the amount of which the financial institution was required under subsection (a)(2) to retain possession or control.

(c) Injunction.—Whenever it appears to the Secretary or the Attorney General that any person is engaged in, or is about to engage in, any act that constitutes, or would constitute, a

---

108. 18 U.S.C. § 2339A (2006).

violation of this section, the Attorney General may initiate civil action in a district court of the United States to enjoin such violation.[109]

Both of these statutes require some modicum of intent, but neither specifies exactly what is required. Especially because MFIs have been identified as being of particular concern as a potential source of terrorist funding, this matter merits further exploration for anyone with an interest in microfinance. As the United States District Court for the Middle District of Florida has noted, in applying the latter statute, 18 U.S.C. § 2339B,

> [T]here are at least three logical constructions of the level of knowledge required by this statute:
>
> (1) knowledge simply that a person is providing something defined as "material support" in the statute;[a]
>
> (2) knowledge, in addition to the first requirement, that the recipient is a FTO or is an entity that engaged in the type of terrorist activity that would lead to designation as a FTO; or
>
> (3) knowledge, in addition to the previous two requirements, that the recipient could or would utilize the support to further the illegal activities of the entity. [110]

As the Crimm excerpt showed, the prevailing current view is that a violation of § 2339B does not require specific intent to further the terrorist activities of the FTO,[111] but does require that the government prove, beyond a reasonable doubt, that the defendant not only knew the organization was a FTO or was designated as such due to illegal activities, but also that the defendant knew it was providing material support and specifically intended that the support further the illegal activities of the FTO.[112]

Question

1. Based on what you have read, which of the three possible interpretations of the intent required by 18 U.S.C. § 2339B have United States federal courts adopted?

PROBLEM 8

How should Beyond Banking, Inc. prepare to weather an economic crisis, and how would you measure its success in doing so?

---

109. 18 U.S.C. § 2339B (2006).

a. This Court is not requiring that the government prove that Defendants knew that what they actually were providing was within the list of items defined as "material support" in Section 2339A. Ignorance of the law is not a defense to Section 2339B.

110. *U.S. v. Al–Arian*, 329 F. Supp. 2d 1294, 1298 (M.D. Fla. 2004).

111. *U.S. v. Warsame*, 537 F. Supp. 2d 1005, 1014 (D. Minn. 2008).

112. *Al-Arian*, *supra* note 100, at 1298.

PROBLEM 9

How should Beyond Banking, Inc. make sure it does not violate 18 U.S.C. § 2339B? Based on what you have read, would adopting a "facilitated lending" model as discussed in Problem 3 insulate it from liability? Why or why not?

Chapter 8

LETTERS OF CREDIT AND DOCUMENTARY SALES

This chapter introduces letters of credit, which one source has called "the lifeblood of international commerce."[1] The chapter begins by introducing a hypothetical illustrating a transaction for which a letter of credit would be a useful and secure means of payment. Later materials in this chapter introduce the legal framework for letters of credit and explain how letters of credit can be part of what is called a "documentary sale" that protects both the buyer and the seller.[2]

THE HYPOTHETICAL—THELMA'S TEA SHOP

Imagine you have been retained by Thelma, who opened Thelma's Tea Shop five years ago in St. Petersburg, Florida. This small shop serves lunch and high tea, sells tea, and also sells teapots and various giftwares imported from England. Thelma is British, and her husband is from India.

For the first several years that she was in business, Thelma served Cosmic Seasonings tea, a well-known tea that is widely available in supermarkets around the country. Business was slow, and Thelma wanted to distinguish her tea shop from several similar shops in town, all of which served mass-market teas such as Cosmic Seasonings, Great Leaf, Splash, or Figelow.

One day, in conversations with her husband's family, all of whom still live in India, Thelma learned that his family has social connections with the owners of Assam Tea Company (ATC), a tea plantation in the northeastern state of Assam. Assam is famous for its teas and produces a significant percentage of the world's tea.

---

1. KING TAK FUNG, LEADING COURT CASES ON LETTERS OF CREDIT 7 (2008).

2. See *infra* Part II.

Based on this information, Thelma has realized she may be able to use this family connection to offer directly imported teas specially blended for her tea shop, and also custom blends for her customers.

Thelma has now enlisted your help to figure out how to design a business model that will make it possible for her to order tea with confidence and security from halfway across the world. During your conversations with Thelma, you have learned two particularly important facts. First, although the owners of ATC have a social connection to her spouse's family, Thelma and ATC's owners have never even spoken. Second, sales of tea and serving high tea generates about thirty percent of the gross revenues from Thelma's Tea Shop. Thelma has told you it would ruin her business reputation if she served poor-quality tea.

In addition to Thelma's concerns as a potential buyer, one should expect that the owners of ATC would have some concerns of their own with respect to Thelma's honesty and solvency. Thus, for obvious reasons, ironing out the payment terms is of tremendous importance before ATC will do business with Thelma. In preparing to advise her, your research has revealed that payment by check, promissory note, credit card, and wire transfer are each less than optimal means of payment for Thelma's initial transactions with ATC; instead, as it turns out, a "documentary sale" involving a letter of credit and a bill of lading as the two key documents will best protect both Thelma and ATC. The following paragraphs explain why.

First, ATC probably would not even seriously consider accepting payment by check from an American business. India follows its own body of negotiable instruments law, the Law of 1881, which is based on the United Kingdom's Bills of Exchange Act. Thus, Indian law may not treat checks exactly the same way that US law does.

As an aside, but an important one, consider for a moment the international landscape of negotiable-instruments law. The two major sources of domestic law addressing promissory notes and drafts (such as checks) are the United Kingdom's Bills of Exchange Act (BEA) and the Geneva Uniform Laws (GUL), which originated in 1930 with the League of Nations. Uniform Commercial Code Articles 3 and 4 are substantially based on the BEA. The GUL is based upon the civil-law tradition. Many countries have adopted some form of the GUL or BEA, and others have developed their own law to govern negotiable instruments. The most important point is that there is no international convention for negotiable instruments comparable to the very popular United Nations Convention on Contracts for the International Sale of Goods (CISG). The United Nations Convention on International Bills of Exchange and Promissory Notes (CIBN), which would address only a limited class of notes and drafts, has not entered into force at this time and perhaps never will.[3] Thus, the domestic law of negotiable instruments governs international transactions by application of the rules of private international law, and there is considerable difference among the various domestic regimes.[4]

Returning to Thelma's situation, even if ATC would accept her check, it would probably hold the tea until the check cleared— which would mean she had to pay for the tea before she could be assured that it was of good quality. Furthermore, there would be some delay in ATC's receiving the check, even using an expensive means of delivery such as FedEx. Even payment by cashier's check is not a particularly good solution. Although the cashier's check would be a more secure means of payment than an ordinary business check insofar as ATC is concerned because such a check would be the bank's payment obligation rather than Thelma's, Thelma would still be paying for tea without any assurance that it is of good quality.

Second, Thelma should not pay for the tea via a promissory note. Although this means of payment could give her the opportunity to pay for the tea in installments over a period of time, ATC would probably refuse her promissory note because it really does not know whether she is creditworthy. Along the same lines, ATC would probably be unwilling to ship tea that Thelma has not paid for yet—what if she never pays? In addition, this form of payment raises the same concerns as a check regarding delay in receipt and differences in applicable law. As previously mentioned, the CIBN is not yet law—and may never be—so there is no international law governing promissory notes.

Third, Thelma should not pay via credit card. This means of payment may have some initial appeal because ATC, assuming it has the capacity to accept credit cards, would not have to rely on its own subjective assessment of Thelma's creditworthiness. Instead, an approval code would be generated right away to indicate that the charge had gone through. Even so, the risk of charge-back would remain in case Thelma later disputed the charge or there was an error in processing.[5] In addition, Thelma would still have to pay for the tea sight unseen, and, because she is a business cardholder, she would not have access to the Truth in Lending Act's dispute-

---

3. For some basic information on the United Nations Convention on International Bills of Exchange and Promissory Notes, visit http://www.uncitral.org/uncitral/en/uncitral_texts/payments/1988convention_bills_promissory.html.

4. For an overview of some of the more important differences between var-

ious civil-law and common-law systems, insofar as the law of payments is concerned, *see generally* Daniel E. Murray, *Drafts, Promissory Notes and Checks: A Comparison of Civilian, Quasi-Civilian and Non-Civilian Suggestions*, 15 LAW. AM. 211 (1983).

5. *See*, e.g., 15 U.S.C. § 1666 (2006).

resolution provisions that protect consumers in the event of dissatisfaction with goods or services purchased by credit card.[6]

Fourth, Thelma should not pay for the tea via wire transfer, at least not at this early stage in the parties' relationship. Once Thelma and ATC have established a relationship, this form of payment has some significant advantages: it is quick, relatively inexpensive, and allows same-day access to cash in many instances. In the meantime, however, it would require her to pay for the tea before she can examine it, and she is unlikely to feel comfortable doing so with a new tea supplier.

Instead of a check, promissory note, credit card, or wire transfer, Thelma should pay for the tea by a commercial letter of credit, at least for now. As this chapter will explain, this means of payment, when coupled with a document of title such as a bill of lading, constitutes a "documentary sale"[7] that protects both ATC and Thelma, such that ATC can be assured it will receive payment, and Thelma can be assured that the high-quality tea she ordered is on its way to her when payment is made. As Dean Gerald McLaughlin has noted, in explaining how a letter of credit protects the seller,

> [C]ommercial letters of payment are alternative, not substitute, bank payment obligations. Contrast a letter of credit with a different form of bank payment obligation—the cashier's check. If [a] seller in Bordeaux were to accept Solid Gold Bank's cashiers check as payment for ... wine, the seller would no longer have recourse against the buyer for the ... purchase price. The cashier's check is a substitute payment mechanism that totally replaces the buyer's payment obligation. The commercial credit, on the other hand, simply adds the issuer's payment obligation to that of the buyer-applicant. The seller-beneficiary still has recourse against the buyer-applicant under [the underlying contract], but only after Solid Gold Bank dishonors its [own contractual] obligation [under the letter of credit].[8]

McLaughlin continues as follows:

> In an international sale contract, the seller who ships goods to the buyer on credit bears the risk that buyer will not be able to pay for the goods when they arrive at their destination point (the so-called insolvency risk). Similarly, the seller who ships

---

6. *See* 15 U.S.C. § 1666 (2006).

7. "A sale in which the buyer pays upon the seller's tender of documents of title covering the goods plus a sight draft requiring the buyer to pay 'at sight.' " BLACK'S LAW DICTIONARY 1364 (8th ed. 2004).

8. Gerald T. McLaughlin, *Remembering the Bay of Pigs: Using Letters of Credit to Facilitate the Resolution of International Disputes*, 32 GA. J. INT'L & COMP. L. 743, 747–748 (2004).

on credit bears the risk that when the goods arrive, the buyer may act fraudulently and demand a reduction in the price of the goods (the so-called dishonesty risk). A commercial letter of credit shifts these risks from the seller to the issuing bank. Once a letter of credit has been opened, the seller need not worry about the financial health of the buyer because issuer Solid Gold Bank, a major banking institution, is obligated to pay for the wine. Once the credit has been issued, the seller also need not be concerned by the buyer's attempts to force seller to accept a price reduction. Again, Solid Gold Bank is obligated to pay the seller-beneficiary for the wine and will not jeopardize its reputation in banking circles by acting dishonestly toward the letter of credit beneficiaries.[9]

McLaughlin's excerpt explains how a letter-of-credit transaction protects the seller. The following section not only further explores this concept, but also explains how a documentary sale transaction, when properly structured, protects a buyer such as Thelma also.

Questions

1. It is interesting that there is a successful international treaty in the area of international sales of goods—the United Nations Convention on Contracts for the International Sale of Goods—but no equivalent in the international payments arena. Why might it be easier to establish international law for sales than for payments?

2. In your own words, what is the difference between an "alternative" bank payment obligation and a "substitute" bank payment obligation, as Dean McLaughlin uses each term?

PROBLEM 1

Imagine that you have just concluded your initial client interview with Thelma, and she has shared with you the facts outlined above. What follow-up questions would you like to ask her? How will the answers to these questions assist you in helping her to craft a business model that will meet her needs?

I. WHAT IS A LETTER OF CREDIT?

Instead of "letter of credit," which is the term commonly used to describe this form of payment in the United States, you may encounter the term "documentary credit" (sometimes abbreviated "credit") in international practice. "Credit" is the term used in the Uniform Customs and Practice ("UCP") promulgated by the Inter-

---

9. *Id.* at 749.

national Chamber of Commerce, which govern most international letters of credit and are more fully introduced in the next section of this chapter. The UCP definition of "documentary credit" is as follows:

UCP Article 2
Definitions

* * *

[A]ny arrangement, however named or described, that is irrevocable and thereby constitutes a definite undertaking of the issuing bank to honour a complying presentation.[10]

* * *

Notably, and as this definition shows, a letter of credit is a bank's agreement to make payment, either on its own behalf or on behalf of one of its customers. Thus, just as a bank's creditworthiness makes a cashier's check a more reliable instrument of payment than a personal check, a letter of credit is a more reliable means of payment than an individual's personal promise to pay would be. The "irrevocability" piece of the UCP definition is crucial.[11] As William Fox has stated, "A revocable letter of credit may be changed or cancelled by the issuing bank at any time with no notice to the beneficiary. This makes the letter of credit almost worthless as a protective device, and as a consequence revocable letters of credit are virtually unheard of in international commercial agreements."[12]

Letters of credit involve "payment against documents." This means that the issuing bank or, where relevant, the confirming bank[13] must make payment when the beneficiary makes what is called a "complying presentation" of the documents named in the letter of credit. UCP Article 7 describes the duties of an issuing bank in relevant part as follows:[14]

UCP Article 7
Issuing Bank Undertaking

(a) Provided that the stipulated documents are presented to . . . the issuing bank and that they constitute a complying

10. INTERNATIONAL CHAMBER OF COMMERCE, UNIFORM CUSTOMS AND PRACTICE FOR DOCUMENTARY CREDITS, ICC Publication No. 600LF, Article 2 (2007 Revision) ("UCP 600").

11. *Id.*

12. WILLIAM F. FOX, JR., INTERNATIONAL COMMERCIAL AGREEMENTS: A PRIMER ON DRAFTING, NEGOTIATING, AND RESOLVING DIS-

PUTES 98–99 (1998). Fox goes on to add, "At the same time, the term *irrevocable* does not mean immutable. Irrevocable letters of credit may be changed or cancelled but only after all parties to the letter give their consent to the modification or cancellation." *Id.* at 99.

13. *See infra* p. 243.

14. *See supra* note 10, Article 7.

presentation, the issuing bank must honour [the credit, unless payment is to be made through another bank, called a "nominated bank"].

(b) An issuing bank is irrevocably bound to honour as of the time it issues the credit.[15]

* * *

As previously explained, a bank involved in a letter-of-credit transaction *must* make payment when the beneficiary tenders conforming documents as outlined in the letter of credit. The bank is not expected to, and indeed *must not*, consider facts or documents outside the letter of credit. This latter point is captured in UCP Articles 4 and 5, which provide as follows:

UCP Article 4

Credits v. Contracts

(a) A credit by its nature is a separate transaction from the sale or other contract on which it may be based. Banks are in no way concerned with or bound by such contract, even if any reference whatsoever to it is included in the credit. Consequently, the undertaking of a bank to honour, to negotiate, or to fulfill any other obligation under the credit is not subject to claims or defences by the applicant resulting from its relationships with the issuing bank or the beneficiary. A beneficiary can in no case avail itself of the contractual relationships existing between banks or between the applicant and the issuing bank.

(b) An issuing bank should discourage any attempt by the applicant to include, as an integral part of the credit, copies of the underlying contract, proforma invoice, and the like.[16]

UCP Article 5

Documents v. Goods, Services or Performance

Banks deal with documents and not with goods, services, or performance to which the documents may relate.[17]

Thus, a bank releasing funds pursuant to a letter of credit is neither required nor permitted to inquire into whether the beneficiary (the party seeking payment) has actually complied with the terms of any contract between the applicant and beneficiary (for example, as a buyer and seller of goods, respectively) entitling the beneficiary to payment under the letter of credit. Instead, the

---

15. UCP Article 8 supplies a similar list of duties for a confirming bank. *Id.* at Article 8.

16. *Id.* at Article 4.

17. *Id.* at Article 5.

bank's role is limited to examining the documents the beneficiary has presented to it, which are intended to provide documentary evidence of its entitlement to payment.[18] This is what is sometimes called the "independence principle" and is a key characteristic of a letter-of-credit transaction.

A limited exception to the bank's payment obligation exists when the beneficiary has engaged in fraud. As one commentator has noted, "The main exception to the substantive independence of credits . . . is fraud, sometimes expressed in Latin in the maxim of *'fraus omnia corrumpit,'* or, fraud corrupts all."[19] Even though the fact that there is a fraud exception that allows the applicant to seek an interlocutory injunction against payment is well established and globally recognized, the kind of conduct that implicates the fraud exception is much more difficult to describe with certainty. In addition, the exception must be construed as narrowly as possible, so as not to undermine the reliability of letters of credit as a means of payment. As Judge Gao Xiang and Professor Ross Buckley have stated,

> The *raison d'etre* of letters of credit is to provide an absolute assurance of payment to a seller, provided the seller presents documents that comply with the terms of the credit. The fraud rule thus goes to the very heart of the letter of credit obligation. The fraud rule is necessary to limit the activities of fraudsters, but its scope must be carefully circumscribed so as not to deny commercial utility to an instrument that exists to serve as an assurance of payment.[20]

The most influential case in shaping the contours of the fraud exception, both in the United States and elsewhere, was *Sztejn v. J. Henry Schroder Banking Corp.*, 31 N.Y.S.2d 631 (N.Y. Sup. Ct. 1941).[21] In denying the defendant bank's motion to dismiss the plaintiff applicant's complaint seeking an injunction against payment of the credit, the *Sztejn* court held in relevant part as follows:

> This is not a controversy between the buyer and seller concerning a mere breach of warranty regarding the quality of the merchandise; on the present motion, it must be assumed that the seller has intentionally failed to ship any goods ordered by the buyer. In such a situation, where the seller's fraud has been called to the bank's attention before the drafts and

18. *Id.* at Article 7 ("Issuing Bank Undertaking").

19. MATTI S. KURKELA, LETTERS OF CREDIT AND BANK GUARANTEES UNDER INTERNATIONAL TRADE LAW 175 (2d ed. 2008) (emphasis in original).

20. Gao Xiang & Ross P. Buckley, *A Comparative Analysis of the Standard of* *Fraud Required under the Fraud Rule in Letter of Credit Law*, 13 DUKE J. COMP. & INT'L L. 293, 293 (2003) (emphasis in original).

21. *Id.* at 295 ("While a U.S. decision, *Sztejn* has influenced and shaped the fraud rule in virtually all jurisdictions worldwide.").

documents have been presented for payment, the principle of the independence of the bank's obligation under the letter of credit should not be extended to protect the unscrupulous seller. It is true that even though the documents are forged or fraudulent, if the issuing bank has already paid the draft before receiving notice of the seller's fraud, it will be protected if it exercised reasonable diligence before making such payment. However, in the instant action [Henry] Schroder [Banking Corp., the issuer] has received notice of [beneficiary] Transea [Traders, Ltd.'s] active fraud before it accepted or paid the draft. . . .

Although our courts have used broad language to the effect that a letter of credit is independent of the primary contract between the buyer and seller, that language was used in cases concerning alleged breaches of warranty; no case has been brought to my attention on this point involving an intentional fraud on the part of the seller which was brought to the bank's notice with the request that it withhold payment of the draft on this account. The distinction between a breach of warranty and active fraud on the part of the seller is supported by authority and reason. As one court has stated: "Obviously, when the issuer of a letter of credit knows that a document, although correct in form, is, in point of fact, false or illegal, he cannot be called upon to recognize such a document as complying with the terms of a letter of credit." *Old Colony Trust Co. v. Lawyers' Title & Trust Co.*, 297 F. 152, 158 (2d Cir. 1924), *cert. denied* 265 U.S. 585 (1924).

* * *

No hardship will be caused by permitting the bank to refuse payment where fraud is claimed, where the merchandise is not merely inferior in quality but consists of worthless rubbish, where the draft and the accompanying documents are in the hands of one who stands in the same position as the fraudulent seller, where the bank has been given notice of the fraud before being presented with the drafts and documents for payment, and where the bank itself does not wish to pay pending an adjudication of the rights and obligations of the other parties. While the primary factor in the issuance of the letter of credit is the credit standing of the buyer, the security afforded by the merchandise is also taken into account. In fact, the letter of credit requires a bill of lading made out to the order of the bank and not the buyer. Although the bank is not interested in the exact detailed performance of the sales contract, it is vitally interested in assuring itself that there are some goods represented by the documents.[22]

Now that these materials have provided some basic background information about letters of credit and documentary sales, it may be useful to examine excerpts from the not-insubstantial paperwork these transactions require. First, consider the following form application for a commercial letter of credit. Note that the word "commercial" is a term of art that distinguishes this kind of letter of credit from a "standby" letter of credit, which will not be covered in these materials.[23] A commercial letter of credit is issued as the intended means of payment in a given transaction, while a standby letter of credit serves much the same function as a performance bond or surety bond.

APPLICATION AND AGREEMENT FOR COMMERCIAL LETTER OF CREDIT[24]

Date: _____

TO: SAEHAN BANK, Int'l Dept.
550 S. Western Avenue, Los Angeles, CA 90020
Swift Address: SAEBUS6L
Fax: 213–389–8255 Tel: 213–389–5550

Please issue your irrevocable letter of credit and advise the beneficiary by: ☐SWIFT[25] ☐ other

IN FAVOR OF (Name and Address of Beneficiary): ____

_____

_____

_____

TEL: _____

FAX: _____

FOR THE ACCOUNT OF (Name and Address of Account Party): _____

_____

_____

_____

---

22. *Sztejn v. J. Henry Schroder Banking Corp.*, 31 N.Y.S.2d 631, 634–635 (1941).

23. A "standby" letter of credit is "[a] letter of credit used to guarantee either a monetary or a nonmonetary obligation (such as the performance of construction work), whereby the issuing bank agrees to pay the beneficiary if the bank customer defaults on its obli-gation." BLACK'S LAW DICTIONARY 923 (8th ed. 2004).

24. This form is available at http://www.saehanbank.com/resources/lc ̈application ̈form.pdf.

25. "SWIFT" stands for The Society for Worldwide Interbank Financial Tele-communication. http://www.swift.com.

TEL: _____

FAX: _____

ADVISING BANK: _____

SWIFT ADDRESS: _____

AMOUNT (Indicate Currency and specify Amount in Words and Figures): _____

EXPIRATION DATE: Documents must be presented at Place of Expiration not later than _____ days after the date of shipment but within the validity of the credit.

PLACE OF EXPIRATION (Unless otherwise indicated, Place of Expiration will be country of Beneficiary): _____

Available with: ☐ any bank OR ☐ nominated bank; by Beneficiary's drafts: ☐ at sight or ☐ days after sight, drawn on Saehan Bank for _____% of the invoice value.

Partial Shipments: ☐ allowed ☐ not allowed

Transshipment:[26] ☐ allowed ☐ not allowed

Shipment From: _____

Shipment To: _____

Latest date of Shipment: _____

PAYMENT AGAINST THE FOLLOWING DOCUMENTS

(Check appropriate boxes)

☐ Signed Commercial Invoice in triplicate

Certifying that goods are in accordance with buyer's purchase order

No._____ dated _____

Covering the following goods with detailed description: __

_____

_____

_____

Terms:[27] FAS FOB CFR CIF C & I Other (circle)

☐ Full set of Clean On Board Ocean Bill of Lading

   ☐ To the order of ☐ Endorsed in blank

---

26. "The act of taking cargo out of one ship and loading it on another." BLACK'S LAW DICTIONARY 1538 (8th ed. 2004).

27. These are all Incoterms, or International Commercial Terms, describing the parties' duties with respect to such important matters as risk of loss and insurance. The Incoterms are published by the International Chamber of Commerce (ICC). For information on the most recent version, which is called Incoterms 2000, *see* http://www.icwbo. org/incoterms/id3040/index.html.

☐ Marked freight ☐ prepaid ☐ payable at destination (collect)

☐ Marked Notify: _____

☐ Air Waybill consigned to: _____

☐ Railroad/Truck Bill of Lading consigned to: _____

☐ Packing List in triplicate

☐ Certificate of Origin in triplicate

☐ Certificate of Inspection in triplicate

☐ Marine ☐ Air insurance policy or certificate in duplicate, endorsed in blank for 110% of the invoice value. Insurance policies or certificates must expressly stipulate that claims are payable in the currency of the draft and must also indicate a claims settling agent in USA. Insurance must include: ☐ Institute Cargo Clauses: (F.P.A./W.A. All Risks) ☐ Institutional War Clauses ☐ Strikes, Riots, Civil Commotions Clauses

☐ Other Documents: _____

☐ This Letter of Credit is transferable by advising bank.

All banking charges other than those of the issuing bank are for the account of

☐ Applicant ☐ Beneficiary

☐ _____ % more or less in quantity and amount are acceptable.

Special instructions: _____

I/we acknowledge and agree that acceptance of this Application by the Bank does not constitute a commitment or agreement by the Bank to issue or open the letter of credit described in this Application and that the opening of the letter of credit is subject to approval by the Bank and receipt by me/us of such approval. I/we further acknowledge and agree that the issuance of the letter of credit described in this Application, or as amended by agreement between the parties hereto, if approved by the Bank, will be governed by the terms and conditions set forth in the Commercial Letter of Credit Agreement, which is on the reverse side of application, which terms shall supersede the terms and conditions of this Application to the extent that the terms of the Commercial Letter of Credit Agreement are inconsistent herewith. The terms of this Application, together with the terms of the Commercial Letter of Credit Agreement, shall constitute the entire agreement between the parties hereto and shall not be subject to change or modification except by written agreement signed by the parties hereto.

Name of Applicant
By Name/Title

FOR BANK USE ONLY

L/C No: _____

L/C Open Date: _____

L/C Amount: _____

OFAC Check: _____

Account Officer's Approval: _____

Operations Manager's Approval: _____

Manager's Approval: _____

After the application has been completed and accepted, the bank will issue a letter of credit. The following fairly typical language is excerpted from a commercial letter of credit that was the subject of litigation in the case entitled *Banco Nacional de Desarrollo v. Mellon Bank, N.A.*, 726 F.2d 87 (3d Cir. 1984).

Mellon Bank N.A.

Documentary Letter of Credit
Irrevocable

Place of issue: Pittsburgh, Pennsylvania.

Date of issue: August 7, 1980.

Letter of Credit Number: of issuing bank 47728.

Advising Bank: Banco Nacional de Desarrollo.

Applicant: I.B.P. Corporation.

Beneficiary: Empresa Nicaraguensa de la Carne, Encar.

Amount: U.S. $98,000.00 (ABOUT).

Expiry: August 31, 1980, in Nicaragua for negotiation.

We hereby issue this documentary letter of credit which is available against beneficiary's draft at SIGHT FOR 100% INVOICE VALUE drawn on Mellon Bank N.A. bearing the clause: "Drawn on documentary letter of credit No. 47728" accompanied by the following documents:

> Signed Commercial Invoice in quadruplicate including statement that all cartons are marked with U.S.D.A. approved markings and that the product is free of any chemicals, additives, and pesticides, and conforms to all regulations of the USDA and country of origin and stating that the original Nicaraguan Meat Inspection Certificate has been airmailed to the broker at the port of discharge,

Special Customs Invoice 5515 in duplicate,

Packing List in duplicate,

One copy Nicaraguan Veterinary [sic] Meat Inspection Certificate,

Copy of your cable addressed to Gurrentz International Corporation dated not later than one week after date of the on board Bill of Lading stating this Letter of Credit Number, quantity, product, name of carrying vessel, and port of discharge,

2/3 set clean on board occan Bills of Lading plus one non-negotiable copy consigned to order and blank endorsed evidencing refrigerated shipment from Nicaragua to Los Angeles, CA dated not later than August 21, 1980,

Copy of beneficiary's cable addressed to I.B.P. Corporation dated no later than one week after date of the on board Bill of Lading stating Letter of Credit Number 47728, quantity, product, name of carrying vessel and port of discharge,

One copy Ministry of Secursos Naturales Nicaragua Meat Inspection Certificate, purporting to cover Fresh frozen boneless beef packed in poly lined fiber carton solid packed in even weight 60 #cartons. Approx. 1200 carton min. 90% C.L. chucks at 1.18 FOB and approx. 124 ctns. 100% lean product at 1.75 FOB Nicaragua _____.

Shipment from Nicaragua to Los Angeles, CA. Partial shipments are not permitted. Transshipments are not permitted.
* * *

We hereby engage with the bona fide holders of all drafts drawn and/or documents presented under and in compliance with the terms of this letter of credit that such drafts and/or documents will be duly honored upon presentation to us. The amount of each drawing must be endorsed on the reverse side of this letter of credit by the negotiating bank.

Indications of the advising bank: This is an irrevocable letter of credit of the above mentioned issuing bank and is transmitted to you without any responsibility or engagement on our part.

Now that these materials have provided a little bit more context to explain how a letter of credit works, the discussion will return to the hypothetical involving Thelma's Tea Shop. As mentioned earlier, when a letter of credit is part of what is called a documentary sale, both parties are protected. ATC can be assured, when it ships the tea, that it will get paid. It can be sure of this because a letter of credit is not Thelma's personal promise to pay;

instead, it is the bank's direct obligation to pay on her behalf. At the same time, Thelma can be assured, if the letter of credit has been thoughtfully constructed, that the tea to be shipped to her will comply with the terms of the parties' contract. This is because the letter of credit will include a list of documents which Thelma specifies that must be tendered to the bank before ATC will get paid.

In other words, if Thelma (and you, as Thelma's attorney) are careful in constructing the letter of credit, the list of documents it contains will be enough to make her feel secure that she is getting high-quality tea before she tenders payment (or rather, before the bank tenders payment on her behalf). For example, because Thelma runs a business in St. Petersburg, Florida, one can fairly assume that she does not have time to fly out to Assam, India, personally oversee the harvesting of the tea she has ordered, and watch it being packed and shipped to her. Even so, if one of the documents listed on her letter of credit is an inspection certificate that must be signed by a reputable inspector (perhaps a government official, or perhaps a private person Thelma has hired), that person will act as her "eyes and ears" in Assam, and his or her representation that the tea has passed inspection would give her some comfort that the high-quality tea she expects and paid for is on its way to her.

Thelma can list as many documents as she wants in her letter of credit, and she and her attorney should have a thorough conversation about what she wants to include—in other words, what documents will serve as a proxy for her ears and eyes in Assam, India. But she needs to remember that, if her list is unreasonable, ATC may refuse to accept her terms, such that she may not be able to go forward with her plans for the custom-blended teas at Thelma's Tea Shop.

Questions

1. What does the concept of "payment against documents" mean and why is this so important to the functioning of a letter of credit?

2. Based on the *Sztejn* excerpt, how can you differentiate in your own words between a case involving allegations of a mere breach of contract or breach of warranty and the kind of fact pattern that would implicate the fraud exception?

3. Consider the last sentence of the *Sztejn* excerpt: "Although the bank is not interested in the exact detailed performance of the sales contract, it is vitally interested in assuring itself that there are some goods represented by the documents."[28] What distinction is the court drawing?

---

28. *See supra* pages 232–233.

4. Take another look at the *Banco Nacional de Desarrollo* letter-of-credit language, and especially the rather lengthy list of documents against which payment is to be made.[29] What can you discern about the goods involved in this transaction and the kinds of potential problems against which the buyer was attempting to guard?

5. Building on the prior question, note the reference to the Ministry of Secursos Naturales Nicaragua Meat Inspection Certificate.[30] Do a little bit of internet research to find out what the "Ministry of Secursos Naturales" is. Why would it make sense, as a practical matter, that the purchaser would not want to pay for the goods without the certificate? If the seller bribed the official who completed the document, such that the official signed the certificate even though the goods in question were of exceedingly poor quality, would you expect the buyer to be able to sue the official? Would you expect the buyer to have a cause of action against the seller or the bank that paid the letter of credit?

6. Because letters of credit are a secure means of payment, one might wonder why they are not used more regularly and informally in daily life. The short answer is that letters of credit are relatively expensive and at least somewhat time-consuming. As William Fox states,

> A letter of credit is not cheap. Banks spend a good deal of time and attention on them both as issuing bank and advising bank. The fee for a typical letter of credit is a percentage of the dollar amount of the letter of credit itself. The fee is increased as the individual letter of credit transaction increases in complexity.[31]

Do a brief internet search on letter-of-credit fees. What seems to be an average fee? Under what circumstances would you advise a buyer client to make payment (or a seller client to insist upon receiving payment) via a letter of credit?

PROBLEM 2

Assume that you have been asked to draft a simple letter of credit for Thelma. Based on what you have read so far, what terms would you want to make sure to include? You will find out more about the parties to a letter-of-credit transaction in Part III and will be able to flesh out this document more fully at that time.

---

29. *See supra* pages 236–237.
30. *See supra* page 237.

31. Fox, *supra* note 12, at 100 (emphasis in original).

II. THE LEGAL FRAMEWORK FOR A DOCUMENTARY SALE

As mentioned in the prior section, many letter-of-credit transactions are governed by the Uniform Customs and Practice (UCP) promulgated by the International Chamber of Commerce (ICC). The UCP are a set of rules that have been characterized as generally favoring banks rather than their customers.[32] Although the ICC began the project that ultimately became the UCP in the 1920s and issued its first final version of the UCP in 1933, it was not until the early 1960s that "the banks of virtually every country in the world—developed and developing, capitalist, socialist, and in-between—adhered to the Uniform Customs and Practice."[33] Since that time, a new version of the UCP has been promulgated approximately once each decade.[34] The most recent version of the UCP is UCP 600, which was finalized in 2007.[35] Like the American Law Institute (ALI) and the Uniform Law Commission (ULC), which are the joint drafters of the Uniform Commercial Code, the ICC is a private organization with no governmental law-making authority. Unlike the UCC or the CISG, the UCP is neither a treaty nor incorporated into a statute by a legislature, but is instead a well-developed international body of commercial norms. In addition, unlike the ALI or the ULC, the ICC is a business organization instead of a legal organization.

When the UCP 600 (or an earlier form of the UCP such as the UCP 500) is incorporated into the parties' contract by agreement, it becomes part of the private law that governs the transaction as a matter of contract law. The UCP has been so successful that UCC Article 5 actually defers to the UCP where it has been chosen by the parties. The specific provision establishing this fact is § 5–116(c), which provides as follows:

32. *Id.* at 100 ("Banks are always skittish about substituting their creditworthiness for that of their customers, and they've written the UCP so that their obligations for handling letters of credit are both clearly spelled out and limited in scope."). For information on how an issuer can decrease its credit risk exposure by using either a "syndicated letter of credit," which is "a credit with multiple issuers, ... each [of which] is liable only for paying the beneficiary its pro rata share of the face amount of the credit," or a "participation credit," which is a credit in which the lead bank undertakes to pay the full amount of the credit to the beneficiary but sells pro rata shares of the credit (participations) to other banks on a non-recourse basis," *see* McLaughlin, *supra* note 8, at 755.

33. ANDREAS F. LOWENFELD, INTERNATIONAL PRIVATE TRADE 142 (3d ed. 1995).

34. *Id.*

35. The UCP 600 is so named because it is the ICC's six hundredth numbered publication. Earlier versions of the UCP were similarly denominated UCP 400, UCP 500, etc.

UCC § 5–116
Choice of Law and Forum

* * *

(c) Except as otherwise provided in this subsection, the liability of an issuer, nominated person, or adviser[36] is governed by any rules of custom or practice, such as the Uniform Customs and Practice for Documentary Credits, to which the letter of credit, confirmation, or other undertaking is expressly made subject. If (i) this article would govern the liability of an issuer, nominated person, or adviser under subsection (a) or (b), (ii) the relevant undertaking incorporates rules of custom or practice, and (iii) there is conflict between this article and those rules as applied to that undertaking, those rules govern except to the extent of any conflict with the nonvariable provisions specified in Section 5–103(c).[37]

* * *

This extraordinary phenomenon—state law deferring to non-law—is a testimony to the great international success of the UCP. In fact, and as a further testament to the esteem with which the various UCP drafts have historically been regarded, the UCP is frequently used even in domestic letters of credit.

Questions

1. Do a little bit of research on the International Chamber of Commerce. You may want to look at its website, http://www.iccwbo.org, among other resources. Based on what you have read, who are the leaders and members of the ICC, and how do you suppose it has become so influential in the area of international letters of credit? In what other subject areas has the ICC affected international policy and practice?

2. In a news release dated June 4, 2007, the ICC made the following statement about the UCP 600:

   The Uniform Customs and Practice for Documentary Credits (UCP) were first published by ICC in 1933. Revised versions were issued in 1951, 1962, 1974, 1983 and 1993. Written into virtually every letter of credit, the UCP are accepted worldwide and are the essential ground rules for billions of dollars in trade transactions every year. They are the most successful private rules for trade ever developed and illustrate the importance ICC attaches to self-regulation.[38]

Based on what you have read so far, in what way do the UCP "illustrate the importance ICC attaches to self-regulation"?

---

36. The terms "issuer," "nominated person," and "adviser" are explained below in Part III.

37. U.C.C. § 5–116(c) (1995).

38. Press Release, International Chamber of Commerce, *ICC Provides Training on UCP 600* (June 4, 2007), *available at* http://www.iccwbo.org/iccbdggg/index.html.

PROBLEM 3

As Question 2 mentions, there were a number of earlier versions of the UCP. Consistent with the notion of contract law as private law, parties remain free to select UCP 400, UCP 500, or even the earlier versions of UCP to govern their transaction if they so choose. Imagine that you were representing Thelma in June of 2007, shortly before UCP 600 became effective on July 1. How would you determine whether to rely on UCP 500 or UCP 600?

III. A BASIC DOCUMENTARY SALE

A basic commercial documentary sale involves both a letter of credit, which has already been introduced, and a carrier's bill of lading, which will be introduced in this part of the chapter. A letter-of-credit transaction involves both an applicant, which is the buyer or other party whose bank is paying for the goods or services, and a beneficiary, which is the seller or other person to whom payment for the goods or services is to be made. The seller and buyer, of course, are commonly also parties to an underlying contract of sale specifying the goods or services to be provided.

The following chart, which illustrates a basic documentary sale, was adapted with permission from Kristen David Adams, *Commercial Transactions: A Survey of United States Law with International Perspective* 18–4 (Thomson/West 2006):

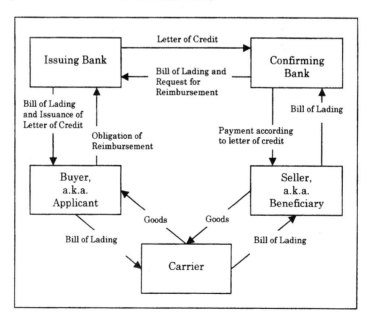

As this chart shows, in addition to the applicant and beneficiary, the transaction will also include at least one bank—and perhaps more. Every letter-of-credit transaction includes an issuing bank. In addition, although the beneficiary will sometimes make present-ment of the required documents directly to the issuing bank, this arrangement would not be convenient when the issuing bank and beneficiary are geographically remote from one another in a trans-action like Thelma's. In such a situation, a second bank, called a confirming bank, would be part of the transaction.[39] The beneficiary would then make presentment of the required documents to the confirming bank, which would be chosen both for its reliability and its proximity to the beneficiary.

The UCP defines each of the parties mentioned above as follows:

UCP Article 2

Definitions

Applicant means the party on whose request the credit is issued.

Beneficiary means the party in whose favour a credit is issued.

* * *

Confirming bank means the bank that adds its confirmation to a credit upon the issuing bank's authorization or request.[40]

* * *

Issuing bank means the bank that issues a credit at the request of an applicant or on its own behalf.

* * *

Up to this point, this chapter has not discussed the extent to which the documents presented under a letter of credit must comply with the terms of the credit, for payment to be released to the beneficiary. The following language from the court's opinion in *Voest-Alpine Trading Co. v. Bank of China*, 167 F. Supp. 2d 940, 946–947 (S.D. Tex. 2000), helps to explain the level of conformity that was required under UCP 500.

39. The UCP also provides for addi-tional banks, denominated "nominated banks" and "advising banks," that will not be discussed in these basic materi-als. *See supra* note 10, Article 2.

40. *Id.*

VOEST-ALPINE TRADING CO. v. BANK OF CHINA

United States District Court for the Southern District of Texas (2000)

167 F. Supp. 2d 940, 946–947

* * *

Section 13(a) of the UCP 500 provides:

> Banks must examine all documents stipulated in the Credit with reasonable care, to ascertain whether or not they appear, on their face, to be in compliance with the terms and conditions of the Credit. Compliance of the stipulated documents on their face with the terms and conditions of the Credit shall be determined by international standard banking practice as reflected in these Articles. Documents which appear on their face to be inconsistent with one another will be considered as not appearing on their face to be in compliance with the terms and conditions of the Credit.

INTERNATIONAL CHAMBER OF COMMERCE, ICC UNIFORM CUSTOMS AND PRACTICE FOR DOCUMENTARY CREDITS, ICC PUBLICATION NO. 500 19 (1993).

The UCP 500 does not provide guidance on what inconsistencies would justify a conclusion on the part of a bank that the documents are not in compliance with the terms and conditions of the letter of credit or what discrepancies are not a reasonable basis for such a conclusion. The UCP 500 does not mandate that the documents be a mirror image of the requirements or use the term "strict compliance."[41]

The Court notes the wide range of interpretations on what standard banks should employ in examining letter of credit document presentations for compliance. Even where courts claim to uphold strict compliance, the standard is hardly uniform. The first and most restrictive approach is to require that the presentation documents be a mirror image of the requirements. *See Banco General Runinahui, S.A. v. Citibank Int'l*, 97 F.3d 480, 483 (11th Cir. 1996) ("This Court has recognized and applied the 'strict compliance' standard to requests for payment under commercial letters of credit . . . '[T]he fact that a defect is a mere technicality' does not matter.' ") (quoting *Kerr-McGee Chem. Corp. v. FDIC*, 872 F.2d 971, 973 (11th Cir. 1989)); *Alaska Textile Co. v. Chase Manhattan Bank*, 982 F.2d 813, 816 (2d Cir. 1992) (noting that documents that are nearly the same as those required by the letter of credit are unacceptable for presentation in a letter of credit transaction).

Second, there are also cases claiming to follow the strict compliance standard but supporting rejection only where the discrepancies are such that would create risks for the issuer if

---

41. "Strict compliance" is the standard to be applied under Uniform Commercial Code Article 5. *See* U.C.C. § 5–108(a) (1995).

the bank were to accept the presentation documents. *See Flagship Cruises, Ltd. v. New England Merchants Nat'l Bank of Boston,* 569 F.2d 699, 705 (1st Cir. 1978) ("We do not see these rulings as retreats from rigorous insistence on compliance with letter of credit requirements. They merely recognize that variance between documents specified and documents submitted is not fatal if there is no possibility that the documents could mislead the paying bank to its detriment"); *Crist v. J. Henry Schroder Bank & Trust Co.,* 693 F. Supp. 1429, 1433 (S.D.N.Y. 1988) (where a party who has succeeded by operation of law to the rights of the beneficiary of a letter of credit, refusal was improper, even though the terms of the credit provided for payment only to the beneficiary); *Bank of Cochin, Ltd. v. Manufacturers Hanover Trust Co.,* 612 F. Supp. 1533, 1541 (S.D.N.Y. 1985) (even under the strict compliance standard, a variance is permitted between the documents specified in a letter of credit and the documents presented there under where "there is no possibility that the documents could mislead the paying bank to its detriment"); *Vest,* 996 S.W.2d at 14 (noting that strict compliance does not demand "oppressive perfectionism").

A third standard, without much support in case law, is to analyze the documents for risk to the applicant. *See* INT'L CHAMBER OF COMMERCE, COMM'N ON BANKING TECHNIQUE AND PRACTICE, PUBLICATION NO. 511, UCP 500 & 400 COMPARED 39 (Charles del Busto ed. 1994) (discussion of a standard that would permit "deviations that do not cause ostensible harm" to the applicant); *see also Breathless Assoc. v. First Savings & Loan Assoc.,* 654 F. Supp. 832, 836 (N.D. Tex. 1986) (noting, under the strict compliance standard, "[a] discrepancy . . . should not warrant dishonor unless it reflects an increased likelihood of defective performance or fraud on the part of the beneficiary").

The mirror image approach is problematic because it absolves the bank reviewing the documents of any responsibility to use common sense to determine if the documents, on their face, are related to the transaction or even to review an entire document in the context of the others presented to the bank. On the other hand, the second and third approaches employ a determination-of-harm standard that is too unwieldy. Such an analysis would improperly require the bank to evaluate risks that it might suffer or that might be suffered by the applicant and could undermine the independence of the three contracts that underlie the letter of credit payment scheme by forcing the bank to look beyond the face of the presentation documents.

The Court finds that a moderate, more appropriate standard lies within the UCP 500 itself and the opinions issued by the International Chamber of Commerce Banking Commission. One of the Banking Commission opinions defined the term "consistency" between the letter of credit and the documents presented to the issuing bank as used in Article 13(a) of the UCP to mean that "the whole of the documents must obviously relate to the same transaction, that is to say, that each should bear a relation (link) with the others on its face ..." INT'L CHAMBER OF COMMERCE, BANKING COMM'N, PUBLICATION NO. 371, DECISIONS (1975–1979) OF THE ICC BANKING COMMISSION R. 12 (1980). The Banking Commission rejected the notion that "all of the documents should be *exactly* consistent in their wording." *Id.* (emphasis in original).

A common sense, case-by-case approach would permit minor deviations of a typographical nature because such a letter-for-letter correspondence between the letter of credit and the presentation documents is virtually impossible. *See* INT'L CHAMBER OF COMMERCE, COMM'N ON BANKING TECHNIQUE AND PRACTICE, PUBLICATION NO. 511, UCP 500 & 400 COMPARED 39 (Charles del Busto ed. 1994) noting the difficulty in attaining mirror-image compliance). While the end result of such an analysis may bear a strong resemblance to the relaxed strict compliance standard, the actual calculus used by the issuing bank is not the risk it or the applicant faces but rather, whether the documents bear a rational link to one another. In this way, the issuing bank is required to examine a particular document in light of all documents presented and use common sense but is not required to evaluate risks or go beyond the face of the documents. The Court finds that in this case the Bank of China's listed discrepancies should be analyzed under this standard by determining whether the whole of the documents obviously relate to the transaction on their face.

* * *

Now that these materials have provided some information on the UCP's compliance standard, at least under UCP 500, the discussion returns to the hypothetical involving Thelma. Up until this point, this chapter has discussed only the letter of credit pursuant to which Thelma would make payment for the tea she purchased from ATC. There is, however, a second major component of a documentary sale: a carrier's bill of lading. Just as the letter of credit governs payment for the tea, the bill of lading controls delivery of the tea. Consider the following form bill of lading.[42]

---

42. BRADFORD STONE, 15 WEST'S LEGAL Forms 449–453 (2D ED. 1985).

| COMBINED TRANSPORT PORT TO PORT BILL OF LADING | MOORE McCORMACK LINES, Incorporated | NOT NEGOTIABLE UNLESS CONSIGNED "TO ORDER" |

SHIPPER/EXPORTER

SKF INDUSTRIES, INC
1100 FIRST AVENUE
KING OF PRUSSIA, PA 19406

DOCUMENT NO.

EXPORT REFERENCES

EXPORT DEC. NO.

CONSIGNEE
ORDER OF

BANCO DO BRAZIL, S.A.
RIO DE JANEIRO, BRAZIL

FORWARDING AGENT - REFERENCES

PIERCE BYRON, INC.   FMC NO.
325 CHESTNUT ST. PHILA., PA

POINT AND COUNTRY OF ORIGIN

NOTIFY PARTY

COMPANHIA IMPORTADORA BRASILEIRA
CAIXA POSTAL 10
RIO DE JANEIRO, BRAZIL

DOMESTIC ROUTING/EXPORT INSTRUCTIONS

DELIVERY TO STEAMER
BY DELAIR TRUCKING CO.

PRECARRIAGE BY	PLACE OF RECEIPT	
PACKER AVENUE		ONWARD INLAND ROUTING
EXPORTING CARRIER (SHIP) USA FLAG	PORT OF LOADING	
S/S MORMACOAK AM	PHILA., PA	
PORT OF DISCHARGE	PLACE OF DELIVERY	
RIO DE JANEIRO		

PARTICULARS FURNISHED BY SHIPPER OF GOODS

MARKS AND NUMBERS	NO. OF PKGS.	SHIPPERS DESCRIPTION OF PACKAGES AND GOODS	GROSS WEIGHT KILOS	POUNDS	MEASUREMENT
C.I.B. RIO DE JANEIRO #1/25	25	(TWENTY-FIVE) CASES OF: STEEL AND ROLLER BEARINGS "IMPORT LICENSE DG-59/10000 EXPIRES FEBRUARY 28, 1984" LETTER OF CREDIT NO E4450/164 "EVIDENCING SHIPMENT OF 1200 BALL BEARINGS NO 187-B AND 2400 ROLLER BEARINGS NO 839-R" FREIGHT PREPAID "ON BOARD" JANUARY 12, 1984 "O R I G I N A L"	2272 KGS	5010 LBS	

FREIGHT TO BE PREPAID IN U.S.A.

ITEM	WEIGHT (2)	CUBIC FEET (3)	@ RATE	FREIGHT CHARGES	TY PC/ RATE	TYPE BRKGE	TYPE CARGO	COMMODITY NO.	PP # COLL.	COLLECT PORT	ACCOUNT CODE
	5010 LBS.		$70.00	156. 50							
		(per 2240 LBS)									
	TERMINAL CHARGE			10. 00							

EXCESS VALUATION (See reverse side)

| Freight to be COLLECTED $ | Freight to be PREPAID $ | $166.50 |

IN ACCEPTING THIS BILL OF LADING, the Merchant expressly accepts and agrees to be bound by all its terms, conditions, exceptions, limitations, exemptions and liberties, whether printed, typed, stamped, endorsed or written, or otherwise incorporated, either on the front or back hereof.

MOORE McCORMACK LINES, Incorporated

	JANUARY	12	1984	5
By	MONTH	DAY	YEAR	[D631]

[Front]

SHORT FORM BILL OF LADING

Received the Goods, or containers, vans, trailers, vehicles, transportable tanks, flats, palletized units, skids, platforms, frames, cradles, sling-loads or other packages said to contain the Goods herein mentioned in apparent external good order and condition, except as otherwise indicated herein, to be transported to the port of discharge named herein and/or such port or place as authorized or permitted hereby or so near thereunto as the vessel can get, lie and leave, always in safety and afloat under all conditions of tide, water and weather and there to be delivered to the Merchant or on-Carrier on payment of all charges due thereon.

This short form Bill of Lading issued for the Merchant's convenience and at its request instead of the Carrier's regular long form Bill of Lading, shall have effect subject to the provisions of the United States Carriage of Goods by Sea Act approved April 16, 1936 or, if this Bill of Lading is issued in any other locality where there is in force a compulsorily applicable Carriage of Goods by Sea Act, Ordinance or Statute of a nature similar to the International Convention for the Unification of Certain Rules Relating to Bills of Lading, dated at Brussels, August 25, 1924, it shall be subject to the provisions of said Act, Ordinance or Statute and rules thereto annexed.

All the terms and conditions of the Carrier's regular long form Bill of Lading, including any clauses presently being printed, typed, stamped, endorsed or written thereon, are incorporated herein by reference with the same force and effect as if they were written at length herein, and all such terms and conditions so incorporated by reference are agreed by Merchant to be binding and to govern the relations, whatever they may be, between all who are or may become parties or holders of this Bill of Lading or owners of the Goods, or containers or other packages covered thereby, as fully as if this Bill of Lading had been prepared on the Carrier's regular long form Bill of Lading.

At all times when the Goods, or containers or other packages are in the care, custody or control of a participating Carrier, such Carrier shall be entitled to all the rights, privileges, liens, limitations of and exonerations from liability, granted or permitted to such participating Carrier under its Bill(s) of Lading, tariff(s) and law compulsorily applicable, and nothing contained in this Bill of Lading shall be deemed a surrender thereof by such participating Carrier.

Each Carrier shall, subject to the terms and conditions of this Bill of Lading and the applicable tariffs, laws, rules and regulations, be responsible for any loss or damage to the Goods, or containers or other packages only during the time the Goods, or containers or other packages are in its actual care, custody and control, except as otherwise expressly provided herein.

In making any arrangements for transportation by participating Carriers of the Goods, or containers or other packages carried hereunder, either before or after ocean carriage, it is understood and agreed that the ocean Carrier acts solely as agent of the Merchant, without any other responsibility whatsoever as Carrier for such transportation.

The Merchant's attention is directed to the fact that the Carrier's regular long form Bill of Lading contains a number of provisions giving the Carrier and participating Carriers certain rights and privileges and certain exemptions and immunities from and limitations of liability additional to those provided by the said United States Carriage of Goods by Sea Act, 1936 and/or Convention and/or such other Act, Ordinance or Statute as may be applicable and, in addition, extends the benefit of its provisions to-stevedores and other independent contractors. The Carrier's regular

long form Bill of Lading is on file with the Federal Maritime Commission and Interstate Commerce Commission in Washington, D.C. and copies can be obtained from the Carrier or from the Federal Maritime Commission or, if covering Intermodal Transportation, from the Interstate Commerce Commission if applicable.

In case of any loss or damage to or in connection with Goods exceeding in actual value the equivalent of $500 lawful money of the United States, per package, or in case of Goods not shipped in packages, per shipping unit, the value of the Goods shall be deemed to be $500 per package or per shipping unit. The Carrier's liability, if any, shall be determined on the basis of a value of $500 per package or per shipping unit or pro rata in case of partial loss or damage, unless the nature of the Goods and a valuation higher than $500 per package or per shipping unit shall have been declared in writing by the shipper before shipment and inserted in this Bill of Lading, and extra freight or charge paid. In such case, if the actual value of the Goods per package or per shipping unit shall exceed such declared value, the value shall nevertheless be deemed to be declared value and the Carrier's liability, if any, shall not exceed the declared value and any partial loss or damage shall be adjusted pro rata on the basis of such declared value.

The words "shipping unit" shall mean and include physical unit or piece of cargo not shipped in a package, including articles or things of any description whatsoever, except Goods shipped in bulk, and irrespective of weight or measurement unit employed in calculating freight charges.

Where containers, vans, trailers, vehicles, transportable tanks, flats, palletized units, skids, platforms, frames, cradles, sling-loads and other such packages are not packed by the Carrier, each individual such container, van, trailer, vehicle, transportable tank, palletized unit, skid, platform, frame, cradle, sling-load and other such package, including in each instance its contents, shall be deemed a single package and Carrier's liability limited to $500 with respect to each such package.

A signed original Bill of Lading, duly endorsed, must be surrendered to the Carrier on delivery of the Goods, or container or other packages.

All agreements with respect to the Goods, or containers or other packages carried hereunder are superseded hereby and none of the terms hereof shall be deemed waived or surrendered unless in writing and signed by a duly authorized agent of the Carrier.   [D632]

Although UCP 600 briefly mentions bills of lading in Article 20, the UCP does not govern bills of lading. Instead,

> [a]s to regulation of the terms of the bill of lading, i.e., the relationship of the carrier and its customers, this is the subject of three international conventions and two United States federal statutes. The three conventions—the Hague Rules,[43] the Hague/Visby Rules,[44] and the Hamburg Rules,[45] respectively—all cover the same subject matter, but are progressively more customer-oriented. The United States has enacted the Hague Rules into its domestic law as the Carriage of Goods by Sea Act (COGSA), but also has non-conforming pre-COGSA legislation (the Harter Act) in force. English law is based on the Hague/Visby Rules.[46]

Note that the sample bill of lading reproduced on the prior pages is negotiable. A negotiable bill of lading allows the goods to follow the paper, in that the bill of lading can be sold while the goods are in transit, giving the bill's new owner the right to either demand delivery of the goods or have them delivered to whomever he or she designates. Thus, in Thelma's case, she could choose to sell the bill of lading to another tea shop.

Questions

1. In Thelma's letter-of-credit transaction, who is the applicant and who is the beneficiary? How might the parties choose the banks to serve as the issuer and confirmer? Assume that Thelma has an extensive banking history with a small local credit union that provides excellent customer service. What would be the benefits and challenges of using a larger national bank for this transaction?

2. After reading the excerpt from the *Voest-Alpine Trading Co.* case, what, in your own words, is the "mirror image" standard and why might it fairly be criticized as absolving banks of the obligation to exercise common sense?[47] How would you describe the standard that the court adopts?

3. The *Voest-Alpine Trading Co.* case was decided under UCP 500, and the excerpt begins with a quote from Article 13(a). The

---

43. The Hague Rules, which date to 1924, can be found on various web sites including http://www.admiraltylawguide.com/conven/haguerules1924.html.

44. The Hague/Visby Rules, which were established in 1968, can be found at http://www.jus.uio.no/lm/sea.carriage.hague.visby.rules.1968/doc.html.

45. The Hamburg Rules, also known as the United Nations Convention on the Carriage of Goods by Sea, date back to 1978 and can be found at http://www.admiraltylaw.com/statutes/hamburg.html.

46. Ralph H. Folsom, et al., International Business Transactions: A Problem-Oriented Coursebook 114 (10th ed. 2009) (part of Problem 4.2, which provides a more comprehensive introduction to bills of lading than the brief materials in this chapter).

47. *See supra* page 245.

corresponding language in UCP 600 is found in Article 14, which reads in pertinent part as follows:

UPC Article 14

Standard for examination of documents

(a) [A] confirming bank, if any, and the issuing bank must examine a presentation to determine, on the basis of the documents alone, whether or not the documents appear on their face to constitute a complying presentation.

* * *

(d) Data in a document, when read in context with the credit, the document itself and international standard banking practice, need not be identical to, but must not conflict with, data in that document, any other stipulated document, or the credit.

(e) In documents other than the commercial invoice, the description of the goods, services, or performance, if stated, may be in general terms not conflicting with their description in the credit.

* * *

(g) A document presented but not required by the credit will be disregarded and may be returned to the presenter.

What differences do you discern between UCP 500 and UCP 600's treatment of the same subject matter? In UCP 600 Article 14(e), why does it make sense to treat the commercial invoice differently from other documents?

4. Based on the form bill of lading provided earlier in this section, who would be listed as the shipper and to whose order should the bill of lading be consigned, in Thelma's transaction?

5. Building on the prior question, read through the "fine print" terms and conditions in the form bill of lading. What should Thelma do to make sure the carrier is liable for the full purchase price of the tea if it is lost or destroyed in transit?

PROBLEM 4

The following are selected terms from a commercial letter-of-credit application used by California Bank & Trust.[48] Imagine that you are an in-house attorney for California Bank & Trust and that the bank, in an effort to simplify its commercial contracts, has asked you to consider shortening this document. What purpose does

---

48. This form is available on the Internet at http://www.calbanktrust.com/ products/products/ibg/jpdfs/LCAPP0906. pdf.

each paragraph currently serve? Is there any language that you would be willing to eliminate? Why or why not?

COMMERCIAL LETTER OF CREDIT AGREEMENT

To: California Bank & Trust

In consideration of your opening at our request a commercial letter of credit (the "Credit"), we hereby agree (the "Agreement") with you as follows:

1. We promise to pay to you, or order, upon demand in lawful money of the United States of America all monies paid by you under or pursuant to said Credit, together with interest, commission and all customary charges: and we agree at least one day before the same is due to provide you with funds to meet all such disbursements or payments. In the event that any sums paid by you hereunder are obtained by you through discount of bills of exchange drawn by us and accepted by you, we promise to pay to you, or order, such sums upon demand or when due in accordance with the terms of each such bill of exchange accepted by you. If any amounts paid or payable under or in respect of said Credit are in any currency other than United States currency, the amount payable or provided by us to you or chargeable by you hereunder may be, at your election, either in such other currency or the equivalent in United States currency computed at the rate you would at the time sell such other currency for United States currency. Past due amounts of any kind shall bear interest at the rate of three percent (3%) per annum above the prime rate. The "prime rate" shall mean the rate of interest established by you from time to time as your prime rate, which may not necessarily be the lowest rate charged by you to your borrowers. You are authorized without prior notice to charge any or all of our deposit accounts with you for all required payments and reimbursements under this Agreement.

2. All goods and documents which shall become into your control or into your possession or that of any of your correspondents as the result of opening or in connection with any transactions under said Credit, are and shall be pledged to you as security (a) for all payments made or to be made by you or your correspondents under said Credit; (b) for any interest, commission or other customary charges in relation to said Credit and (c) for any other obligations of us to you. Upon any default by us in any of the undertakings set forth in this Agreement, you are authorized to sell, without notice to us, at public or private sale, any of such pledged goods or documents: in the event of any deficiency, we will pay the same to you

immediately or in the event of any surplus, you shall pay the same to us or to the persons entitled thereto.

* * *

4. We will obtain, or will cause to be in existence: insurance on any goods described in said Credit against fire and other usual risk and against any additional risks which you may request. You are hereby authorized and empowered to collect the amount due under any such insurance and apply the same against any of our obligations to you arising under said Credit or otherwise.

* * *

7. You and your correspondents shall be entitled to make payments under said Credit if the documents presented there under appear on their face to be in accordance with the terms and conditions of said Credit; and neither you nor your correspondents shall be liable or responsible for the form, sufficiency, accuracy, genuineness, falsification or legal effect of any documents, or for the authority of any persons signing the documents, or for the good faith or acts or omissions, solvency, performance or standing of the beneficiary or any other person whomsoever, including performance of the underlying contract or other transaction between us and the beneficiary. Furthermore, you and your correspondents shall not have any liability or responsibility for the consequences arising out of delay or loss in transit of any messages, drafts or documents, or for any delay, interruption, mutilation or other error arising in the transmission of any telecommunication, or for errors in translation or interpretation of any message or documents relating to said Credit. You and your correspondents shall not be liable for any failure to pay or accept any draft under the Credit resulting from any law or restriction exercised by any domestic or foreign government, any court order, or any other cause beyond your control. Any and all claims by us for improper payment, dishonor or other actions or inaction by you shall be made by written notice within sixty (60) days of the contested action or inaction or such claim is waived. Any and all proceedings to recover from you or your correspondents must be made within one (1) year from the date of said notice or said claim shall be deemed waived.

* * *

11. You may, in your discretion, arrange for the direct or indirect participation by other financial institutions in the issuance of said Credit or provide for the assignment or transfer to and assumption by other financial institutions of all or some portion of your liability under said Credit; and you may

assign or transfer this Agreement or all or any portion of your rights hereunder, and any instrument(s) evidencing all or any portion of your liability under said Credit, and you may deliver all or any of the property then held as security for our obligations hereunder, to the assignee(s) or transferee(s), who shall thereupon become vested with all the powers and rights in respect thereto given you herein or in the instrument(s) assigned or transferred, and you shall thereafter be forever relieved and fully discharged from all liability or responsibility with respect thereto, but you shall retain all rights and powers hereby given with respect to any and all instrument(s), rights or property not so assigned or transferred.

* * *

14. You shall not be liable for any failure by your correspondents to pay or accept any draft under the Credit resulting from any law or restriction exercised by any domestic or foreign government or from any other cause beyond your control or your correspondents', and we agree to indemnify and hold you harmless from any claim, loss, liability or expense arising by reason of any such failure to pay.

Chapter 9

BANKRUPTCY

Bankruptcy can result from two different types of insolvency. One is simply owing more in debt than one possesses in assets. The more common type of insolvency is having an inadequate cash flow to meet obligations as they come due. An individual or an entity might have more assets than liabilities, but if the principal assets are illiquid, this can lead to the situation where that party cannot meet its current obligations.

There are several dangers in this situation. When assets are foreclosed upon or levied upon to enforce liens or judgments, they are subject to a forced sale which for various reasons is not calculated to produce a fair market price. For example, there is no standard warranty of title (*see* UCC § 2–312(2)), and third parties are generally unwilling to participate in such auctions unless they believe they are getting an outstanding bargain. When numerous creditors are scrambling to find assets upon which to execute or trying to enforce security interests in property in which other creditors also have or claim an interest, a great deal of energy and expense can be devoted to these creditors' disputes. One purpose of bankruptcy law is to provide procedures for orderly and efficient assembly and sale of assets and distribution of proceeds.

The Federal Bankruptcy Act (11 U.S.C.A. § 101 et seq.) provides for two distinct outcomes for business entities. In a Chapter 7 proceeding, the debtor is liquidated with all assets being collected and used to pay expenses and make distributions to creditors. In a Chapter 11 proceeding a business entity debtor may be "reorganized," shedding liabilities and unwanted executory contracts so that it might continue as a going business and emerge from bankruptcy with a better net cash flow and debt to asset ratio. These Chapter 11 proceedings permit the use of the bankruptcy law as a business planning tool.

To see how this might work in practice, assume the following hypothetical.

THE HYPOTHETICAL—HARRY'S CAFÉ'S

Harry successfully opens and operates a café which he modestly calls "Harry's." Success leads to expansion and soon Harry has leased ten locations in which he has opened "Harry's" cafés. Convinced that he has the touch, Harry opens an upscale white-table-cloth restaurant which he calls "Upscale." Harry hires a renowned chef whom he attracts by giving him a three-year contract at a high salary. After opening four "Upscale" restaurants in leased premises, it becomes apparent that while nine of the ten "Harry's" operations are doing well, the "Upscale" operations are bleeding cash in part due to the extravagance of the new chef. As the level of debt piles up, it becomes time to consider bankruptcy.

The goal is to keep nine of the ten "Harry's" cafés. (The tenth one operates in what has turned out to be a bad location.) This involves keeping the nine leases, all of the "Harry's" employees and most of the supply contracts for items such as food. The party who has a long-term contract for linen services has proved difficult and it would be nice to get rid of that contract. The goal is to close all of the "Upscale" restaurants cancelling the leases and terminating the expensive chef and those employees who cannot conveniently be moved to a "Harry's" operation. Various creditors have security interests in personal property and fixtures which gives them the right to repossess these items if provision is not made for the payment of these loans. Of course, there are also numerous general unsecured trade creditors.

Upon filing bankruptcy under Chapter 11, Harry seeks appointment as a debtor in possession (DIP), meaning that he can continue to run his business subject to approval by the bankruptcy court of any actions that are outside the ordinary course of business. He also gains protection from an automatic protective order that enjoins creditors from proceeding to take possession of property, attach accounts or otherwise attempt to enforce their claims. Under a Chapter 11 bankruptcy, the debtor in possession has all of the rights that a trustee would have, including the power to assume or reject executory contracts. (11 U.S.C.A. §§ 365(a) and 1107). The next step will be to present to the court a list of those leases and contracts that Harry wishes to continue which includes such things as the nine leases for "Harry's" locations, the purchase contracts for necessary fixtures and equipment at these locations, and the desired contracts such as those described above for food. The list of contracts and leases to be terminated includes all those relating to the other locations that Harry wishes to close. It also includes the chef and the linen supply company.

While the Act allows the debtor in possession to continue to carry on his business using his own judgment, the rejection of executory contracts and unexpired leases requires court approval (11 U.S.C.A. § 365(a)). The most commonly used test for approval of rejection is the "business judgement" test in which the focus is upon whether or not rejection would benefit the pool of unsecured creditors who seek a dividend from the estate. The alternative test is the "burdensome" test. The difference is apparent in the example of an executory contract to sell a property at a price that exceeds its book value but is below its current market value. Sound business judgement would dictate that one cancel this contract whereas it is not technically burdensome since the property is being sold at a profit. These were the facts in the matter of *In re Chi-Feng Huang*, 23 B.R. 798 (9th Cir. 1982) where the court stated:

> We believe rejection of the burdensome test in favor of the 'business judgment' rule is dictated by logic as much as by precedent. We agree with Professor Krasnowiecki's view of the burdensome test:
>
>> Whatever the support for that view, it does not seem to be too persuasive. The purpose of the power to reject is to augment the estate of the debtor. For this purpose, there seems to be no difference between an obligation which consumes cash, and an obligation which, because of its depressive effect on a particular asset or because of its undervaluation of that asset consumes a part of the value of that asset. In the end the latter will turn up as a net reduction in cash to pay the creditors.
>
> Krasnowiecki, The Impact of the New Bankruptcy Reform Act on Real Estate Development and Financing, 53 Am. Bankr. L.J. 363.382 (1979).

(*Id.* at 800–801.) In some jurisdictions rejection of executory contracts will be disallowed where the party whose contract is to be rejected would be damaged disproportionately to any benefit to be derived by the general creditors of the estate. For an example of this unusual situation, see *In re Petur U.S.A. Instruments*, 35 B.R. 561 (W.D. Wash. 1983). The party whose contract or lease is terminated can file a creditor's claim for the damages suffered due to the cancellation. Per the facts of the hypothetical, Harry would likely be able to reject any unprofitable lease or service contract, as well as terminate an employee.

Harry will present the court with a plan whereby his business can be brought out of bankruptcy protection. This might include an extended period of time in which the nine "Harry's" cafés will continue to operate and earn profits from which existing creditors will gradually be paid. It may involve the court ordering that creditors be paid only a percentage of the total amount owing to them, and their claims may also be repaid without interest. Harry can negotiate with an existing creditor or with a new lender for a DIP loan. New lenders or existing creditors will be willing to loan the debtor more money notwithstanding his bankruptcy because the court can give the new loans priority over existing secured and unsecured claims.

There are two justifications for a law that permits Harry to continue a going business while creditors are at least temporarily left without payment and perhaps ultimately repaid only a fraction of what is owing to them.

First, had Harry's business been liquidated, assets of the restaurants such as equipment would likely be sold for a small fraction of cost or market value and what was received would go first to those creditors who had a security interest in those goods and fixtures, and they most likely would not be paid in full. The potential cash flow of the nine profitable "Harry's" cafés would be lost if the entire business is terminated. Liquidation could thus leave all creditors worse off than the results of the bankruptcy proceedings.

Second, the effect of keeping the nine "Harry's" restaurants operating is that many employees retain their jobs and the community continues to enjoy the services that these restaurants provide. There are various societal benefits that result from keeping a local business in operation. There is also an obvious benefit to Harry.

Expertise in bankruptcy law is a necessary aspect of a business law practice in the US today. In a real sense it is a necessary aspect of business planning for Harry. It certainly allows Harry to take risks that he might not take if the benefits of bankruptcy proceedings were not available to him. Planning for the possibility of bankruptcy proceedings is also a necessary activity for merchants or lenders who extend credit and for landlords who might themselves borrow money and erect buildings in reliance upon long-term leases. Because of the numerous examples of small and large businesses that have gone into bankruptcy and survived to continue their operations in the community, the stigma that was once attached to a bankruptcy proceeding in the US has largely disappeared. People have accepted the fact of flying on bankrupt airlines and will presumably also buy cars or other durable goods from manufacturers in bankruptcy.

Much is written about the entrepreneurial spirit of individuals in the US. We have a history of start up businesses that expand overnight into major enterprises. One factor that permits this risk taking conduct is the fact that the worst that can happen is that one loses the investment, and perhaps other personal assets, but comes out debt free and able to try again.

Contrast to Other Systems

To understand a fundamentally different societal approach to bankruptcy, it is informative to consider the law in Germany before 1999. The purpose of bankruptcy proceedings was to assemble the assets of the debtor, liquidate those assets, and pay creditors. If the creditors of a business entity were not satisfied as to 100% of their claims, the claims remained owing and the entity was simply terminated or abandoned. Assuming no personal liability, this would effectively end the chances of enforcing the obligations. However, if the obligations of an individual who became bankrupt were not 100% satisfied, the individual debtor remained liable for the rest of his or her life. The result was that this individual was often frozen out of the regular job market, living in a shadow economy where cash is the only currency. Not only did German law not provide for the continuation of a bankrupt business, there was not even an acceptance of the notion of discharging the debtor from further liability.

The potential societal benefits of preserving a continuing business in the community were lost. Jobs were lost. In fact, creditors suffered in circumstances where the monies made available in a liquidation were less than what might have been received had a restructured business continued in operation. The profits of the nine remaining "Harry's" cafés could be used to satisfy at least partially some creditors' claims that might have gone wholly unpaid had the whole little restaurant chain been completely closed.

One can readily appreciate the impact of the pre-1999 law upon risk taking in Germany. When the German citizen with the talents of a Steve Jobs or Bill Gates considered the possibility of starting a new business in a new industry, the threat of a lifetime spent as a debtor might discourage all but the most daring. On the other hand, the US concept of "piercing the corporate veil" to hold individual shareholders or executives liable for corporate debt was not a German practice. This difference may be in part compensation for the concept of non-dischargeable obligations.

THOMAS J. SALERNO, "REORGANIZATION OF THE FINANCIALLY DISTRESSED BUSINESS IN THE US—JUST HOW FAR AFIELD IS IT FROM THE REST OF THE WORLD?"

Global Insolvency & Restructuring Yearbook 2008/2009 at page 71
Published by Euromoney Institutional Investor PLC (London).
Republished with permission

Overview of US chapter 11 reorganization

The US Bankruptcy Code, as it applies to businesses, is perhaps the most "debtor friendly" in the world. That may not be surprising, given the proclivities of the US's founding fathers, persecuted English colonists residing in the miscreant caste of English society. Many of the original English settlers had themselves spent time in debtors prisons and came to view the hardships of the New World as, at worst, an even exchange for the English penal system. From this tradition, the US developed arguably the world's most liberal bankruptcy laws. Many commentators describe US insolvency law as embodying a "rescue culture" approach to bankruptcy—*i.e.* US bankruptcy laws aim at rescuing the financially distressed business so that it can continue as a productive economic unit rather than punish those who allowed the business to flounder in the first place.[1] Chapter 11 in the US, is, ideally, judicially supervised negotiation between and among debtors and creditors, not litigation or debt-collection.

What of "Bad Debtors"?

US bankruptcy law does still contemplate punishment for those who abuse the bankruptcy laws, lie to the court, or commit bankruptcy crimes (either before or after filing the bankruptcy). Such "bad debtors" are dealt with not only within the federal Criminal Code (Title 18 of the US Code) but also under state statutes and common law. Lawsuits and criminal prosecutions for fraud, embezzlement, securities and tax fraud, and other similar misdeeds are more common than an outsider might believe. US newspapers follow closely the criminal prosecutions of the masterminds behind the Enron, Adelphia, Tyco, and Qwest debacles (involving "creative" financing mechanisms to mask the companies' true financial condition and egregious examples of corporate looting). Bankruptcy crimes are prosecuted by the US Department of Justice and include

---

1. The very word "bankruptcy" has a penal connotation. "Bankruptcy" is derived from the Latin *banca rota*, meaning "broken bench," and is used to signify financial distress because of a peculiar practice in ancient Rome. Merchants unable to pay their debts were prohibited from selling their wares in the marketplace. When their creditors complained, the authorities would physically break the bench or stall from which the financially troubled merchant would conduct his business.

filing bankruptcy petitions without disclosing all one's assets, hiding assets, or filing numerous bankruptcy petitions for improper purposes. These crimes carry monetary penalties (such as fines and sanctions) and, for some, criminal penalties (such as incarceration).

US bankruptcy law does not punish the "wrongdoer" at the expense of saving the business. Such an approach—throwing the "baby out with the bath water"—would result in protracted liquidations that often harm the very constituency (the creditors) the process should protect. The counterintuitive nature of such an approach is self-evident. If a business owes creditors but is legally precluded from making money to repay at least some of what it owes, creditor recoveries are obviously minimised. Perhaps the creditors feel vindicated when the debtor has been punished, but with no financial recovery, that vindication is hollow. Fraudulent or grossly incompetent management is displaced in a Chapter 11 reorganisation—just not (necessarily) at the very outset and certainly not automatically.

When is a "Bankruptcy" not a "Bankruptcy"?

Although most nations strictly differentiate between a "reorganisation" proceeding and a "bankruptcy" proceeding—the primary difference being liquidation as a foregone conclusion versus an attempt to negotiate some business workout plan that allows the business to survive as a going concern—US bankruptcy law considers all formally commenced proceedings under the US Bankruptcy Code as "bankruptcy" proceedings. Within that broad category, a financially distressed business may seek a straight liquidation, run by a third party fiduciary trustee (a Chapter 7 bankruptcy), or a "reorganisation" proceeding, run under Bankruptcy Court supervision by existing management (a Chapter 11 proceeding). Many nations' laws would not consider, at the outset, a reorganisation proceeding as a "bankruptcy proceeding" because of the intense stigma associated with "bankruptcy."

Over the last 30 years, that stigma has abated in the US such that a reorganisation proceeding has come to be viewed as a viable and responsible business tool. The larger recent US bankruptcies demonstrate both the breadth of industries involved in bankruptcy proceedings and the extent to which the traditional "stigma" of bankruptcy has fallen away in the US. Since 1980, there have been over 30 Chapter 11 bankruptcies involving over US$1bn in assets. Although the number of Chapter 11 filings is presently down, many cases (in terms of both debt and assets) are enormous. For example, in the relatively good economic times of 2005 and 2006, the ten largest bankruptcy filings of public companies involved businesses with combined annual revenues of US$102.8bn, total liabilities of over US$140bn, and over half a million employees.[2]

Chapter 11 Reorganisation under US Law

In contrast to a Chapter 7 bankruptcy, in which the debtor liquidates its assets for the benefit of its creditors and terminates its business operations, a Chapter 11 proceeding permits a business to continue operating despite its inability to meet its current obligations to its creditors. A Chapter 11 proceeding is most often used to restructure a business's debts (by satisfying or extending existing debt in one fashion or another), enabling the business to continue operating after the bankruptcy proceeding concludes.

How is it started?

Although individuals may qualify for relief under Chapter 11, the typical Chapter 11 debtor is a business, which can be organised as a corporation, partnership, limited liability company, or other type of business entity. A Chapter 11 proceeding is commenced with the filing of a petition for relief. The business to be reorganised may file the petition itself (a "voluntary petition"), or a group of creditors may file a petition on the business's behalf (an "involuntary petition"). Voluntary filings are most common.

The automatic stay

The filing of a voluntary petition (or an order for relief following an involuntary petition) invokes the "automatic stay," a judicial injunction prohibiting all creditors and parties from proceeding against the debtor or its assets outside of the bankruptcy proceeding without the bankruptcy court's express consent. The automatic stay stops all lawsuits against the debtor (at least temporarily) and stops all collection activity against the debtor's assets and pledged collateral. The automatic stay binds all creditors, even those unaware of the bankruptcy filing, all creditors within the US, and even those creditors outside of the US with material business operations in the US. The automatic stay is intended to give the distressed debtor a "breathing spell" so that it may concentrate on reorganising its financial affairs without the time and expense of defending litigation in various jurisdictions.

Who controls the business?

Once the bankruptcy court issues an Order for Relief (which is automatic on the filing of a voluntary petition), the debtor is typically permitted to continue running its business as a "debtor-in-possession" or "DIP." The bankruptcy court may appoint a trustee to replace the DIP only if there is evidence of the debtor's

---

2. *See* 2007 Bankruptcy Yearbook & Almanac (New Generation Research 17th Ed.) at 44–45.

existing management's fraud or gross incompetence. The Bankruptcy Code presumes that existing management can best maximise the value of the troubled business' assets and that bringing in a trustee does not usually maximise value, and may reduce it.

To ensure that creditors and the debtor's equity holders are adequately represented, the bankruptcy court may appoint one or more committees to advocate for the interests of similarly-situated parties (such as an Unsecured Creditors Committee), and whose professional fees (attorneys, financial advisors, etc.) are typically paid out of the debtor's assets. Chapter 11 proceedings usually require heavy professional involvement. Where a debtor has more than US$5m in unsecured debt, or where cause exists, the bankruptcy court may also appoint an examiner who is not a trustee but who has powers (enumerated by the court) to investigate certain aspects of a debtor.

Interim operations in Chapter 11

How does a DIP operate its business while it negotiates with creditors concerning a plan of reorganisation (discussed below)? Existing management continues to run the business and make business decisions for the debtor. So-called "ordinary course" types of transactions (such as ordinary sales if the debtor's business is to make such sales) and operations are permitted without bankruptcy court approval. Extraordinary transactions (such as major sales of assets outside of the ordinary course of business, retention of professionals, settlement of claims) are subject to approval by the bankruptcy court after notice to all parties.

Creditors with a security interest in the debtor's cash, or cash-equivalent types of collateral such as accounts receivable or contract rights, have a say in how that cash is spent during the proceeding. The debtor company may only use such cash (called "cash collateral" in the Bankruptcy Code) with the secured creditor's consent and under appropriate budgets and other safeguards or, absent consent, the debtor may get bankruptcy court approval to use the cash by showing that the secured creditor will not be materially harmed by the cash collateral use.

"DIP financing"

If cash collateral use is not sufficient for the continued operation of the debtor's business, the Bankruptcy Code allows a debtor to borrow from lenders post-bankruptcy. This is commonly referred to as "DIP financing." DIP financing is an extraordinary tool. If a debtor does not have otherwise unencumbered collateral, the bankruptcy court may approve a post-bankruptcy lender making a loan secured by a first lien against the debtor's assets even without the consent of existing lien holders. This is known as "super-priority financing." This is not done lightly, but in appropriate circumstances it is done to save a business.

While observers outside of the US marvel that any lender would lend to a company in bankruptcy, in fact, with the proper asset base and bankruptcy court protections, a debtor often has its choice of several potential DIP financing sources who may compete to make the loan. The reason is simple: unlike lending to a financially distressed business that has not yet gone into a bankruptcy (where no one knows what will happen), a lender that lends to a DIP will have a court-adjudicated lien and first right to all of the assets in the bankruptcy. There are institutions that have been established for the sole purpose of lending to DIPs and investing (through the plan of reorganisation) in companies emerging from Chapter 11.

Sales free and clear of liens

Finally, US bankruptcy laws permit a DIP to sell encumbered assets even if the sale would not result in sufficient proceeds to satisfy all creditors with a lien against the sold asset. This is known as "sales free and clear of liens," and can only be done on bankruptcy court approval with the liens attaching to the sales proceeds in the same order of priority as they exist on the asset. The secured lenders have the right to "credit bid" in such a sale— *i.e.* they can offer to buy the asset from the debtor by giving a credit against their liens instead of paying cash. This is a way for a DIP to maximise asset value as part of a reorganisation without having a "fire sale" liquidation, which tends to minimise value.

The plan of reorganisation

The primary goal of a Chapter 11 proceeding is the formulation and court approval of a "plan of reorganisation," which provides a blueprint for the satisfaction of all the debtor's existing debts using the Bankruptcy Code's method of classifying different types of creditors. Under such a plan, creditors of similar type (for example, unsecured trade creditors) are placed in a "class" and every member of that class must receive the same treatment under the plan. Holders of equity interests, such as shareholders, are placed in a separate class from all creditors. Certain types of debts are given priority over others (such as certain tax and employee claims), and Chapter 11 requires that all debts in a class with priority over a second class must be satisfied in full before the second class may receive any return on account of its debts.

Types of reorganisations

Chapter 11 places no restrictions on the type of reorganisation a debtor may pursue, as long as it is otherwise lawful. For example, a debtor's plan may provide that some or all of its assets—unprofitable divisions or product lines—will be sold. Those proceeds will be paid to creditors holding liens against those assets and any remaining proceeds will go to the reorganised debtor to make payments on unsecured debt over time. There is no statutorily required repayment period or amount. In essence, the only prohibition on what a debtor proposes to do in a plan is that the bankruptcy court must find the plan "feasible."

Feasibility means that the bankruptcy court must be convinced that the debtor will be able to make the payments under the plan. The longer the payments go under a plan, the more speculative future payments become, and the heavier the feasibility burden of proof is on the debtor. Having a statutorily prescribed minimum repayment amount or payment term would be to legislate economics. Better that the payment amount be the subject of negotiation with interested parties and the economics of the particular industry. If the law were to require that no plan could be confirmed unless there was a minimum of, say, 30% repayment to creditors within a two-year period, that law, while on its face appearing to protect creditors, would in fact hurt creditors. Perhaps the particular industry and prevailing economics could only support an 18% payment over a three-year period. The going concern nature of the distressed business (and the jobs that go with it) should not be lost because a legislature has arbitrarily set minimum recoveries or prescribed payments periods.

The "exclusivity period"

For a limited period, only the debtor has the right to propose a plan of reorganisation, solicit accepting votes from creditors and equity interest holders, and seek approval of the plan from the bankruptcy court (called "confirmation"). If this "exclusivity period" expires without the debtor having obtained an order confirming a plan, other parties, including one or more creditors, may propose and solicit votes on another plan. There is no set deadline by which any party must propose a plan or obtain confirmation of a plan. On average, Chapter 11 proceedings last approximately 22 months, with some lasting many years.

The confirmation process

In order to obtain confirmation of a plan, the debtor must follow a two-step process. First, the plan proponent must draft and file with the bankruptcy court a disclosure statement, which acts as a sort of prospectus given to all creditors to solicit their vote on the plan. The disclosure statement must contain "reasonably adequate information," and the parties in the Chapter 11 proceeding have a right to review and comment on the disclosure statement before the bankruptcy court approves it. It is not unusual in a Chapter 11 proceeding for the debtor to file a disclosure statement and for parties (such as official committees or others) to complain to the bankruptcy court that the disclosure statement does not contain adequate information. If so, the bankruptcy court usually requires the debtor to amend or supplement the disclosure statement as a condition to its approval.

Second, once the disclosure statement is approved, the debtor then solicits votes on its plan of reorganisation. The debtor mails the plan (and the disclosure statement, along with a ballot, to all creditors whose rights are impaired by the plan and are, therefore, entitled to vote to accept or reject the plan. Voting is by class. A secured creditor is usually classified by itself, whereas other creditors (such as general unsecured creditors) are usually classified together in one large class.

Creditor votes received by the deadline set by the bankruptcy court are the only votes counted for purposes of determining acceptance or rejection of a plan. A creditor may not vote "no" simply by failing to vote. A class vote is tallied in two ways: in order for a class to accept a proposed plan, more than one-half in number of those voting and more than two-thirds in amount of claims must vote to accept the plan. Voting is always conducted by paper ballot; voting is never conducted in person.

Example: Assume that a class under a plan consists of 1,000 unsecured creditors. When voting is completed, only 10 of the 1,000 creditors actually submitted a ballot. Of those 10, nine creditors are owed US$10.00 each, and the last creditor voting was owed US$100.00. The nine creditors owed US$10.00 each all voted to accept the plan, and the one creditor owed US$100.00 voted to reject plan. When the class' votes are tabulated, the plan obviously received accepting votes of more than one-half in number of the creditors—here, nine out of 10 of creditors voted to accept the plan. The class would not be deemed to have accepted the plan, however, because the class must also contain accepting votes of more than two-thirds in amount of claims. Here, a total of US$190.00 in claims voted. US$90.00 of the US$190.00 voted to accept, but two-thirds of US$190.00 is US$126.54. Accordingly, the class would not be deemed to have accepted the plan.

"Cramdown"

What happens if a debtor's plan is accepted by some, but not all, classes of creditors? The debtor may still seek bankruptcy court approval of the plan even though all creditor classes have not voted to accept it. As long as the debtor has the acceptance of at least one class of creditors whose rights are impaired by the plan, the debtor can still seek confirmation of the plan using what is known as "cramdown." Cramdown refers to confirmation of a plan in circumstances where not all classes of creditors have voted to accept the plan.

"Cramdown of secured creditors" is accomplished by showing that the secured creditor, despite its rejection of the plan, will eventually be paid the amount of its allowed secured claim in full, with a market rate of interest, secured by the original lien collateralising its claim. "Cramdown of unsecured creditor" classes that do not vote to accept the plan is accomplished by showing that the plan is "fair and equitable," does not discriminate unfairly against the rejecting class of creditors, and does not provide anything on account of claims or interests junior to that class. This last requirement is referred to as the "absolute priority rule." The class junior to unsecured creditors usually comprises the debtor's equity holders. Therefore, absolute priority rule requires that if unsecured creditors are not going to be paid 100% of their claims plus interest, and they do not, as a class, vote to accept the plan that provides for lesser treatment, the stockholders of the debtor may not retain their stock and some third party may have to acquire the new stock in the debtor once it emerges from bankruptcy. At that point, the debtor is known as a "reorganised debtor."

Discharge

On confirmation of a plan, the debtor is freed or "discharged" from all debts and claims of all parties treated under the plan or arising before confirmation of the plan. The debtor's only obligations to pre-bankruptcy creditors are those the debtor assumes under the plan. By way of example, assume that before bankruptcy a debtor had US$1m of total debts. As a result of a confirmed plan, the debts have now been reduced to US$400,000, which the debtor is going to pay over, say, six years. The discharge is granted as of the time the plan is confirmed, and the US$600,000 in debt that is not being paid has been discharged—it has gone away and the debtor is no longer legally bound to pay it. At that point, the debtor's balance sheet has been "deleveraged" in that it has US$600,000 less debt.

How many Chapter 11s succeed and why?

Given the number of Chapter 11 filings that occur in the US, how many of them succeed? The answer could depend on the definition of "succeed." For example, if a Chapter 11 is filed to maintain the going concern nature of a business, and the assets are sold as a going concern (thereby maximising value), and the case then converts to a straight liquidation for the sole purpose of distributing sale proceeds to creditors, is that a successful case or not? If the goal was to maximise value for creditors and maintain a going concern, it would be. That notwithstanding, statistics kept over the last 10 years suggest that, of the cases studied, approximately 17% of all Chapter 11 cases filed resulted in confirmed Chapter 11 plans of reorganisation.[3] Of that 17%, how many go on to become thriving businesses? One study suggested that only 7% continue to be thriving businesses after five years.[4] Of course, a case that might have been liquidated at the outset and survives for five years, employing people and otherwise paying taxes, would qualify as a success in the author's opinion.

Such perspectives aside, however, not a large percentage of Chapter 11 cases result in confirmed plans, and most eventually feature liquidations through the bankruptcy process. Why? Financially distressed companies fall into two broad categories—those with too much debt on their balance sheets (sometimes called "overleveraged companies"), and those that do not make enough money after paying normal operating expenses to pay debt (that is, they have no positive net income after paying general operating expenses exclusive of debt—the "operationally challenged companies"). Chapter 11 can work very well for overleveraged companies, but does nothing to help (and in fact may quicken the demise of) the operationally challenged companies. If the distressed company does not have positive cash flow after it pays its operational expenses to make some debt service, unless it has a clearly-defined exit strategy (such as an imminent sale to a third party or a coherent, attainable operational turnaround plan), the operationally challenged companies will not survive a Chapter 11 bankruptcy, and the filing of a Chapter 11 bankruptcy will only lead to a protracted liquidation.

Creditors can be (and usually are) very vocal about these things in the bankruptcy proceeding. At the outset of a case, the bankruptcy court will usually give the debtor the benefit of the doubt on these issues. If it becomes apparent through the actual operating results during the case that the debtor is truly an operationally challenged company with no bright prospects on the horizon, the bankruptcy court can and usually will shut the business down or replace management with a trustee.

Why hasn't "reorganisation" been adopted in other countries throughout the world?

If reorganisation and the "rescue culture" is such a laudable end, why don't all countries adopt some form of it? Why is it that certain western European countries which have, in fact, adopted a type of reorganisation proceeding, find that it is largely unused in those countries? A notable example is Germany, which has adopted a reorganisation law, yet it is rarely used. Why? The German *"Insol-*

3. *See* Jensen-Conklin, "Do Confirmed Chapter 11 Plans Consummate? The Result of a Study and Analysis of The Law," 97 Comm. L.J. 297 (Fall 1992).

4. "How To Identify The Seven Percent That Succeed After A Chapter 11 Bankruptcy," *IOMA Report On Managing Credit* (April 1, 2004).

venzplan" and *"Eigenverwaltung".*[5] The reorganisation scheme (*"Insolvenzplan"* and *"Eigenverwaltung"*) pursuant to the German Insolvency Act (*Insolvenzordnung*, in force since 1999) is only rarely used despite that these provisions were intended to represent big improvements in German insolvency law.

The main reasons are two-fold: First, German bankruptcy receivers and bankruptcy courts still have little experience in applying the new provisions (despite that German law before 1999 had a type of reorganisation in a separate act—the *"Vergleichsordnung"*—which had a overly complicated and formalistic approach and was rarely used). As such, bankruptcy receivers and courts tend now to do what they have always done—liquidate insolvent companies rather than reorganise them.[6]

Second, together with the passage of the new Insolvency Act in 1999, the German Civil Code was changed with regard to one important provision: the deletion of § 419 BGB (German Civil Code), which attached liability for the seller's debtors against those who acquired a business in its entirety (or any of its major parts). This provision made it rather risky for investors to acquire "healthy" parts of the business from insolvent companies, since doing so carried the risk that the acquirer would be liable for the debts of the entire business. Since the law changed in 1999, reorganisation in Germany mostly occurs through the creation of new companies instead of applying the reorganisation provisions of the Insolvency Act. The "healthy" parts of the business (including brands, trademarks, patents) are sold to a newly-founded company (often through a Management Buyout) which will continue (with a slightly changed name) the business of the insolvent company, often from the same address. The old company is liquidated, and its debt (partly) satisfied with the proceeds from the sale of the "healthy" parts of its business.

"Reorganisation" in the proper sense (*i.e.* under the new law) has been used only in a very limited number of cases. Prominent examples are the Kirch Media Group[7] (formerly Germany's leading

---

5. The author expresses his gratitude to Dr. Jan Curschmann of Taylor Wessing in Hamburg and Dr. Andreas Fillmann of Squire Sanders in Frankfurt for their input and insight into this portion of the materials.

6. As quoted in the *Süddeutsche Zeitung* in its article of March 29, 2004 entitled *"Insolvenzen helfen zucht beim Uberleben"*: Eberhard Baum, senior partner with Schulze & Brauer, thinks that the acceptance of the new possibilities under Germany insolvency law are going to start slow. People still see insol-

vency as time consuming, costly and risky procedures. Since the new law has been used so little, for right now there is a social stigma about insolvency. The old law firms are not well versed in the insolvency field, which can be a liability in itself.

7. *See "Insolvenzen helfen nicht beim Uberleben," Süddeutsche Zeitung* at 7 (March 29, 2004) ("As the media entrepreneur Leo Kirch pulls off a spectacular insolvency, he paves the way for Germany bankruptcy.")

movie trader and private TV company) as well as Babcock (a former major group of companies whose main business was plane engineering).

Why does chapter 11 work?

If one believes that US-style Chapter 11 works as a means to rehabilitate and otherwise rescue financially distressed businesses, is it possible to isolate some of the reasons why it works in the US and does not (or in all events is rarely used) in such places as Germany? The author asserts that Chapter 11 works as a result of the following five factors:

The US has a specialised bankruptcy bench

There are 351 bankruptcy judges in the US. They are judges who are appointed by the Circuit Courts of Appeal for 14–year terms, and hear only bankruptcy matters. As such, they are extremely specialised and, either by virtue of their experience in the law before being appointed to the bankruptcy bench or as a result of their actions on the bench, they know and understand bankruptcy law and fundamental business dynamics. In the US, judges are usually lawyers with many years of practice before being appointed to the bench. Bankruptcy judges see bankruptcy issues every day, some more than others depending on the jurisdiction in which they sit. For the most part, there are very few jury trial rights with respect to disputes that arise in bankruptcy cases. As such, disputes are resolved by bankruptcy judges through "bench trials" on issues in which the bankruptcy judge is well versed (such as valuation of collateral, feasibility of projected financial operations, etc.). Bankruptcy judges tend to be very sophisticated triers of fact.

There are specialised professionals in the US system

Like specialised judges, the last 20 years has seen the development of an entire specialty in US professions relating to bankruptcy and insolvency matters. Indeed, there are subspecialties within the specialty, and there are many lawyers (the author included), and indeed certain lawfirms, that do nothing but Chapter 11 business reorganisation cases. In addition to lawyers, there are other professional groups that have developed over the last 20 years to assist in Chapter 11 cases. They include financial advisors and investment bankers (such as Houlihan Lokey and Chanin Capital), large accounting firms (such as Ernst & Young Corporate Finance and KPMG), "turnaround consultants" and management companies (such as Alix Partners, Alvarez & Marsal, and FTI Consulting) who are hired to advise either the distressed company, lenders, or committees and otherwise monitor the financial aspects of Chapter 11 cases. In addition, there are public relations firms that specialize in assisting financially distressed businesses (such as Sitrick & Co. in Los Angeles).

It is important to note that the specialised bench and specialised professional groups did not arise overnight. The Bankruptcy Code as it is known today only came into existence in 1978. Certainly for the first five to eight years, lawyers and professionals were struggling to find their way with respect to the new law. Over time, and after the transition period was over, professionals found that there was money to be made in this new area, and competent professionals were attracted to the field in the legal and financial areas. The expertise of bankruptcy judges also grew with the level of sophistication of the cases.

Transparent systems

The nature of bankruptcy proceedings in the US is that they are public, and creditors and other interested parties can easily obtain information about bankruptcy cases (which for the most part are public records). The obligations to list all creditors, and notify creditors of important hearing dates, is put on the debtor (usually with the help of its legal and financial advisors), and that obligation is taken seriously by debtors in bankruptcy. There are companies hired by debtors to do nothing but ensure that notices are properly given to creditors in larger cases. Having a transparent system provides public confidence in the bankruptcy system, which helps with respect to its efficiency.

The system assumes parties will watch out for their own interests

The US system assumes that, if there is a transparent system and proper notification is given to creditors and interested parties in cases, parties that do not object to developments in the bankruptcy case are well-informed and do not object on purpose. Accordingly, silence under the US bankruptcy system (again assuming proper notice is given to parties) is deemed an implied consent to what is happening. With proper notice, lack of objection is deemed to be a consent to what is being sought (at least as far as the parties in the case are concerned). This is particularly true in the voting protocol with respect to Chapter 11 plans. It is not necessary to get a requisite number or percentage of all claims to vote in the case; the only votes that count are those actually cast. Parties that do not vote are deemed not to be sufficiently interested in the outcome and, as such, their lack of participation is not counted for or against the debtor.

In addition, with the constituencies having competent legal and financial advisors, the US system is premised on the assumption that the parties with the financial stakes will negotiate honestly and efficiently with each other.

The system creates a level playing field

Finally, US reorganisation proceedings work because the laws are designed to level the playing field. At the outset of Chapter 11 cases, there is a presumption that the distressed business deserves an opportunity to catch its breath and to attempt to devise a restructuring plan without being picked apart by creditors. Existing management is presumed to be competent in making reasoned business judgments. This presumption, however, is rebuttable in the sense that if parties bring to the bankruptcy court evidence to the contrary, bankruptcy judges can and do take action to remedy that (which could include displacing management with a trustee under appropriate circumstances). Also, the longer a case goes on without resolution, the less credibility debtor's management might have in the case unless there is some reason why it is taking a long time to reach resolution.

Because of these presumptions, there is a more level playing field with neither the debtor nor the creditors having the ability to bury the other. As long as both parties realise that, absent very unusual circumstances, there will not be an unduly quick end to the case, the parties will negotiate with one another, and a collaborative approach will result in a plan that is the ultimate goal of a Chapter 11 case. Even banks and secured lenders, who frequently assert that they just want their collateral back, are often benefited by a Chapter 11 bankruptcy, in that a stabilised business, even if it is to be liquidated, can result in greater values for secured creditors such as banks. In addition, if there are claims that other creditors or the debtor may wish to raise against a bank, those can be (and frequently are) resolved in the context of a resolution in the Chapter 11 case, such as through a plan of reorganisation. In essence, a "successful" Chapter 11 is one in which each party feels like it left something on the table, got a meaningful recovery, but didn't necessarily get everything it could have got.

Conclusion

For these troubled times, the way to economic strength is to have an insolvency law that allows a financially distressed business a chance to catch its breath, operate without being buried by its creditors, and without artificial constraints (on time or recoveries). At the same time, the law must give creditors rights to seek redress before the court expeditiously to ensure that the debtor is playing by the rules. In essence, a working insolvency law must create an even playing field that facilitates and encourages negotiation. Giving any constituency too much leverage will not, ultimately, result in an effective reorganisation law.

Author:

Thomas J. Salerno, Esq., Chair
International Insolvency Practice Group

Squire, Sanders & Dempsey L.L.P
Adjunct Professor, University of Pacific McGeorge School of Law

---

In recent years, many countries have revised their bankruptcy laws in an attempt to permit the survival of more of the firms that are in financial distress. Countries have adopted concepts such as debtors remaining in possession to continue operating the business during bankruptcy proceedings and bankrupt entities being permitted to choose what contracts to continue and which ones to terminate. Mr. Salerno, author of the article quoted above, and Jeffrey A. McGehee, Esq. advised the Government of the Czech Republic in the drafting of its new bankruptcy law permitting reorganizations. They describe the resulting Czech law as the most advanced of the new European laws on this subject. (Act On Insolvency And Its Resolution (No.182/2006) effective January 1, 2008.) Yet in their article "The Czech Republic's long awaited overhaul of its insolvency code arrives" published in Global Insolvency & Restructuring Review 2007/2008 these lawyers describe various weaknesses in the new law that will likely preclude its effective operation. Items they mention include:

1.   Post-bankruptcy financing for the DIP may be difficult to arrange since the new loans are given priority over unsecured creditors but only equal status with secured creditors.

2.   Voting by creditors registers those not voting as a "no" vote.

3.   An early vote of creditors is required on the issue whether the debtor should even be permitted to present a plan which the authors describe as the product of a general attitude that debtors are to be punished unless the creditors acquiesce in letting them try to develop a reorganization plan.

4.   The law provides for a creditors committee consisting of both secured and unsecured creditors and may include employee representatives. Committee members can be held liable for failing to act with due diligence in pursuit of their common interest. Of course, the interests of these three diverse groups are not "common" with respect to many issues

5.   There is no provision for allowing the debtor to get out of unfavorable contracts.

6.   A reorganization plan cannot be implemented until a final order is entered; the filing of an appeal precludes the court's order from becoming final; and, any creditor may appeal with-

out posting bond or incurring liability for the delay that is caused.

It is apparent that in many societies it will take a change in attitudes toward insolvent parties before there can be adoption and balanced enforcement of laws that give debtor businesses a reasonable opportunity to reorganize.

Index

References are to Pages

†